# MAKING

# ENTERPRISE RISK

# MANAGEMENT PAY OFF

Thomas L. Barton

William G. Shenkir

Paul L. Walker

Prentice Hall PTR
One Lake Street
Upper Saddle River, NJ 07458
www.phptr.com

Editorial/Production Supervision: KATHLEEN M. CAREN
Executive Editor: JIM BOYD
Marketing Manager: BRYAN GAMBREL
Manufacturing Manager: MAURA ZALDIVAR
Cover Design: TALAR BOORUJY

 ©2002 Financial Executives Research Foundation, Inc.

 Published by Financial Times/Prentice Hall PTR
Pearson Education, Inc.
Upper Saddle River, NJ  07458

Prentice Hall books are widely used by corporations and government
agencies for training, marketing, and resale.

The publisher offers discounts on this book when ordered in bulk quantities.
For more information, contact: Corporate Sales Department, Phone: 800-382-3419; Fax:
201-236-7141; E-mail: corpsales@prenhall.com; or write: Prentice Hall PTR, Corp. Sales
Dept., One Lake Street, Upper Saddle River, NJ  07458.

Printed in the United States of America

10  9  8  7  6  5  4  3  2  1

ISBN 0-13-008754-8

Pearson Education LTD.
Pearson Education Australia PTY, Limited
Pearson Education Singapore, Pte. Ltd.
Pearson Education North Asia Ltd.
Pearson Education Canada, Ltd.
Pearson Educación de Mexico, S.A. de C.V.
Pearson Education—Japan
Pearson Education Malaysia, Pte. Ltd.
Pearson Education, Upper Saddle River, New Jersey

# ADVISORY COMMITTEE

# FINANCIAL TIMES PRENTICE HALL BOOKS

*For more information, please go to www.ft-ph.com*

Thomas L. Barton, William G. Shenkir, and Paul L. Walker
*Making Enterprise Risk Management Pay Off:*
*How Leading Companies Implement Risk Management*

Deirdre Breakenridge
*Cyberbranding: Brand Building in the Digital Economy*

William C. Byham, Audrey B. Smith, and Matthew J. Paese
*Grow Your Own Leaders: How to Identify, Develop, and Retain*
*Leadership Talent*

Jonathan Cagan and Craig M. Vogel
*Creating Breakthrough Products: Innovation from Product Planning*
*to Program Approval*

Subir Chowdhury
*The Talent Era: Achieving a High Return on Talent*

Sherry Cooper
*Ride the Wave: Taking Control in a Turbulent Financial Age*

James W. Cortada
*21st Century Business: Managing and Working*
*in the New Digital Economy*

James W. Cortada
*Making the Information Society: Experience, Consequences,*
*and Possibilities*

Aswath Damodaran
*The Dark Side of Valuation: Valuing Old Tech, New Tech,*
*and New Economy Companies*

Henry A. Davis and William W. Sihler
*Financial Turnarounds: Preserving Enterprise Value*

Sarvanan Devaraj and Rajiv Kohli
*The IT Payoff: Measuring the Business Value*
*of Information Technology Investments*

Jaime Ellertson and Charles W. Ogilvie
*Frontiers of Financial Services: Turning Customer Interactions*
*Into Profits*

Nicholas D. Evans
*Business Agility: Strategies for Gaining Competitive Advantage through Mobile Business Solutions*

Kenneth R. Ferris and Barbara S. Pécherot Petitt
*Valuation: Avoiding the Winner's Curse*

David Gladstone and Laura Gladstone
*Venture Capital Handbook: An Entrepreneur's Guide to Raising Venture Capital, Revised and Updated*

David R. Henderson
*The Joy of Freedom: An Economist's Odyssey*

Philip Jenks and Stephen Eckett, Editors
*The Global-Investor Book of Investing Rules: Invaluable Advice from 150 Master Investors*

Thomas Kern, Mary Cecelia Lacity, and Leslie P. Willcocks
*Netsourcing: Renting Business Applications and Services Over a Network*

Frederick C. Militello, Jr., and Michael D. Schwalberg
*Leverage Competencies: What Financial Executives Need to Lead*

Dale Neef
*E-procurement: From Strategy to Implementation*

John R. Nofsinger
*Investment Madness: How Psychology Affects Your Investing... And What to Do About It*

Tom Osenton
*Customer Share Marketing: How the World's Great Marketers Unlock Profits from Customer Loyalty*

Stephen P. Robbins
*The Truth About Managing People...And Nothing but the Truth*

Jonathan Wight
*Saving Adam Smith: A Tale of Wealth, Transformation, and Virtue*

Yoram J. Wind and Vijay Mahajan, with Robert Gunther
*Convergence Marketing: Strategies for Reaching the New Hybrid Consumer*

**FINANCIAL TIMES**

Prentice Hall

In an increasingly competitive world, it is quality
of thinking that gives an edge—an idea that opens new
doors, a technique that solves a problem, or an insight
that simply helps make sense of it all.

We work with leading authors in the various arenas
of business and finance to bring cutting-edge thinking
and best learning practice to a global market.

It is our goal to create world-class print publications
and electronic products that give readers
knowledge and understanding which can then be
applied, whether studying or at work.

To find out more about our business
products, you can visit us at www.ft-ph.com

Pearson
Education

# CONTENTS

# Introduction

*Risk—let's get this straight up front—is good. The point of risk
management isn't to eliminate it; that would eliminate reward.
The point is to manage it—that is, to choose where to place bets,
and where to avoid betting altogether.*

Thomas Stewart, *Fortune*[1]

As businesses worldwide enter the twenty-first century, they face an
assortment of risks almost unimaginable just 10 years ago. E-commerce
has become ingrained in society with amazing speed: Companies that
cannot keep up are doomed to obsolescence in record time. Technology
is driving business models to be retooled in months instead of years.
The traditional gatekeepers of information are being supplemented
with the Internet democracy in which anyone with a PC can disseminate
information widely and quickly—for good or bad.[2] Derivatives, which
were originally intended to help manage risk, have themselves created
whole new areas of risk.

It is probably axiomatic that well-managed businesses have successful risk management. Over time, a business that cannot manage its key
risks effectively will simply disappear. A disastrous product recall could
be the company's last. A derivatives debacle can decimate staid old institutions over a long weekend. But historically, risk management in
even the most successful businesses has tended to be in "silos"—the insurance risk, the technology risk, the financial risk, the environmental
risk, all managed independently in separate compartments. Coordina-
tion of risk management has usually been nonexistent, and the identification of new risks has been sluggish.

This study looks at a new model—enterprise-wide risk management—in which the management of risks is integrated and coordinated
across the entire organization. A culture of risk awareness is created.

Farsighted companies across a wide cross section of industries are successfully implementing this effective new methodology.

## An Abundance of Uncertainty

Uncertainty abounds in today's economy. Every organization is, to some extent, in the business of risk management, no matter what its products or services. It is not possible to "create a business that doesn't take risks," according to Richard Boulton and colleagues. "If you try, you will create a business that doesn't make money."[3] As a business continually changes, so do the risks. Stakeholders increasingly want companies to identify and manage their business risks. More specifically, stakeholders want management to meet their earnings goals. Risk management can help them do so. According to Susan Stalnecker, vice president and treasurer of DuPont, "Risk management is a strategic tool that can increase profitability and smooth earnings volatility."[4] Senior management must manage the ever-changing risks if they are to create, protect, and enhance shareholder value.

Two groups have recently emphasized the importance of risk management at an organization's highest levels. In October 1999, the National Association of Corporate Directors released its *Report of the Blue Ribbon Commission on Audit Committees,* which recommends that audit committees "define and use timely, focused information that is responsive to important performance measures and to the key risks they oversee."[5] The report states that the chair of the audit committee should develop an agenda that includes "a periodic review of risk by each significant business unit."

In January 2000, the Financial Executives Institute released the results of a survey on audit committee effectiveness. Respondents, who were primarily chief financial officers and corporate controllers, ranked "key areas of business and financial risk" as the most important for audit committee oversight.[6]

With the speed of change increasing for all companies in the New Economy,[7] senior management must deal with a myriad of complex risks that have substantial consequences for their organization. Here are a few of the forces creating uncertainty in the New Economy:

- Technology and the Internet

- Increased worldwide competition

- Freer trade and investment worldwide

- Complex financial instruments, notably derivatives

- Deregulation of key industries

- Changes in organizational structures resulting from downsizing, reengineering, and mergers

- Higher customer expectations for products and services

- More and larger mergers

Collectively, these forces are stimulating considerable change and creating an increasingly risky and turbulent business environment. Perhaps no force on the list is having as great an impact on business as the Internet. As the Internet comes of age, companies are rethinking their business models, core strategies, and target customer bases. "Getting wired," as it is often called, provides businesses with new opportunities, but it also creates more uncertainty and new risks.[8] In his book *The High Risk Society,* Michael Mandel states, "Economic uncertainty is the price that must be paid for growth." To be successful, businesses must seek opportunities "where the forces of uncertainty and growth are the strongest."[9]

The mismanagement of risk can carry an enormous price. In recent years, the business community has witnessed a number of risk debacles that have resulted in considerable financial loss, decreased shareholder value, damaged company reputations, the dismissal of senior management, and in some cases the destruction of the business. Consider the impact of the following events:

- Companies selling poor-quality or defective products, or unnecessary service, coupled in some cases with severely mishandling the crisis surrounding the product recall or service problem

- Environmental disasters and inadequate attention to the resulting crisis

3

- Rogue traders lacking oversight and inadequate controls assuming enormous risks

- Organizations trading in complex derivative instruments without understanding the risks involved

- Mergers destroying shareholder value

- Insurance salespeople churning customers' accounts

- Sexual harassment of employees

- Racial slurs by management and discrimination against employees

This increasingly risky environment, in which a debacle can have major and far-reaching consequences, requires that senior management adopt a new perspective on risk management. The new perspective should be one that not only prevents debacles but also enhances shareholder value. Indeed, the New Economy calls for a new risk management paradigm.

## New Risk Management Paradigm

In thinking about a shifting paradigm for risk management, the recipe for boiling a frog is instructive. If you drop a frog into a pan of boiling water, it will jump out. But if you put the frog in a pan of cold water and gradually raise the temperature, the frog will stay in until the water boils, not realizing that its paradigm is shifting. In a similar fashion, the risk management paradigm has been shifting gradually for some organizations. Some of them may not have recognized the paradigm shift and the advantages of the new perspective on risk management.

Traditionally, most organizations have viewed risk management as a specialized and isolated activity: the management of insurance or foreign exchange risks, for instance. The new approach has its basis in keeping managers and employees at all levels sensitized to and concerned about risk management. Table 1.1 identifies three key aspects of this shift to an organization-wide perspective for risk management.

As noted in table 1.1, the risk management perspective for some organizations is shifting from a fragmented, ad hoc, narrow approach to an integrated, continuous, and broadly focused approach. The question

*Table 1.1*
*Key Features of the New Risk Management Paradigm*

| Old Paradigm | New Paradigm |
|---|---|
| ■ Fragmented—department/function manage risk independently; accounting, treasurer, internal audit primarily concerned | ■ Integrated—risk management coordinated with senior-level oversight; everyone in the organization views risk management as part of his or her job |
| ■ Ad hoc—risk management done whenever managers believe need exists to do it | ■ Continuous—risk management process is ongoing |
| ■ Narrowly focused—primarily insurable risk and financial risks | ■ Broadly focused—all business risks and opportunities considered |

Source: Economist Intelligence Unit, *Managing Business Risks,* 10. A similar analysis is presented in DeLoach, *Enterprise-Wide Risk Management,* 15–16.

is whether senior management will make the shift consciously now or make it after the water heats up and a debacle occurs.

This new perspective on risk management is sometimes referred to as integrated, strategic, business, or enterprise-wide risk management, and we use these terms interchangeably. The term "risk" includes any event or action that "will adversely affect an organization's ability to achieve its business objectives and execute its strategies successfully."[10] The scope of risk covers all risks, internal and external, that may prevent an organization from achieving its objectives. Adding the word *management* to integrated, business, or enterprise-wide risk implies a "structured and disciplined approach" that "aligns strategy, processes, people, technology and knowledge with the purpose of evaluating and managing the uncertainties the enterprise faces as it creates value."[11] Hence, the goal of an enterprise-wide risk management initiative is to create, protect, and enhance shareholder value by managing the uncertainties that could either negatively or positively influence achievement of the organization's objectives.

# Studies of Risk Management

Enterprise-wide risk management is an emerging concept that has gained in popularity over the past decade. The recognition of a more risky business operating environment and, at the same time, increased accountabilities has led several professional organizations to address control and risk assessment in major publications. In addition, several of the Big Five accounting firms have produced documents expounding the value of enterprise-wide risk management.

In 1992, the Committee of Sponsoring Organizations of the Treadway Commission (COSO) issued *Internal Control—Integrated Framework* (ICIF).[12] This pathfinding document departed from the traditional internal accounting control model by presenting a broad control framework of five interrelated components: control environment, risk assessment, control activities, information and communication, and monitoring. According to the document, control is the responsibility of the board of directors, management, and other personnel within the organization, not just the accountants. Particularly relevant is the identification of risk assessment as a vital component of control.

The growing importance of risk management is evidenced by the following major publications issued by professional groups since ICIF was published:

- Economist Intelligence Unit (in cooperation with Arthur Andersen & Co.), *Managing Business Risks—An Integrated Approach* (1995).

- Canadian Institute of Chartered Accountants Criteria of Control Board, *Guidance for Control* (1995).

- The Conference Board of Canada (by L. Nottingham), *A Conceptual Framework for Integrated Risk Management* (1997).

- American Institute of Certified Public Accountants, *Report of the Special Committee on Assurance Services* (1997).

- Canadian Institute of Chartered Accountants Criteria of Control Board, *Learning About Risk: Choices, Connections and Competencies* (1998).

- Institute of Internal Auditors Research Foundation (by D. McNamee and G. M. Selim), *Risk Management: Changing the Internal Auditor's Paradigm* (1998).

- International Federation of Accountants Financial and Management Accounting Committee (prepared by Pricewaterhouse-Coopers), *Enhancing Shareholder Wealth by Better Managing Business Risk* (1999).

- Joint Australian/New Zealand Standard, *Risk Management* (1999).

- Canadian Institute of Chartered Accountants Criteria of Control Board, *Guidance for Directors—Dealing With Risk in the Boardroom* (1999).

- The Institute of Chartered Accountants in England and Wales Internal Control Working Party, *Internal Control: Guidance for Directors on the Combined Code* (1999).

- American Institute of Certified Public Accountants/Canadian Institute of Chartered Accountants Risk Advisory Services Task Force, *Managing Risk in the New Economy* (2000).

While a few of these publications include case studies analyzing companies' experiences implementing risk management, most of the studies tend to advocate a particular generalized framework for risk management. Each of the publications listed, as well as others, appears in the annotated bibliography in appendix C.

## Objectives and Approach of This Study

The objectives of this study are as follows:

- To present in-depth case analysis of several companies' risk management practices

- To identify emerging patterns in risk management that could be useful to companies in developing an enterprise-wide risk management system

The research is not intended to deduce from the case studies a uniform framework for risk management. If anything, the research indicates that when it comes to risk management, one model does not fit all companies.

With these objectives in mind, we identified five companies that were at various stages of developing an enterprise-wide risk management approach. At each company, we conducted in-depth interviews on site with senior management and other key employees. An interview protocol containing a list of questions guided the interviews (see appendix A). The case studies are based on the transcribed interviews, company-provided materials, and published information.

In selecting the companies, we sought a cross section from different industries. The five firms chosen are all public companies. They represent the agriculture (United Grain Growers), chemical (DuPont), energy (Unocal), financial services (Chase Manhattan), and technology (Microsoft) industries. Table 1.2 lists the study companies and key statistics for each.

## Organization of This Study

Chapter 2 discusses the lessons learned from the five case studies. Chapters devoted to each case study follow that analysis. The last chapter gives overall conclusions drawn from the research.

*Table 1.2*
*Case-Study Companies*

| Study Company | Industry | Revenues[1] | Employees |
|---|---|---|---|
| Chase Manhattan Corp.[2] | Financial Services | $22,982 | 74,800 |
| DuPont | Chemical | $26,918 | 94,000 |
| Microsoft Corp. | Technology | $19,750 | 31,575 |
| United Grain Growers Ltd. | Agriculture | C$1,832 | 1,600 |
| Unocal Corp. | Energy | $6,057 | 7,550 |

[1] Most recent fiscal year in $ millions U.S. (except for United Grain Growers, which is in $ millions Canadian).

[2] J.P. Morgan Chase & Co. as of December 31, 2000

# Endnotes

1. Thomas A. Stewart, "Managing Risk in the 21$^{st}$ Century," *Fortune* (February 7, 2000): 202.

2. This was illustrated strikingly by the case of a 15-year-old New Jersey boy who manipulated the prices of 11 stocks he owned by posting false messages on Internet bulletin boards and in chat rooms. In September 2000, the Securities and Exchange Commission charged the boy with stock fraud. He paid $285,000 to the U.S. Treasury to settle the case (Kevin Peraino, "A Shark in Kid's Clothes," *Newsweek* (October 2, 2000): 50.).

3. Richard E. S. Boulton, Barry D. Libert, and Steve M. Samek, *Cracking the Value Code—How Successful Businesses Are Creating Wealth in the New Economy* (New York: HarperBusiness, 2000): 181.

4. See the DuPont case study in chapter 4.

5. National Association of Corporate Directors, *Report of the Blue Ribbon Commission on Audit Committees* (Washington, DC: National Association of Corporate Directors, 1999): 2–3.

6. Financial Executives Institute, "Survey: Audit Committees Should Focus on Key Business Risks," FEI Press Release, January 12, 2000.

7. New Economy companies are leaders in innovations (Internet, microprocessors, etc.) and include technology, information services, media, telecommunications, and life science companies.

8. "New Challenges Arise as All Business Becomes E-Business," *Washington Post* (September 20, 2000): G1.

9. Michael Mandel, *The High Risk Society* (New York: Times Business, 1996): 9.

10. Economist Intelligence Unit, written in cooperation with Arthur Andersen & Co., *Managing Business Risks—An Integrated Approach* (New York: The Economist Intelligence Unit, 1995): 2.

11. James W. DeLoach, Jr., *Enterprise-Wide Risk Management—Strategies for Linking Risk and Opportunity* (London: Financial Times, 2000): 5.

12. The National Commission on Fraudulent Financial Reporting, known as the Treadway Commission, was created in 1985. The commission is sponsored by the American Institute of Certified Public Accountants, American Accounting Association, Financial Executives Institute, Institute of Internal Auditors, and the Institute of Management Accountants.

# Lessons Learned From Case Studies

*Risk, then, encompasses the uncertainty of future reward in terms of both the upside and the downside. And opportunity in business arises from managing the future. Companies today must face (and manage) the future knowing that they cannot simply carry on with business as usual.*

Richard E. S. Boulton, Barry D. Libert, and Steve M. Samek,
*Cracking the Value Code—How Successful Businesses
Are Creating Wealth in the New Economy*[1]

*I also need my CFO to be a risk-management wizard, ahead of the pack in figuring out all the things that could possibly go wrong…and finding ways to limit those risks.*

Marcia Vickers, "Up from Bean Counter,"
in "The 21st Century Corporation," *Business Week*[2]

Enterprise-wide risk management represents a paradigm shift in the way businesses manage the uncertainties that stand in the way of achieving their strategic, operational, and financial objectives. While the old paradigm was a silo approach to risk management—with each risk considered in isolation—the new approach is holistic, integrating the risks across the organization and designing risk response strategies. Some organizations have recognized the need to change and are incrementally implementing the new paradigm. This chapter synthesizes the lessons learned from the five case-study companies.

The case studies demonstrate, in as much detail as the companies would publicly share, how they manage risk. One common theme emerged. Each company believed it was creating, protecting, and enhancing value by managing enterprise-wide risks. Value can be created, protected, and enhanced by knowing risks, knowing how those risks relate to each other and whether offsets occur, and knowing the risk tolerance level of the company and its stakeholders. Value can also be created, protected, and enhanced by knowing the effect risks have on both financial position and earnings, knowing the probabilities of achieving an earnings goal, and knowing the likelihood and significance level of each risk. In addition, knowing whether inconsistencies exist across the company in risk management and knowing whether resources are being efficiently allocated based on risk strengthens the likelihood of creating, protecting, and enhancing value.

Finally, value can be created, protected, and enhanced by managing risk to reduce earnings volatility, by building risk-based incentive systems, by seeking new opportunities to finance and/or transfer risk, and by having infrastructure in place to manage and oversee the entire effort. We highlight some of these "value" lessons below.

At the outset, there is one overriding lesson from these five studies:

---

*Value Lesson 1*

*A cookbook recipe for implementing enterprise-wide risk management is not feasible because so much depends on the culture of the company and the change agents who lead the effort.*

---

## Risk Identification Process

Before a company sets out to manage risks, it must know what risks to manage. To some companies, this seems obvious at first. In DuPont's early days, everyone understood and respected the risk of making dynamite. To United Grain Growers (UGG), weather was clearly a risk that had a significant effect on the company's performance. In Chase's early years, the risk in the loan portfolio could dramatically alter the corporation's earnings. For Unocal, the risk is to find more oil or go broke. For Microsoft, it is to innovate continuously before someone else replaces you and takes your market share. Yet in today's rapidly changing, complex, and global-based businesses, risk is not always quite so apparent.

While ultimately the chief executive officer (CEO) is the company's chief risk management officer, decision makers at all levels should consider risk management as a critical part of their job. For that to occur, they must be aware of the risks their organizational unit faces as well as the risks that confront other units and the organization as a whole.

*Value Lesson 2*

***To manage effectively in today's business environment, companies should make a formal, dedicated effort to identify all their significant risks.***

The study companies used no single method to identify risks but did follow several common approaches. In Microsoft, the risk management group continually promotes risk management to the business units. Microsoft's risk managers say that they "evangelize" the business units about the importance of identifying risk and considering its potential impact and its likelihood in business decisions. In addition, Microsoft's risk management group emphasizes face-to-face time with business units. This approach allows the risk management group to be aware of "perhaps 90 percent of the risks facing Microsoft," according to Microsoft's treasurer.

Microsoft also uses scenario analysis to identify its material business risks. As Brent Callinicos, treasurer and head of Microsoft's risk management group, states, "In the past, we have looked at silos of risk. For example, we may have looked at property insurance when we considered the risks of an earthquake and thought about protecting equipment, damage to buildings, and that type of thing." But as Callinicos notes, "The real risk is not that buildings get damaged but that it causes business interruption in the product development cycle and that you cannot do business." The risk management group identifies various risk scenarios and initiates the thinking about those scenarios. This group also benchmarks its scenarios against events that actually took place at other companies.

Another common risk identification approach is for business units to undertake self-assessments. At Chase, managers at various levels complete self-assessment scorecards to identify their unit's risks. Similarly, Unocal requires annual risk assessments in each business unit. Unocal emphasizes the dramatic change in its new risk-based approach this way: "Instead of worrying about 800 check marks in an auditor's workpaper, management would, through dynamic self-assessment, identify the areas of greatest risk and devise steps to manage those risks." Another lesson can be seen in Unocal's emphasis on "dynamic." Risk identification is not a one-shot solution. Businesses change and so do their risks. UGG acknowledged that the list of risks it had identified was already outdated.

*Value Lesson 3*

*Various techniques are available to identify risk, and once identified, the process of identification should be dynamic and continuous.*

In addition to risk identification through self-assessments, both Unocal and UGG use team meetings of key employees or brainstorming sessions to identify their risks. Unocal encourages each business unit to establish a team and have the team meet to systematically list risks. These meetings are not just about financial risks; they seek to identify *all* risks—everything from government regulations, technology, and competition to risks facing each business process.

The risk identification sessions also include a risk-ranking component. The rankings are based on dollar effects, severity, or impact. This analysis helps management learn two things. First, it shows the perceived importance of the risk. Second, by sorting risks according to their importance, management can use the list to develop a risk management strategy and to allocate resources efficiently.

*Value Lesson 4*

*Risks should be ranked on some scale that captures their importance, severity, or dollar amount.*

Another aspect of risk identification includes assigning probabilities to the risks. For example, after Unocal's business units list risks, they rate them on probability. Microsoft also assesses risks on more than the dollar level. Instead of probability, Microsoft assigns a frequency to each risk. The combined importance level (or significance level) and probability (or frequency) can be projected on a risk map (see figure 5.4, page 137, for Microsoft's map). Even though DuPont does not generate risk maps, the company does acknowledge the value of knowing the frequency and severity of risks: "Our concern [in how we manage risk] was more focused on staying away from the high frequency–low severity risks because we think that is managed quite well. We wanted to focus on the low frequency–high severity risks because those are the ones that tend to have perhaps a big hit. We still need to refine that and start thinking more quantitatively." Risk lists and maps help management to visually grasp all risks and know which are the most important.

*Value Lesson 5*

*Risks should be ranked on some scale of frequency or probability.*

Rankings of risk importance levels may or may not be accurate. For example, UGG had one risk ranked high but later measured the risk quantitatively and found that it was not nearly as high as UGG had thought. Risk measurement can assist companies in knowing the true importance of a risk. Managers should strive to make conscious decisions about risk. Risk measurement can help them make those decisions.

## Risk Measurement

The only way to know that a company is not wasting resources, allocating capital inefficiently, or spending time on the least risky areas is to measure risk. Measuring risk can be as simple as ranking it. For some risks, a subjective ranking is all the measurement that can be done. Microsoft and UGG acknowledge that some risks just are not measurable. Microsoft states, "The approach we have taken in financial risk and business risk is to try to quantify what we can and not necessarily worry that we are unable to capture everything in our measurement." Unfortunately, in many instances data are available for the high frequency–low impact events, while few data are available for the low frequency–high impact events. When it can be done, however, risk measurement helps to validate the real level of risks. Otherwise, companies may be operating on intuition and experience only.

## Value at Risk and Stress Testing

The most developed areas for risk measurement are in financial risks, and the most common approaches for measuring and assessing financial risk are value at risk (VAR) and stress testing. VAR was originally developed for use in financial institutions to enable them to assess their capital at risk in different financial market transactions and their risk-adjusted rates of return. The technique is now finding much wider application. (See figure 2.1 for an overview of VAR.) Chase

*Figure 2.1*
*Value at Risk (VAR)*

As noted in the Microsoft case (chapter 5), "VAR measures the worst expected loss over a given time interval under normal market conditions at a given confidence level." VAR is a monitoring tool, not a forecasting tool.

The use of VAR began in the banking industry. VAR allows market risk to be reported at the instrument, portfolio, and aggregate fund levels across different asset and security levels.

VAR is an easily understood, single reporting figure. For example, VAR will tell the user that losses are not expected to exceed $X in more than X out of the next X months with X percentage confidence. It is most useful in actively traded liquid markets and can be used for information reporting and trading limit allocation. To calculate VAR, one needs the current market value, the volatility or standard deviation of that market value for a marketable instrument, an assumed risk horizon, and a required confidence level.

VAR relies on historical data and can take into account only risks that can be measured quantitatively. Therefore, it cannot consider drastic events or risks such as political, liquidity, personnel, or regulatory risks. Because each component of the portfolio must have large amounts of historical data related to it in the system, less actively traded instruments do not provide the volume of transactions needed or the constant valuation of the investment. Another consideration is the difficulty in unwinding the investment when something goes wrong, which may cause additional losses beyond those predicted by the VAR model. VAR assumes that the portfolio is held constant over a period of time. It is not a measure of the largest loss that will occur but of the level of loss that has X percentage probability of occurring.

uses VAR and stress testing to measure its market risk. To Chase, "VAR is a measure of the dollar amount of potential loss from adverse market moves in an everyday market environment. The VAR looks forward one trading day and is the loss expected to be exceeded with a 1 in 100 chance." Stress testing examines the impact of worst-case scenarios on the trading portfolio. Microsoft uses VAR and stress testing to manage market risks. To measure VAR, Microsoft uses three separate systems to generate the numbers. The company wants "to make sure at least directionally the risk is the same and, hopefully, from an order of magnitude standpoint the risk is the same as well," says Callinicos. The VAR calculation provides a way to respond when someone asks, "How much risk is Microsoft taking?"

It is important to recognize that a measure of financial risks may have implications for managing nonfinancial or general business risk. Microsoft ensures that financial risk wears a "business hat" by using the information on financial risk to improve decision making regarding other business risks.

*Value Lesson 6*

*Measure financial risk with the most sophisticated and relevant tools available, such as VAR and stress testing.*

## Earnings at Risk

VAR may be one of the more advanced techniques, but it is not the only one. DuPont admits that VAR was not much help to its risk managers. It was not always clear how to manage VAR and notional amounts,[3] and management throughout the organization did not always understand VAR. As an alternative, DuPont chose to use earnings at risk (EAR), which measures the effect of a risk on DuPont's earnings. DuPont comments on how the company views earnings at risk:

> We can quantify earnings at risk in any given quarter just from market movements. To do so, we first look at all cash flows with an identifiable market risk factor and then aggregate exposures to validate any natural offsets. Next, we run thousands of simulations integrating market risk factors, volatilities, and correlations and how

they could potentially impact earnings. For this exercise, we look at the extreme left tail of the potential earnings distribution. Let's say, for illustration purposes, that total earnings at risk for all of our market exposures is potentially $100 million. Now that we have it quantified, let's talk about what our appetite [for risk] is. It's similiar to what we did with the insurance side—what do we think the company can live with? Is $100 million right or should we manage the risk in a way that brings it down to $50 million? We can then run all different kinds of scenarios and strategies to see what's the most effective way to manage the risk to bring it down to $50 million.

By using EAR, DuPont manages risk to a specified earnings level based on the company's risk appetite and the potential appetite of investors. That is, the company can decide how much risk it is willing to accept (after controls and transfers[4]) and have a measure of how that risk affects not notional amounts, but earnings. This information allows managers to see the big-picture relationship between earnings, risk, and expected earnings and the likelihood of meeting certain earnings levels (something that may be considered critical in today's stock market).

*Value Lesson 7*

*Develop sophisticated tools and measures that meet the organization's needs and that management can easily understand.*

*Value Lesson 8*

*Know your company's and your shareholders' appetite for risk.*

But can companies use sophisticated techniques to measure nonfinancial risk? According to Chase's vice chairman, Marc Shapiro,

[The management of] operating risk is newer, and much less advanced. We've just set up a group to do what we're doing in credit risk and market risk. In credit risk, we probably have a 20-year credit history, in market risk we have a 10-year history, and in operating risk, we've got a no-year history but our thought is, we need to do much of the same thing.

I'm not a believer that you can quantify operating risk in exactly the same way [as the other two]. In other words, I think that a lot of operating risk is so random that it is hard to develop models that are reasonable predictors. But I think what you can do is share best practices, look at an overall, executive-level view of the system for controlling operating risk, develop the metrics that you need in each business, and then have an overall monitoring for those metrics. And probably do a better job of allocating capital than we're doing. That's what the goal is.

This "share best practices" concept came up at other companies also. DuPont's experience with measures such as VAR led it to examine its traditionally insurable risks with a more rigorous and quantitative process. DuPont tries to get risk profiles and worst-case scenario probabilities (similar to stress testing) even for nonfinancial risks. Microsoft also sought to bring the financial risk management discipline to its business risk areas.

UGG states, "It is much harder to try to get a handle on the less easily measurable business risks. How do you identify a value at risk model for those kinds of situations?" However, UGG did apply more rigor to some nontraditional financial risks by using a variation of VAR. Using historical data, UGG calculated gain/loss probability curves for some key risks. Such curves reflect the likelihood of losing or gaining money from a risk. UGG also used those data to plot the effect of risks on earnings per share. Again, this analysis was done on what are traditionally considered nonfinancial risks. The company further used these data to determine the actual effect of risks on revenues over a certain time period—learning along the way that certain risks contribute as much as 50 percent of the variance in revenue.

*Value Lesson 9*

*Apply more rigor to measuring nonfinancial risks whenever possible.*

It is clearly valuable to know the real level of risks facing a company. That knowledge comes first by ranking risks and next by measuring risk (if possible). Only on the basis of that knowledge can value-maximizing decisions be made. Although some limitations in risk measurement exist, innovations are occurring in this area. Armed with the knowledge of risks, managers can set out to manage them more effectively.

## Risk Response Strategies

"What can you do to improve the way this risk is being managed?" is a question on a Unocal risk document. It is a question that all companies should ask themselves. In effect, companies can choose to accept, transfer, or mitigate risks. A company's risk appetite (or that of its stakeholders) may influence its approach. For example, companies accept risks because they can bear the burden or because they have either mitigated the risk or transferred it to a level that the company is willing to accept.

---

*Value Lesson 10*

*Companies are choosing various combinations of acceptance, transfer, and mitigation to manage risk.*

---

Building controls in response to risk is a form of mitigation. A Unocal document states that after a unit identifies risks, it should evaluate existing controls to mitigate the high-priority risks. DuPont chooses a balanced approach in some areas. For example, the company accepts certain operational safety risks by self-insuring because it believes it has extensive controls over that area that allow it to accept a higher level of risk. However, DuPont's Bruce Evancho warns, "I've always said if you're doing that, you need to continue to monitor to be sure that you are investing in prevention, because if you ever let down, you're setting yourself up for a problem."

---

*Value Lesson 11*

*Decisions regarding control (an application of mitigation), acceptance, and transfer are dynamic—they must be continuously reevaluated.*

---

Chase has used a combination of acceptance, transfer, and mitigation to change the shape of the risk in its loan portfolio. Chase's loan portfolio is more diversified than ever, and the company now relies less on the interest spread. In fact, Chase states that it makes money if rates go up and if rates go down. Chase also places 90 percent of its commercial loans with investors in the market to help transfer the credit risk. Chase adds another dimension to risk management by linking risk management to employee incentives through shareholder value-added (SVA). Doing this reinforces the importance of managing risk, because a decision maker is evaluated based on his or her SVA metric. This metric calculates a profit amount by subtracting a charge for invested capital from cash operating earnings.

Some risks are inevitably hard to control. The weather has a significant effect on grain-handling volumes and, ultimately, on UGG's performance. However, UGG's risk measurement and analysis revealed that an integrated risk financing solution was an alternative. The solution was unique in that the company integrated a previously uninsurable business risk (grain-handling volume) with insurable risks. This solution allowed UGG to reduce earnings volatility, reduce the long-term cost of risk, and increase its leverage capacity.

---

*Value Lesson 12*

*Seek creative solutions and transfer risk where economic opportunities exist.*

---

## Risk Integration

How do companies attempt to integrate risk and adopt an enterprise-wide approach to risk management? How wide is enterprise-wide risk management? A first step in answering these questions is to know all of the risk—that is, build a portfolio of risks. The case-study companies do so to varying degrees. A risk map, a list of risks, or a model that highlights the company's assessment of risks is a major step in the right direction. A second step is to integrate best practices and tools. Some companies take tools and methods to manage financial risk and adapt them to nonfinancial risks.

A third step is for companies to take what risk information they have and attempt to look at enterprise-wide management of those risks.

For example, although DuPont has not yet integrated all risks, it can now get a greatly improved analysis of how all risks that have been quantified affect earnings. Perhaps more important, the company has quantified how those risks affect the likelihood of meeting earnings targets. Similarly, by examining risks enterprise-wide, UGG saw dramatic inconsistencies in the level of risks it was taking, and it saw that a small group of risks had a major influence on revenue variability. Further, UGG saw opportunities for savings and risk transfer: By integrating noninsurable business risks with traditionally insurable risks, it could reduce the long-term cost of risk. (See table 2.1 for a summary of the three steps to risk integration.)

Chase looked enterprise-wide and realized it needed an operations risk committee, similar to its other risk committees. DuPont and Microsoft looked enterprise-wide and realized that they simply had not considered or adequately managed all risks. Unocal looked enterprise-wide and found it was not allocating adequate resources to the riskiest areas.

*Value Lesson 13*

*Organizations should adopt an enterprise-wide view of risk management.*

*Table 2.1*
*The Three Steps to Risk Integration*

| Step | Action | Methods |
|------|--------|---------|
| 1 | Identify all significant risks. | List risks, assess risk, map risk |
| 2 | Measure risk and integrate best practices and tools. | Value at risk (VAR) and stress testing; earnings at risk (EAR) |
| | | Apply financial tools to nonfinancial risks |
| 3 | Look enterprise-wide. | Look for— |
| | | ■ Inconsistencies |
| | | ■ Natural offsets |
| | | ■ Transfer/financing opportunities |

# Use of Consultants

Several of the companies used outside consultants to assist them with aspects of the risk management process. Two used consultants from Big Five accounting firms, but they used them in different ways: UGG commissioned a treasury department review by a Big Five consultant, while Unocal used a Big Five firm in its risk management adoption process. DuPont codeveloped a risk management solution with another company, and UGG used a consultant to assist it with the entire process, including seeking an integrated financing solution. Microsoft used consultants in two areas: to provide information on how other companies were managing specific risks, and to provide data on incidents for the risk management group to analyze. The risk management group at Microsoft has used consultants as a "fresh set of eyes" to make sure that the company does not go very far down the road on an issue if it has not considered some relevant piece of information. In all the cases, the consultants did not replace senior management involvement but rather supplemented the organization's own knowledge and skills.

*Value Lesson 14*

*Consultants, if they are used, should supplement, not replace, senior management involvement in the risk management effort.*

# Driving Risk Awareness Throughout the Organization

Companies that embrace enterprise-wide risk management face the daunting task of instilling a risk awareness in a corporate culture focused on other objectives. Unocal Chief Financial Officer (CFO) Tim Ling was especially frustrated by the common view in his company that risk management was adjunct to the normal course of business—a staff function having incidental ties to the effective management of the company: "I think sometimes when we say 'risk,' we tend to try to segment risk as something different than just running our business. To me, running a business is all about managing risk and managing returns, whether on the financial side or the balance sheet side, or running a field operation."

In the fast-paced world of securities trading, the trader at Chase is something of a solo pilot, making multimillion-dollar decisions in a matter of minutes with very little direct oversight, yet responsible for assessing risk–return trade-offs in a flash. Chase Executive Vice President Lesley Daniels Webster says, "It's a business that's open pretty much 24 hours a day now, and it's a business where people work incredible hours with incredible amounts of information on incredible and mind-boggling deadlines. You need to put a price on a huge amount of risk in 10 minutes, and so you're always reinventing." There simply is not time to check with a home office risk manager on routine trades. Microsoft's Bill Gates is an evangelist on the empowerment of people through information, and this is reflected in Microsoft's extensive use of an intranet. Information is available to rank-and-file employees across the company to an extent that new hires find surprising. Gates explains the rationale: "A company's middle managers and line employees, not just its high-level executives, need to see business data.... Companies should spend less time protecting financial data from employees and more time teaching them to analyze and act on it." How better to spread risk awareness among Microsoft's some 32,000 employees than to use an information system so ingrained in company culture?

Historically, corporations were forced to manage silos of key risks or go out of business. If Unocal had not managed the risks of its expensive and dangerous oil drilling ventures, it would not be the world's largest investor-owned, independent oil exploration and production company. Chase could not have become the world's number one derivatives trader if it could not manage its exposure to some of the most volatile securities ever devised. Microsoft would not be the provider of operating systems to 90 percent of the world's personal computers if it had not managed the technological risk that changes the PC landscape literally overnight.

Almost by definition, successful companies are good at managing their most pressing risks. But enterprise-wide risk management is another matter. Companies are not adopting this paradigm out of desperation—because they are inept at risk management. Rather, they are adopting it because it offers even greater potential success—better control of risks along with some surprising efficiencies. UGG was able to finance its greatest risk, grain volume fluctuations, in an insurance package that cost no more than its old package. That type of success is almost impossible to believe—it appears to be a free lunch, something for nothing. But it really is completely logical and is merely the result of a creative, innovative application of enterprise-wide risk management.

---

*Value Lesson 15*

*Successful companies are good at managing silos of risk. Enterprise-wide risk management offers them more effective risk management at potentially lower costs.*

---

The study companies have chosen different routes toward their goal of permeating their organizations with the risk awareness needed to make enterprise-wide risk management work for them. Table 2.2 summarizes each study company's approach to the problem. Of course, these approaches could change as systems mature over time.

In 1998, Chase introduced SVA as a mechanism to connect performance evaluation and incentives to manage risk. Chase was concerned that it was not being sufficiently compensated for its risks. Chase vice chairman Marc Shapiro explains it this way:

> Under the old system, as a person in the lending area, you were always incented to make loans you thought were good—even if they had marginal profitability—because you were paid on that income, and generally there is a positive spread. So if you'd made a loan, you'd generated more net income.

> The current system says, "OK, you've made a loan. We're going to assign this much capital to it, and the loan spread may or may not cover the cost of that capital."

Under SVA, profit is calculated by subtracting a charge (currently 13 percent) on risk-adjusted capital from revenues. The more risk a decision maker takes on Chase's behalf, the higher the capital charge. If a decision maker takes more risk without a commensurate increase in revenue, his or her profit goes down. Shapiro adds, "We're in the business of taking risks, but we're in the business of getting paid for the risks that we take."

SVA has been a stunning success in driving risk awareness throughout the organization and in aligning the interests of decision makers

*Table 2.2*
*Approaches to Instilling Risk Awareness*

| Study Company | Approach | Description |
|---|---|---|
| Chase | Shareholder value-added (SVA) | Measure profit across operating units by subtracting a charge for risk-adjusted capital from revenues |
| DuPont | Risk philosophy | Tie risk to business strategy and set controls |
| | Earnings at risk (EAR) | Maximize potential earnings loss within confidence interval —intuitive, and provides common risk language |
| Microsoft | Intranet | Web-based knowledge tools; data sharing |
| | Face-to-face time | Risk management group consultation; leveraging wisdom |
| United Grain Growers (UGG) | Communication | Articulate policies and tolerances |
| | Analytical tools | Quantify risks and develop scenarios |
| Unocal | | Mandated annual risk assessments within business units |
| | Risk Assessments | Replace compliance-based approaches to internal audit and health, environmental and safety with risk assessments—risk "peer reviews" |

with those of shareholders. Asset growth has been dramatically reduced under SVA, from 15 percent per year to 2 percent.

DuPont relies on its risk philosophy to drive risk awareness. A component of this philosophy is the link between risk management and strategy: "The company is expected to manage risk at a level consistent with business strategy and not engage in activities that are inconsistent with the Corporate Financial Risk Management Policy." DuPont emphasizes that risk must be managed with a full understanding of what the company wants to achieve, not in isolation. This way, risk management is a natural outgrowth of operating the business and not an adjunct to it.

In addition, DuPont's adoption of earnings at risk helps ensure that all business units are speaking the same "risk language." EAR is a concept that has intuitive meaning for managers and therefore gives them a frame of reference for identifying and managing their key risks.

Microsoft's extensive intranet creates a seamless integration of risk management and everyday business management. Microsoft's risk management group offers Web-based knowledge tools for the management of risk. The intranet includes risk checklists, best practices, and other factual information for managers to consult in their day-to-day operations and for special projects. In addition, members of the risk management group are evaluated on the amount of face-to-face time they spend working with managers on risk issues. Not only is the risk management group seeking to instill a risk awareness in managers, it is also seeking insights from them—"leveraging wisdom." Risk Group Manager Lori Jorgensen describes it this way: "The job of the risk management group is to learn from them and see how we can leverage the wisdom gained across the enterprise and share best practices. Further, perhaps we can add some incremental value by providing information they have not considered."

The focus at UGG is on communication and the use of analytical tools. As the company has made enterprise-wide risk management a priority, the risk management committee has expended considerable effort in ensuring that everyone understands UGG's risk policies and the risk tolerances it is willing to accept. Communication is enhanced through more extensive use of analytical tools that can quantify a wider cross section of risks than ever before.

Unocal's risk assessments have become an important way to create risk awareness in the organization. Originally, these risk assessments were something of an experiment, but they have evolved into a required annual exercise within the business units, which are located all over the world. Participation in the business-unit risk assessments is broad, and the discussion and prioritization of the risks is thorough. The assessments are instrumental in changing the mind-set of managers and employees toward building risk into everyday decision making versus viewing risk management as the responsibility of staff people looking to see if they are in compliance with rules and regulations. Internal audits and health, environment, and safety audits are now structured around the assessment of risk and in some ways are looked on as peer reviews.

Each study company has its own methodology for creating an awareness of risk and risk management at all levels of the organization. Most key business risks were being controlled before the advent of enterprise-wide risk management, but the level and breadth of control appear much stronger now, and some significant cost efficiencies have been achieved. Risk management is no longer merely an adjunct to good overall business management but rather is an integral component.

*Value Lesson 16*

*Making risk consideration a part of the decision-making process is an essential element to enterprise-wide risk management.*

## Risk Infrastructure

As noted in chapter 1, the new paradigm assumes that enterprise-wide risk management will become part of strategic and operational decision making throughout the organization. The infrastructure that the case study companies use to accomplish that goal varies. For example, Microsoft does not see the need for a chief risk officer position but does have a risk management group headed by the treasurer. The group communicates the importance of taking a broad view of risk when making operational decisions. The internal reporting process provides timely information to the CFO and other senior management on the VAR measurement for financial risk. Microsoft's infrastructure may be characterized as driven by technology via the intranet and ongoing personal communication between the risk management group and operating management.

The Chase infrastructure is composed of committees in five risk areas: credit, market, capital, operating, and fiduciary (see figure 3.5, page 48). These five committees report to an executive committee, which provides a strategic and integrated view on risk management. The executive committee, in turn, reports to the risk policy committee of the board of directors, which has the ultimate responsibility for risk management. The committees use regular and timely reports to monitor their risk management responsibilities. Chase's infrastructure may be characterized as a highly organized committee structure to communicate and drive risk management considerations into operating decisions.

DuPont's infrastructure includes a risk management committee composed of high-level officers (see table 4.1, page 98). This committee assists the chief executive officer in setting risk management policies and guidelines. The committee maintains close contact with the businesses and has the authority to execute any financial instruments necessary to manage risks.

UGG's approach includes a risk management committee composed of high-level corporate officers. At both DuPont and UGG, the CFO is a member of the committee. In addition to recommending policy and process, the UGG risk management committee is responsible for reporting to the audit committee of the board of directors on risk management performance. The board of directors assigned responsibility for the Strategic Risk Management Project, which was the precursor to its enterprise-wide risk management approach, to the risk management committee.

At Unocal, enterprise-wide risk management has emanated from the Internal Audit Department and the Corporate Health, Environment, and Safety (HES) Department. Both groups strive to promote throughout the organization the idea that a good manager is a good *risk* manager and that risk management is a line function, not a staff function. The efforts of the internal audit department and HES provide the infrastructure to promote enterprise-wide risk management.

A summary of the risk management infrastructures appears in table 2.3.

*Table 2.3*
*Risk Infrastructures*

| Study Company | Risk Infrastructure |
|---|---|
| Chase | Highly organized committee structure to communicate and drive risk management considerations into operating decisions. |
| DuPont | Risk management committee assists CEO in setting risk management policies and guidelines. Committee maintains close contact with business units. |
| Microsoft | Driven by technology via intranet and ongoing personal communication of risk management group with operating management. |
| United Grain Growers | Risk management committee recommends policy and process; reports to audit committee on risk management performance. |
| Unocal | Efforts of internal audit and health, environmental and safety promote enterprise-wide risk management throughout operating management. |

*Value Lesson 17*

*Risk management infrastructures vary in form but are essential to driving throughout the organization the idea that decision makers should consider risks.*

## Champions of Enterprise-wide Risk Management

Adopting enterprise-wide risk management is a major cultural change for a company. To succeed, it needs commitment from the highest levels of management. It is not enough for senior management to merely begin the process and then go on to other things. The last thing most businesses need is another mandate from on high that is imposed, then left to wither and fade away. "People don't want another corporate initiative," says

General Auditor Karl Primm of Unocal, describing employees' aversion to "just another program from corporate."

In each of the study companies, enterprise-wide risk management is championed at the highest ranks. Unocal CFO Tim Ling, who had previously been a consultant with McKinsey & Co., believed strongly in the importance of viewing risk management as a primary component of good management. The rapid, successful introduction of enterprise-wide risk management at Unocal was possible only because of his personal commitment. Karl Primm in Internal Audit, and George Walker in Health, Environment, and Safety at Unocal spearheaded the risk management efforts in their areas and provided the cooperation and synthesis between the two corporate functions that was essential to the integration of the process.

Brent Callinicos, treasurer and a senior Microsoft "Risk Champion," makes it clear where risk management begins in his company: "At the end of the day, the chief risk officer is Bill Gates. He is the one who ultimately takes the risk of do we develop this product or go into this market." Lori Jorgensen, risk management group manager, and several other senior treasury officers, along with Callinicos, comprise the Risk Management Group at Microsoft.

At DuPont, Bruce Evancho observes, "The ultimate risk manager of any company is the CEO. What we're in business to do is to take risks and get rewards. If you don't have any risks then you're probably not going to have any rewards." DuPont's CEO, CFO, and treasurer have all played roles in the risk management integration process and were instrumental in shaping its success.

Chase's Shapiro is on the front line of risk management. He personally championed the development of shareholder value-added, the enormously successful effort that slowed Chase asset growth from 15 percent to 2 percent while maintaining profitability. SVA is at the heart of Chase's enterprise-wide risk management program. Senior officers Lesley Daniels Webster, Robert Strong, and Joseph Sclafani, representing the three major risk areas at Chase, play instrumental roles in advancing risk management as a major strategic focal point.

UGG's CEO Brian Hayward and CFO Peter Cox have advanced their company to the vanguard of enterprise-wide risk management best practices in North America. Although UGG is the smallest of the study companies, the risk management system there is state-of-the-art and reflects Cox's imaginative and strategic thinking in the field. Hayward is up-front about his own role: "My job is to protect the corporation so that we're in business the next day." George Prosk, treasurer; Brian Brown, head of internal audit; and Michael McAndless, corporate risk manager, form the remainder of the senior risk management team and have individually and collectively advanced UGG's efforts in significant ways.

Enterprise-wide risk management will succeed only in organizations where senior management is ready to put its full faith and effort into the program. The integration process requires a delicate balancing of various interests and skills and may affect some well-ensconced fiefdoms. Technical readiness and formal processes are important, but only high-level champions will make enterprise-wide risk management live up to its enormous potential.

---

*Value Lesson 18*

*A prerequisite for implementation of enterprise-wide risk management is the commitment of one or more champions at the senior management level.*

---

## Concluding Comments

Each of the five case-study companies has made considerable strides on the long journey of implementing enterprise-wide risk management. In this chapter, we have drawn 18 lessons from the case studies that follow. The individual case studies provide more detail on how these lessons have played out at each company.

We emphasize that senior managers cannot just delegate the task of implementing enterprise-wide risk management; they must be the champions of the effort. In particular, as one of the opening quotes to this chapter noted, a CFO who sees his or her role as a "risk-management wizard" can add immeasurably to the successful implementation of enterprise-wide risk management.

# Endnotes

1. Richard E. S. Boulton, Barry D. Libert, and Steve M. Samek, *Cracking the Value Code—How Successful Businesses Are Creating Wealth in the New Economy* (New York: HarperBusiness, 2000): 182.

2. Marcia Vickers, "Up from Bean Counter," in "The 21st Century Corporation," *Business Week* (August 28, 2000): 118.

3. The notional amount of a derivative contract is a stated amount upon which the contract's payments are based. The notional amount can be likened to the principal amount of a bond.

4. "Transfer of risk occurs when the firm passes a risk through to an independent financially capable third party at a reasonable economic cost under a legally enforceable arrangement. Transfer can be accomplished in many ways, e.g., through the insurance markets, by hedging risk in the capital markets, by sharing risk through joint venture investments or strategic alliances, through an outsourcing arrangement accompanied by a contractual risk transfer and by indemnifying risk through contractual agreements." (DeLoach, *Enterprise-Wide Risk Management,* 274).

# Chase Manhattan Corporation[*]

*Under the old system, as a person in the lending area, you were always incented to make loans you thought were good—even if they had marginal profitability—because you were paid on that income, and generally there is a positive spread. So if you'd made a loan, you'd generated more net income.*

*The current system says, "OK, you've made a loan. We're going to assign this much capital to it, and the loan spread may or may not cover the cost of that capital." In the two years before we introduced shareholder value-added (SVA), assets were growing at the rate of 15 percent per year. In the two and a half years since we introduced SVA, assets are growing at 2 percent per year. If you believe in incentive systems, this is the greatest proof that it works. SVA clearly puts in the incentive to reduce risk. People get paid to reduce risk.*

*We're in the business of taking risk, but we're in the business of getting paid for the risks that we take.*

Marc Shapiro, vice chairman

## Company Background

Chase Manhattan Corporation is the third-largest bank in the United States, behind Citigroup and Bank of America. In mid-2000, it had total assets of $400 billion and a market capitalization of $45 billion.[1] *Forbes* lists Chase as the fourth-largest company in the United States in total assets and as the 13th largest in its composite ranking of public companies based on sales, profits, assets, and market capitalization.

Chase earnings grew by 44 percent during the 1999 fiscal year, resulting in a 24 percent return on equity, compared with Citigroup's

[*] J.P. Morgan Chase & Co. as of December 31, 2000

22.7 percent and Bank of America's 17.5 percent returns. Chase is number one in syndicated loans (34 percent share), derivatives trading, U.S. dollars fund transfer, and mortgage origination. The company ranks number two in foreign-exchange trading, number three in investment-grade bonds, and number six in merger and acquisition counseling. Chase is the world's largest raiser of debt capital.[2]

The Chase Manhattan of 2000 is the result of two separate mergers in the 1990s involving three large banks: the merger of Chemical Bank and Manufacturers Hanover Trust in 1991, and the merger of Chemical and Chase in 1996. All three banks trace their roots to some of the earliest banking enterprises in the nation. In fact, Chase Manhattan dates back 200 years, to a public health crisis in New York City.

In 1799, there was a general outcry about the quality of the public water supply following an attack of yellow fever that struck hundreds of New Yorkers. Alexander Hamilton and Aaron Burr[3] were leaders of a group that lobbied for the establishment of a private company to provide water to New York. In March 1799, the New York State Legislature passed a bill to create such a water company, the Manhattan Company. Included in the bill was a provision that unexpended capital could be used for "any other...operations not inconsistent with the Constitution and laws of the United States." This provision enabled the board of the Manhattan Company to establish its own bank. Six months later, the Bank of the Manhattan Company opened its doors at 40 Wall Street with capital left over from the $2 million raised for the water company.[4]

A similar pattern would be repeated in the cases of Manufacturers Hanover Trust and Chemical Bank—companies were formed for industrial purposes, and later, subsidiary banks were started under the corporate umbrella. In 1812, New York Manufacturing Company was founded, and its operations eventually included a bank. Decades later, this bank became Manufacturers Hanover. In 1823, six businessmen, including a druggist and a wholesale grocer, formed the New York Chemical Manufacturing Company to produce dyes, medicines, and paint. A year later, banking was added to the product line. This bank became Chemical Bank.

Until 1838, banks were viewed as quasi-public institutions, and it could be difficult to obtain a charter for a stand-alone bank. It was considerably easier to apply for a charter to engage in other forms of business but with a charter broad enough to permit a banking operation to be started as a unit of the initial business. In addition, it was common for import-export firms to offer banking services such as the exchange of banknotes and stocks and bonds.

Chase National Bank was chartered in 1877 and named in honor of Salmon P. Chase, Treasury Secretary in Abraham Lincoln's administration.[5] Chase National Bank's founder, John Thompson, seemed to choose an unfortunate time to start the bank, soon after the Panic of 1872. Thompson responded to his critics with these words: "This is just the time to start a new bank. Everything has touched bottom. If there is any change at all, it must be for the better. A bank which has no real estate, not a debt in the world, no lawsuits and plenty of cash need fear nothing." The words proved to be prophetic. By the late 1920s, Chase National had accumulated assets of $1 billion and was the largest bank in the United States. In the 1930s, when thousands of other banks were closing during the Great Depression, Chase National did not lay off even a single employee.[6]

The three major banking companies that merged in the 1990s to form the present-day Chase Manhattan were themselves the products of scores of smaller mergers over almost 200 years. Over the years, they pioneered many of the innovations in financial services that are common today: check endorsements, bank credit departments, check-clearing houses, automated teller machine networks, and home electronic banking. Figure 3.1 displays timelines of the three banks from their nineteenth-century roots to today, and figure 3.2 shows a graph of the stock price of Chase Manhattan from 1987 to May 2000.

## Figure 3.1
## Chase Manhattan Timeline

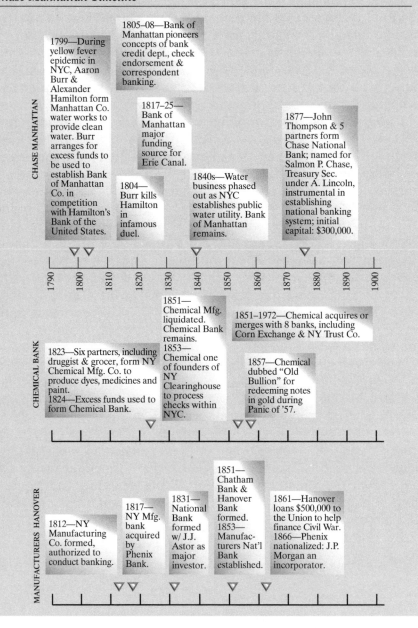

*Figure 3.1*
*Chase Manhattan Timeline (Continued)*

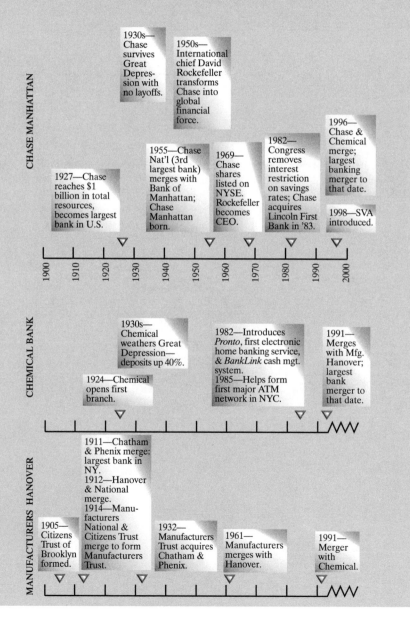

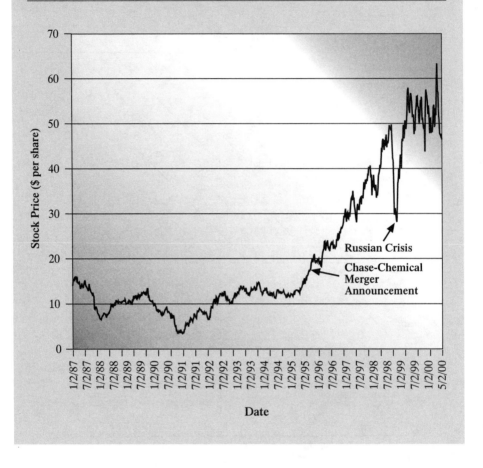

*Figure 3.2*
*Chase Stock Price, January 1987 to May 2000*

## Chase Manhattan Today

We see the fear of higher interest rates driving down stock prices across all financial companies. And yet the way we manage our company today, we're indifferent to which way interest rates move. We can make money in a rising environment or in a falling environment.

We think a balanced bank is the right answer because it provides a diversification you have to have, as long as you have leadership in each of your businesses. The key to reducing risk is to have diversification across your businesses and have leadership positions. I think the old banks were very spread out. Our predecessors didn't have leadership positions in each of [their] businesses. That's the biggest change in the new Chase. We're a 200-year-old company, but really we're a two-year-old company since the merger between Chase and Chemical has created a brand-new company.[7]

Marc Shapiro

For very large banks like today's Chase Manhattan, banking extends far beyond the historical function of taking in customer deposits and lending the money to borrowers. In the traditional approach, banks generated net income from the spread between the interest earned from loans and the cost of the funds loaned out. Bank failures were typically caused by an excess of bad loans or a "run," in which customers wanted their funds on deposit back and the bank did not have sufficient funds available to meet those demands. The primary risks were credit risk (borrowers cannot repay their obligations) and liquidity risk (the bank cannot repay depositors). Over time, federal and state governments enacted strict regulations and monitoring plans to ensure that banks controlled these risks.

Chase Manhattan is a prototype of the large, modern, global banking institution. While Chase still lends money and makes a profit on the interest spread, this part of its operations is small in relation to the other, more profitable services it provides. Figure 3.3 displays the elements of the three major businesses that comprise Chase: Global Bank, National Consumer Services, and Global Services.

*Figure 3.3*
*Segment Composition*

**GLOBAL BANK**

| | |
|---|---|
| Global Markets | Sales, trading, origination, underwriting and research covering foreign exchange, derivatives and fixed-income capital markets |
| Chase Capital Partners | Private equity investments |
| Global Investment Banking | Syndicated financing, M&A advisory, high-yield securities underwriting, private placements |
| Corporate Lending and Portfolio Management | Credit and lending services emphasizing origination with distribution |
| Global Private Bank | Banking services for high-net-worth individuals |

**NATIONAL CONSUMER SERVICES**

| | |
|---|---|
| Chase Cardmember Services | Credit card issuance and servicing; merchant processing |
| Regional Consumer Banking | Consumer and small business banking in New York and Texas |
| Chase Home Finance | Origination and servicing of residential mortgage loans |
| Diversified Consumer Services | Origination of auto loans and leases; student loans; investment products |
| Middle Markets | Financial services to middle-market companies in New York and Texas |

**GLOBAL SERVICES**

| | |
|---|---|
| Global Investor Services | Custody and other investor services to mutual funds, investment managers, etc. |
| Chase Treasury Solutions | Treasury, cash management, and other services to companies, governments, etc. |
| Capital Markets Fiduciary Services | Processing services for securities issuers |

| **REVENUE BY SEGMENT 1999** | **CASH PROFIT BY SEGMENT 1999** |
|---|---|
|  | 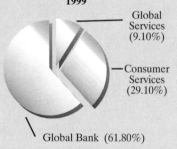 |

REVENUE BY SEGMENT 1999: Global Services (13.30%), Consumer Services (42.20%), Global Bank (44.50%)

CASH PROFIT BY SEGMENT 1999: Global Services (9.10%), Consumer Services (29.10%), Global Bank (61.80%)

Source: Adapted from 1999 Chase Manhattan 10-K Filing.

Global Bank provides an array of services that centers on securities, investments, and syndications. Chase is one of the world's largest capital markets trading organizations, and that function is included in Global Bank's Global Markets unit. Chase Capital Partners is the world's largest private equity investor, investing primarily in New Economy companies.[8] The lending of money through Global Bank is centered on the origination and syndication of loans[9] and the subsequent servicing of loans. Chase actually holds very few of these loans as assets in its own portfolio.

National Consumer Services provides credit cards and auto and mortgage loan origination to individuals and small businesses in the United States. Global Services focuses on furnishing an array of investor, cash management, and processing services to investment companies and other businesses.

As figure 3.3 shows, Global Bank and National Consumer Services generate almost the same amount of revenue, about 42 to 44 percent each, but Global Bank is immensely more profitable. In 1999, Global Bank earned about 62 percent of Chase cash profit, compared with National Consumer Services' share of 29 percent. Table 3.1 shows a breakdown of revenues and profits by major business and units within the two larger businesses, as well as other metrics. It is striking to realize that almost half of Chase's profits derive from its capital market activities and private equity investments. (See shaded portion of table 3.1.)

Loans receivable on Chase's balance sheet dated December 31, 1999, were $173 billion out of total assets of $406 billion, or 43 percent. Consumer loans comprise less than half of loans outstanding. Over 90 percent of the commercial loans initiated by Chase end up being placed with investors and other institutions. Chase earns money on these loans mainly through origination and servicing fees. This "laying off" of loan capital on others is a key component of Chase's overall risk management strategy.

*Table 3.1*
*Segment Results ($ in millions)*

| | Global Bank | | National Consumer Services | | Global Services | | Support/Corporate | | Total | |
|---|---|---|---|---|---|---|---|---|---|---|
| | 1999 | 1998 | 1999 | 1998 | 1999 | 1998 | 1999 | 1998 | 1999 | 1998 |
| Operating revenue | $10,379 | $7,955 | $9,847 | $9,149 | $3,120 | $2,826 | ($364) | ($317) | $22,982 | $19,613 |
| Cash operating earnings | 3,564 | 2,387 | 1,677 | 1,445 | 525 | 486 | (75) | (41) | 5,691 | 4,277 |
| Average common equity | 12,616 | 11,976 | 7,823 | 7,643 | 2,855 | 2,183 | (1,317) | (474) | 21,977 | 21,328 |
| Average managed assets | 235,197 | 251,363 | 129,314 | 119,046 | 16,540 | 14,336 | 6,807 | 6,477 | 387,858 | 391,222 |
| Shareholder value added | 1,885 | 776 | 636 | 418 | 145 | 193 | 97 | 19 | 2,763 | 1,406 |
| Cash return on common equity | 27.9% | 19.4% | 21.1% | 18.5% | 18.1% | 21.8% | | | 25.6% | 19.6% |

**Detail for 1999, Global Bank & National Consumer Services**

| Global Bank | Operating Revenues 1999 | Cash Operating Earnings 1999 |
|---|---|---|
| Global Markets | $4,090 | $1,369 |
| Chase Capital Partners | 2,330 | 1,383 |
| Global Investment Banking | 1,576 | 335 |
| Corporate Lending/Portfolio Mgt. | 1,546 | 548 |
| Other | 837 | (71) |
| Total Global Bank | $10,379 | $3,564 |

| National Consumer Services | Operating Revenues 1999 | Cash Operating Earnings 1999 |
|---|---|---|
| Chase Cardmember Services | $4,004 | $523 |
| Regional Consumer Banking | 2,410 | 420 |
| Chase Home Finance | 1,212 | 284 |
| Diversified Consumer Services | 1,125 | 187 |
| Middle Market and Other | 1,096 | 263 |
| Total National Consumer Services | $9,847 | $1,677 |

| Major Contributors to Earnings | 1999 | |
|---|---|---|
| Chase Capital Partners | $1,383 | 24.0% |
| Global Markets | 1,369 | 23.7% |
| Corp. Lending/Portfolio Mgt. | 548 | 9.5% |
| Global Services | 525 | 9.1% |
| Chase Cardmember Services | 523 | 9.1% |
| All Other | 1,418 | 24.6% |
| Cash Operating Earnings* | $5,766 | 100.0% |
| *Before support/corporate | | |

Source: Adapted from 1999 Chase Manhattan 10-K Filing.

## Risk at Chase Manhattan

The two biggest ways I get comfortable with risk are diversification and controls. We're extremely diversified, and we're diversified because of the size and the scope of the institution and the diversity of businesses that we're in. And we're diversified within the main risks, which are credit and market risk, because we have so many different transactions. We have fairly low limits in terms of what any one transaction can do, and in that diversification, there's enormous protection.

The second way I get comfortable is the quality and institutionalization of the controls at the micro level. The credit approval process and the trading monitoring process—we are probably the most vigilant about those two processes, and that's where I think we have very good systems.

Marc Shapiro, vice chairman

Chase splits its overall risk into three basic components: market risk, credit risk, and operating risk. Market risk is the risk of losing money because the market price of an asset or a rate changes unfavorably. For example, suppose Chase holds a short position in French francs and the price of the franc increases.[10] Appendix 3.1 contains a discussion of market risk at Chase and the management of those risks, drawn from the company's 1999 annual report (10-K). Market risk is covered in some detail later in this chapter.

Credit risk is the risk of loss because a counterparty to a contract does not perform, such as when a customer defaults on a loan. This is the type of risk most closely associated with the traditional banking function of loaning money and collecting principal and interest. Figure 3.4 discusses the nature and management of credit risk at Chase.

Operating risk is the "risk of loss due to fraud by employees or outsiders, unauthorized transactions by employees, and errors relating to computer and telecommunications systems."[11] To a large extent, it results from deficiencies in internal control systems. For example, Christopher Goggins, a trader in the foreign exchange and interest rate markets, reportedly overstated the value of his foreign exchange forwards positions by some $60 million over a period of about a year. Chase's internal processes identified and captured this overstatement, but it caused Chase

*Figure 3.4*
*Company Description of Credit Risk and Its Measurement*

## CREDIT RISK MANAGEMENT

Credit risk is the risk of loss due to borrower or counterparty default. Credit risk is managed at both the transaction and portfolio levels. Risk management processes are disciplined and designed both to preserve the independence and integrity of risk assessment and to integrate effectively with business management.

## CREDIT RISK MANAGEMENT PROCESS

### Risk Measurement

Chase's credit risk management discipline begins with an assessment of the risk of loss resulting from default by an obligor or counterparty. All credit exposures are assessed, whether on or off balance sheet. These exposures include loans, receivables under derivative and foreign exchange contracts, and lending-related commitments (e.g., letters of credit and undrawn commitments to extend credit).

Using statistical techniques, estimates are made, for each segment of the portfolio, of expected losses (on average, over a cycle) and unexpected losses. The latter represent the potential volatility of actual losses relative to the expected level of loss. These estimates drive the credit cost allocations to business units, which are incorporated into the business unit SVA measurement. Consequently, a unit's credit risk profile is an important factor in assessing its performance.

Credit losses are not the most significant indicator of risk. If losses were entirely predictable, the expected loss rate could be factored into product prices and covered as a normal and recurring cost of doing business. It is the volatility or uncertainty of loss rates around expected levels that creates risk and is the primary concern of credit risk management.

The risks of the consumer and commercial portfolios are markedly different. Broadly speaking losses on consumer exposures are more predictable, less volatile and less cyclical than losses on commercial exposures. For the latter, the loss volatility can be much greater over the course of an economic cycle.

### The Cost of Credit Risk-Loss Provisions and Capital Allocation

Chase uses its estimates of expected loss and loss volatility, respectively, to set risk-adjusted loss provisions and allocate credit risk capital by portfolio segment. Within the consumer businesses, allocations are differentiated by product and product segment. In the commercial portfolio, allocations are differentiated by risk rating, maturity and industry. Off-balance sheet exposures are converted to loan equivalent amounts, based on their probability of being drawn, before applying the expected loss and capital factors.

*Figure 3.4*
*Company Description of Credit Risk and Its Measurement (Continued)*

**Risk Management Processes**

Chase's credit risk management process is guided by policies and procedures established by the Chief Credit Officer. At both the business unit and corporate levels, disciplined processes are in place that are intended to ensure that risks are accurately assessed and properly approved and monitored.

 In addition to establishing corporate-wide policies and procedures, the Chief Credit Officer has the primary responsibility for the credit risk measurement framework, allocating the cost of credit, assessing concentration risks, setting limits to provide for adequate portfolio diversification, delegating approval authorities and managing problem assets.

Within each major business unit an independent credit risk management function reports jointly to the business executive and the Chief Credit Officer. These units are responsible for the tactical credit decision making. They approve significant new transactions and product offerings, have the final authority over credit risk assessment and monitor the credit risk profile of the business unit's portfolio.

**Credit Risk Management for Consumers Assets**

Consumer credit risk management uses sophisticated portfolio modeling, credit scoring and decision support tools to project credit risks and establish underwriting standards. Risk parameters are established in the early stages of product development, and the cost of credit risk is an integral part of the pricing and evaluation of a product's profit dynamics. Consumers portfolios are monitored to identify deviations from expected performance and shifts in consumers' patterns of behavior.

**Credit Risk Management for Commercial Assets**

Within the commercial sector, credit risk management begins with the client selection process. Chase's global industry approach helps Chase to be aware of an industry's developing risk so that exposures can be reduced where risk is increasing. Overseas, client selection is especially important. Chase's international strategy, especially in emerging markets, is to focus on the largest, leading firms with cross-border financing needs.

Concentration management is critical to managing commercial credit risk. Chase manages concentrations by obligor, risk grade, industry, product and geographic location. Concentration management is also facilitated by Chase's strategy of origination for distribution.

Source: Adapted from 1999 Chase Manhattan 10-K Filing.

to restate its fourth quarter 1999 revenues downward by the $60 million amount.[12] In isolated cases, the impact of operating risk can be ruinous. In 1995, Barings Bank, one of the world's oldest and most respected financial institutions, was destroyed by the unauthorized trades of a Singapore-based futures trader named Nick Leeson.[13]

As Marc Shapiro says, Chase believes that the keys to managing its major risks are diversification and strong controls. An integral part of the control process is the risk management committee structure. This structure begins with the risk policy committee of the board of directors, continues to the executive committee, and then flows to the committees on credit risk, market risk, and capital, and two new committees, operating risk and fiduciary risk. (The recent establishment of a separate fiduciary risk committee reflects a decision to manage fiduciary risk separately from other forms of operating risk.) This structure is depicted in figure 3.5.

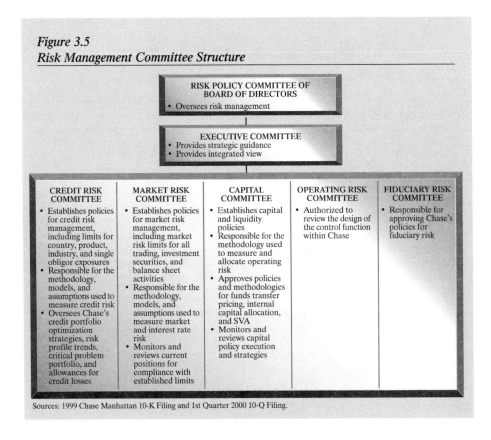

**Figure 3.5**
**Risk Management Committee Structure**

| RISK POLICY COMMITTEE OF BOARD OF DIRECTORS | | | | |
| --- | --- | --- | --- | --- |
| • Oversees risk management | | | | |

| EXECUTIVE COMMITTEE | | | | |
| --- | --- | --- | --- | --- |
| • Provides strategic guidance<br>• Provides integrated view | | | | |

| CREDIT RISK COMMITTEE | MARKET RISK COMMITTEE | CAPITAL COMMITTEE | OPERATING RISK COMMITTEE | FIDUCIARY RISK COMMITTEE |
| --- | --- | --- | --- | --- |
| • Establishes policies for credit risk management, including limits for country, product, industry, and single obligor exposures<br>• Responsible for the methodology, models, and assumptions used to measure credit risk<br>• Oversees Chase's credit portfolio optimization strategies, risk profile trends, critical problem portfolio, and allowances for credit losses | • Establishes policies for market risk management, including market risk limits for all trading, investment securities, and balance sheet activities<br>• Responsible for the methodology, models, and assumptions used to measure market risk<br>• Monitors and reviews current positions for compliance with established limits | • Establishes capital and liquidity policies<br>• Responsible for the methodology used to measure and allocate operating risk<br>• Approves policies and methodologies for funds transfer pricing, internal capital allocation, and SVA<br>• Monitors and reviews capital policy execution and strategies | • Authorized to review the design of the control function within Chase | • Responsible for approving Chase's policies for fiduciary risk |

Sources: 1999 Chase Manhattan 10-K Filing and 1st Quarter 2000 10-Q Filing.

While diversification and controls are critical, in early 1998, Chase introduced a concept that quickly became a cornerstone of its enterprise-wide risk management effort: shareholder value-added.

## Shareholder Value-Added

I was worried that assets were growing too fast and people weren't making those [risk-reward] trade-offs. There were various convoluted models being tossed around, and I thought they were all too complicated to understand. Value-added is a pretty simple concept when you get down to it, and if it's a pretty simple concept, people can understand it. And there were some problems in the company because people didn't trust the financial systems, so they were all making up their own standards by which they ought to be judged and adjusting the numbers and that sort of thing.

So we said, "Look we're going to go with one standard and it's going to apply to everybody in the corporation. You can't adjust the numbers; these are the numbers we're going to judge you by no matter what numbers you come up with." And it worked.

It was a desire to have a simple, accountable system that people could understand and that would have the desired benefit of helping us control the amount of capital we use because we were using too much capital.

Marc Shapiro

To put it simply, Chase's SVA calculates a profit amount by subtracting a charge for invested capital from cash operating earnings. It is Chase's refinement of the tried-and-true concept of residual income, used for decades by corporate America for internal reporting purposes.[14] The importance of SVA lies in its automatic linkage of risks and rewards through the use of *risk-adjusted capital.*

At Chase, decision makers are evaluated on the basis of their individual SVA metric. If the decision maker approves a loan or takes a trading position, his or her SVA will increase if the cash return exceeds the capital charge (currently 13 percent of risk-adjusted capital). A decision maker who consumes proportionately more capital is expected to earn a higher cash return and is rewarded accordingly. Chase's 1999 annual report explains it this way: "SVA measures the dollar benefit (or cost) of employing capital to the business units versus returning capital to shareholders. Management measures each business unit on its contribution to long-term growth in SVA."

In one move—the introduction of SVA—Chase solved two major problems:

1. It found a way to make all business decisions incorporate an explicit consideration of risk. Line decision makers across a very broad spectrum of diverse businesses are evaluated on the basis of their success or failure in managing the risks unique to their environments. The evaluation is done routinely and automatically, and everyone understands the ground rules.

2. It found a way to reduce asset growth. Invested capital was growing too rapidly, at a compounded rate of 15 percent per year. Chase was profitable, but this growth rate by itself created enormous incremental risk. Shapiro is proud of a graph (see figure 3.6) that shows the highly positive impact of the introduction of SVA: Risk-adjusted assets were growing at 15 percent in the period preceding SVA. In the post-SVA period, the graph flattens out to a 2 percent growth rate, while cash income is at a healthy 17 percent growth rate. Shapiro credits SVA with this turnaround.

Another advantage of SVA is the way it aligns the interests of decision makers throughout the company with the interests of the company's shareholders. Shapiro explains,

We believe what the shareholders want is growth of free cash flow. They may also want revenue growth. But at the end of the day, economic theory teaches us that stock prices reflect discounted value of future free cash flow. Effectively, we define SVA as free cash flow. At a corporate level, you can say earnings per share is a pretty good proxy for that, because if you don't need to grow capital, then you can reduce shares and therefore you can grow earnings per share faster.

If you do need capital, you issue shares and if that's a good transaction, that's OK, and the share count kind of rationalizes that. The problem is that at a divisional level, we don't have a share count. So we have to do something that rewards people for retiring capital. At the corporate level we had that. It's called repurchasing stock, making our share count go down. At the divisional level we didn't have any way to encourage people to retire capital. So the way I see it, SVA aligns divisional management with shareholder interest in a way no other thing can because we don't have the equivalent of earnings per share at a divisional level.

*Figure 3.6*
*Shareholder Value-Added Impact*

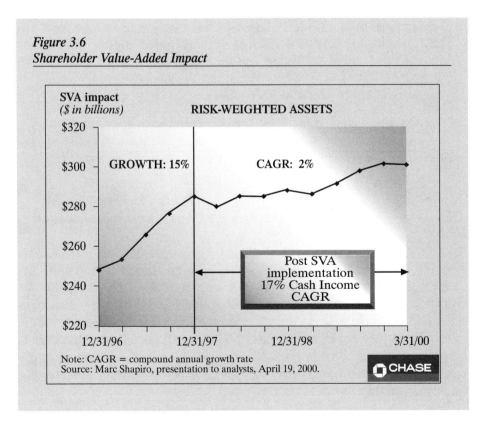

Note: CAGR = compound annual growth rate
Source: Marc Shapiro, presentation to analysts, April 19, 2000.

# Market Risk

There's nothing that stands static in this business. It has great analogies to Silicon Valley in a sense. It's a business that's open pretty much 24 hours a day now, and it's a business where people work incredible hours with incredible amounts of information on incredible and mind-boggling deadlines. You need to put a price on a huge amount of risk in 10 minutes, and so you're always reinventing.

Generally speaking, as a trader, you share in the gains in the position but do not share in the losses once your P&L [profit and loss] is zero for the year. Because of the structure of the incentives, it's very important that traders and businesses be allocated capital proportionately to their real risk. They're allocated capital, they're charged for capital, and their capital charge comes off the top in terms of business risks. Their incentives are aligned closely [to the company's] but it's not a perfect system.

So what that means is the capital has to push the risk. It means [the measurement of capital] has to be plausible. But it also means that risk calculations have to take into account the unlikely situations. That's why stress tests become very important.

Lesley Daniels Webster,
executive vice president, market risk management

The management of market risk at Chase is grounded in two methodologies that are complementary but reflect different approaches to risk measurement: value at risk (VAR) and stress testing. Business units and decision makers are charged for invested capital under SVA based on 13 percent of the *higher* of VAR or stress test results. This is how the capital becomes risk-adjusted. VAR and stress testing apply conservative what-if scenarios to some 250,000 positions outstanding on any given day.

## Value at Risk

VAR can be defined differently for different applications, but here is how Chase defines it for the purpose of managing market risk: "VAR is a measure of the dollar amount of potential loss from adverse market moves in an everyday market environment. The VAR looks forward one trading day and is the loss expected to be exceeded with a 1 in 100 chance." This approach is based on historical simulation and assumes that the most recent one-year historical changes in interest rates, foreign exchange rates, and equity and commodity prices are good indicators of future changes. The simulation is applied to trading positions at the end of each trading day. The results are reported by individual position and also aggregated across businesses, geographies, currencies, and type of risk. Table 3.2 shows Chase's VAR results for its trading portfolio, as reported in its 1999 annual report, broken down by major components.

## Stress Testing

Stress testing is a process of applying worst-case scenarios to the trading portfolio in what Chase describes as "plausible events in abnormal markets." These scenarios fall into two categories:

1. Reenactments of historical crises such as the Russian currency collapse of 1998 and the 1987 stock market crash.

2. Carefully chosen hypothetical situations such as geopolitical turmoil causing a "flight to quality" in stable countries.

Chase's 1999 stress test dollar amounts are shown in table 3.3.

The stress tests are performed weekly on random dates and resemble the VAR calculations, as Webster explains,

> One of the interesting things about stress testing is that it uses the same architecture that we use for value at risk: the same systems, the same fact assumptions, same *modus operandi* in terms of calculation. Some stress tests are similar to doing a very narrow cut of value at risk, only a stress test does not point to the past. But it uses the same set of positions from a randomly selected date that we would run through value at risk.

*Table 3.2*
*Value-at-Risk (VAR) Disclosures*

**Value-at-Risk**

The table that follows represents Chase's average and period-end VARs for its total
trading portfolio and for each of the major components constituting that portfolio.

| (in millions) | Marked-to-Market Trading Portfolio | | | | |
|---|---|---|---|---|---|
| | Year Ended December 31, 1999 | | | At December 31, 1999 | At December 31, 1998 |
| | Average VAR | Minimum VAR | Maximum VAR | VAR | VAR |
| Interest Rate | $20.2 | $10.7 | $36.5 | $20.0 | $20.1 |
| Foreign Exchange | 7.0 | 2.3 | 21.3 | 3.0 | 2.3 |
| Equities | 6.3 | 3.4 | 10.1 | 7.2 | 4.6 |
| Commodities | 3.5 | 1.9 | 9.0 | 3.4 | 2.6 |
| Hedge Fund Investments | 4.1 | 3.1 | 4.6 | 3.3 | NA |
| Less: Portfolio Diversification | (17.0) | NM | NM | (13.7) | (8.9) |
| Total VAR | $24.1 | $12.3 | $41.8 | $23.2 | $20.7 |

NM—Because the minimum and maximum may occur on different days for different
risk components, it is not meaningful to compute a portfolio diversification effect.
In addition, Chase's average and period-end VAR is less than the sum of the VARs of
its market risk components due to risk offsets resulting from portfolio diversification.

NA—Not available. Chase started reporting in 1999 its market risk exposure to hedge
fund investments as a separate VAR category.

Source: 1999 Chase Manhattan 10-K Filing.

The hypothetical scenarios for stress testing are carefully chosen for
their relevance to the types of businesses in which Chase operates. Poor-
ly selected stress test scenarios would be at best of little value, and at
worst, misleading. Webster describes Chase's thinking on the hypothetical scenarios:

We construct hypothetical scenarios because history repeats itself,
but not always the same way. There are nuances to how the markets
develop; there are nuances to how market participants interact.
They change over time: the leverage in the system may change or
risk appetite of other dealers may change. So it [scenario construc-
tion] is something that you need to come back to and evaluate, and
so we do hypothetical scenarios.

**Table 3.3**
*Stress Testing Disclosures*

**Stress Testing**

The following table represents the potential stress test loss (pre-tax) in Chase's trading portfolio predicted by Chase's stress test scenarios. This is the first year that Chase is providing this stress testing information. Chase's average potential trading-related stress test loss was predicted to be approximately $186 million pre-tax in 1999. Chase's largest potential stress test loss of $302 million was observed under a replay of the historical 1998 Russian crisis scenario. At the date of this stress test, Chase had a larger-than-usual exposure to interest rates in Latin America and Asia. In addition to the 1998 Russian crisis scenario, the historical 1994 bond market sell-off scenario frequently is a scenario that produces potential large stress test losses in Chase's trading portfolio.

| | Marked-to-Market Trading Activities Largest Monthly Stress Test—Pre-Tax | | | | |
| | Year Ended December 31, 1999 | | | At December 1999 | At December 1998 |
| (in millions) | Average | Minimum | Maximum | | |
|---|---|---|---|---|---|
| Stress Test Loss–Pre-tax | $(186) | $(112) | $(302) | $(231) | $(150) |

Source: 1999 Chase Manhattan 10-K Filing.

The Market Risk Committee has the responsibility of approving these scenarios. Periodically, we have a very full discussion in the committee about these scenarios. We talk about them and their relevance. There are really two things we ask from the scenarios. First, they have to be pertinent to our risks. There's not much sense in running a stress test on a hypothetical scenario if it doesn't really have any import in terms of the risk—something like an earthquake in Japan. It has some pertinence, but it's not really a big event for us.

Second, hypothetical scenarios have to be unlikely but plausible. What does it mean for something to be unlikely? It means *ex ante* not being forecastable. It's very hard to form a model with such and such probability that this is likely to happen because you're in an area of stress testing where things are impossible to predict. The best you can do is form some sort of judgment about what makes them happen. So they have to be unlikely, but they also have to be plausible. There has to be a story. It can be a political story, it can be an economic story, it could have any of those footings but there has to be a story, a logic that makes the scenario compelling, believable. The scenarios have to be believable but they have to be unlikely, and that's the test.

In the management of market risk, VAR and stress testing are augmented by nonstatistical measures of the size and direction of an exposure. They typically will involve a sensitivity analysis to gauge the impact of, say, a change in market rates.

This approach to managing market risk, with its reliance on VAR, stress testing, and SVA, has worked well for Chase. Webster gives some additional insights on the system's strengths in the highly decentralized world of trading:

> What it's done is allow us to cut our risk profile by about 50 percent from what it was in '97. These businesses take risk in a very decentralized fashion because trading has a very decentralized decision-making structure. We have about 1,200 to 1,300 traders scattered around the world. It's very decentralized. If you look at a loan decision, you will usually find a hierarchy of approval signatures. If you look at a trading ticket, it will normally just have the trader's initials on it—so it's a very different form of risk taking. There is an understanding all the way down to the trader of how much risk to take. There's tremendous dovetailing of interest. Traders would like to *retire* from their jobs [as opposed to losing them].

## Credit Risk

> We're very explicit because we have very clear, open models of how we allocate the capital. We take credit risk by grade, by tenor, by a variety of factors that we can put into a pricing model so that somebody, when they're making a loan decision, can tell exactly what SVA is being created or destroyed by that loan decision.
>
> Marc Shapiro

Chase has managed its credit risk in recent years through two mechanisms:

1. Transferring much of the risk to other institutions via syndication.

2. Applying the SVA methodology to performance evaluation within the credit extension units.

Chase originates about $500 billion in syndicated loans each year but retains only about 7 percent for its own portfolio. Chase earns interest income on the retained portions of the loans and income on origination and servicing. This reinvention of the credit issuance function dramatically alters Chase's credit risk profile. Chief credit officer Robert Strong explains the results when the current loan portfolio is stress tested:

> We put our portfolio against a very deep recession scenario. We take our two portfolios that historically have had the biggest loss components and we crush those. We take our defaults up to the highest they've been in any recession and we run it out on a two-year basis and say, "How bad can it get? How ugly can this be?" It's relatively ugly, but what is interesting is it's an *earnings issue* as opposed to a safety and sound-capital issue. That's the fundamental difference today.

Strong's point is that while bad economic conditions will no doubt have a negative effect on earnings, the bank's capital base will still be secure. But even the earnings impact is not as severe as might be expected. Strong continues:

> Our most volatile is our wholesale side. We have roughly 50 percent wholesale and 50 percent retail. On the retail piece [for stress testing], we take a deep recession scenario in the United States; we take personal bankruptcy up over 2 million. It peaked at about 1.35 million a year or so ago. So we really crush that. But you still don't get as much draw on your charge-offs because the retail piece is much more of a diverse pool. You've got a big impact on your wholesale charge-offs but when you add them all together, you still don't get all that big an impact on the corporation given our total earnings.
>
> The biggest reason is we've significantly taken risk out of the consolidated balance sheet. In 1986, our wholesale risk assets were about 10 times our capital, post-reserves. Today they are 4.4. And so the one portfolio that has the most volatility has been significantly isolated. We used to be 80 percent wholesale and 20 percent consumer, with the three [predecessor] banks combined. We're now 50/50. That was a very conscious move to take the risk profile down.

The syndication process is the tactic by which we've achieved the strategic objective of significantly bringing down the wholesale risk portfolio while growing wholesale revenues. We have fewer wholesale loans on our books today than we had 12 years ago. So we set out to "de-risk" the place by reducing concentrations—industry and obligor—and by reducing the aggregate concentration of wholesale in our portfolio. Not only did we reduce it relatively, we reduced it in absolute terms to less than half of what it used to be.

SVA has had a dramatic effect on Chase's efforts to communicate its credit risk appetite to line management. Since SVA is calculated using a charge for risk-adjusted capital, two behaviors are reinforced:

1. Retain less of the outstanding loan because it reduces the capital charge.

2. Ensure that loan pricing includes a sufficient premium for risk because riskier loans will be charged higher risk-adjusted capital.

Strong gives an example of the first point:

[For SVA,] we add a 50 percent premium to each dollar of capital over $3 million. We don't like big exposures. So if the model says you're going to have $4 million in capital, we hit you with $4.5 million because that $1 million increment gets an extra 50 percent. So $3 million in capital is a fairly modest amount, and we have $26 billion in capital; $3 million tends to be a pretty granular part of our portfolio. And that's the way we like it.

David Pflug, managing director of Global Bank Credit, elaborates on the second point: "It's probabilistic. Grade 1 [least risky] attracts a certain amount of capital; a grade 10 attracts a much higher amount of capital. [For a $1 million loan with 20 percent retention] at a grade 10, you would have to provide probably $400,000 to $500,000 [in capital]. It's very mechanistic." Yet even with the risk charges under SVA, Chase really has little interest in loans with a significant default probability. Pflug explains,

Internally the risk rating is less important than "should we do it or shouldn't we." Yes if you're doing it, there are very few loans that from the get-go are not profitable. So it's more the size risk: how much do we underwrite, and how much do we sell down? Those are much more the decisions.

I have very few arguments over whether something is a grade 5 or a grade 6 since our philosophy is to underwrite and sell. So we're pretty aggressive in underwriting, meaning we're awfully unaggressive in retaining. And where the capital charge will really bite is if you hold that asset for its duration. We should sell down as far as we can go. I would say the worse the grade, the more interested we are in selling it. But if there's a pretty good risk of default, then you can't really do that anyway.

But even with all the emphasis on distributing loans to others to carry, Chase always retains some portion of each loan it syndicates. Strong describes the reasoning for this:

Our basic model for wholesale [lending] was "you originate, you distribute, you get paid for the origination and the structuring." The less you hold, the less capital you need and the more those [origination and structuring] fees leveraged the return on capital. If we hold you responsible for maximizing return on capital, you [as a manager] have a natural desire to hold as little as possible in that transaction.

Now at the same time—and we think this in an important issue for us, which on the surface seems to go against credit but in fact is supportive of credit—we hold a piece of everything we do. We do not believe in the model of selling anything we can in the market; we don't sell, wash our hands, and get out of there. We think it's important to the client to know we're there. We know it's critical to our investors to know we're going to be there with them and when things do happen and problems occur, we have a world-class group of problem solvers in our special loan group who can get in and professionally manage these things.

## Mark-to-Market[15]

When Russia had its meltdown [in 1998], we announced that we thought we might lose $250 million in Russia. But in the next few weeks, we lost $30 *billion* of market [capitalization]. People were saying that seemed like an extreme reaction. The credit spread blew out tremendously at that time: our emerging market deals went up to LIBOR plus 10.[16] You take that environment and you mark-to-market a $120 billion loan portfolio, and you're going to have $30 billion of loss.

Robert Strong

I think on credit risk, we're moving to a mark-to-market world, whereas credit risk has historically been a non-mark-to-market world. I think there's a lot of work to be done on the credit side in terms of how you go to a mark-to-market world: the credit spreads become important, whereas historically, banks have earned credit on the basis of expected loss.

Marc Shapiro

Strong cited the stock market's reaction to the news of Chase's $250 million in Russian losses in August and September 1998. (See the notation on the graph in figure 3.2.) His point was that the market was implicitly adjusting all of Chase's emerging markets loan portfolio downward to incorporate the higher risk premiums. The traditional approach to credit risk focuses on expected losses, not market valuations. Yet in the world in which Chase operates, a mark-to-market approach to the loan portfolio makes sense for two reasons:

1. As a public company, Chase's shares are constantly revalued based on existing market conditions, which include the market variables affecting the value of the loan portfolio.

2. Chase relies heavily on selling off large pieces of its loan portfolio as a basic risk management tool. The marketplace cannot be expected to pay more than the current market price for the portfolio pieces.

Current accounting and regulatory requirements concentrate on expected losses for the balance sheet valuation of loans receivable. Still,

Shapiro and Strong recognize that an even better alignment of incentives would be possible if SVA included measures based on variables other than just risk-adjusted capital as currently defined—variables that would capture other market-related phenomena. Strong expresses the sentiment this way:

> So conceptually, we may not be perfect. Maybe right now we think we're not getting our proper share prices. We've got to find a way to more accurately measure what that change is in the market value [of the loans] and then ultimately use that to reinforce the behavior we want on people's part to do the right thing. What we need to do is to build models and processes that provide that reinforcement.

## Operating Risk

[The management of] operating risk is newer, and much less advanced. We've just set up a group to do what we're doing in credit risk and market risk. In credit risk, we probably have a 20-year credit history, in market risk we have a 10-year history, and in operating risk, we've got a no-year history but our thought is, we need to do much of the same thing.

I'm not a believer that you can quantify operating risk in exactly the same way [as the other two]. A lot of operating risk is so random that it's hard to develop models that are reasonable predictors. But I think what you can do is share best practices, look at an overall, executive-level view of the system for controlling operating risk, develop the metrics that you need in each business, and then have an overall monitoring for those metrics. And probably do a better job of allocating capital than we're doing. That's what the goal is.

Marc Shapiro

The systems for managing market risk and credit risk at Chase are well developed and have stood the test of time. Managing operating risk is another matter. Because so much of operating risk relates to the strength of the control structure, a condition that can be gauged only through subjective assessment, the development of elaborate VAR or stress test models is simply not feasible. Losses in operating risk tend to be unpredictable and not subject to quantitative modeling. Chase's 1999 annual report includes the following discussion of operating risk:

> Chase, like all large corporations, is exposed to many types of operating risk, including the risk of fraud by employees or outsiders, unauthorized transactions by employees, or operational errors, including clerical or record keeping errors or errors resulting from faulty computer or telecommunications systems. Given the high volume of transactions at Chase, certain errors may be repeated or compounded before they are discovered and successfully rectified. In addition, Chase's necessary dependence upon automated systems to record and process its transaction volume may further increase the risk that technical system flaws or employee tampering or manipulation of those systems will result in losses that are difficult to detect. Although Chase maintains a system of controls designed to keep operating risk at appropriate levels, Chase has suffered losses from operating risk and there can be no assurance that Chase will not suffer losses from operating risks in the future.

The case of the trader's apparent overstatement of the value of his forward contracts caused Chase to write down its reported revenue in 1999 by $60 million, but the actual incremental cost to the company is probably not quantifiable. The following control flaw was discussed in Chase's 1999 annual report under "Operating Risk." The issues are critical and the potential consequences are significant since the flaw affects fiduciary responsibilities to customers and conformance with Securities and Exchange Commission (SEC) regulations. Again, Chase's incremental cost of the control deficiency, except for nominal out-of-pocket costs to fix the system, is probably not quantifiable.

> Chase has identified some deficiencies in the computerized bond record keeping system in the bond paying agency function within Chase's Capital Markets Fiduciary Services group. These deficiencies include an overstatement by the computer system of the amount of outstanding bonds and matured unpresented bonds and other items.

Because of these deficiencies, Chase is currently unable to totally confirm through a complete reconciliation of the relevant accounts that the value of bonds that could potentially be presented for payment does not exceed the amount of cash on hand for payment of such bonds. Chase has under way a project to correct the system's deficiencies and to reconcile the affected accounts.... The Securities and Exchange Commission has commenced an investigation relating to the question of whether, in connection with this matter, there have been violations of its transfer agency record keeping or reporting regulations and whether Chase's disclosure regarding these issues have been adequate and timely.

Operating risk affects a manager's SVA calculation just as market and credit risks do, but not surprisingly, the methodology is not nearly as advanced. Currently, capital is adjusted quarterly for operating risk only at the line-of-business level, and the adjustment is based on three factors, equally weighted: expense dollars, audit scores, and risk evaluation rankings. A manager who receives an audit score of A, for example, would be assigned less capital than one who receives a C, thereby increasing the first manager's SVA and incentive compensation. Appendix 3.2 shows an example of operating risk guidelines used in the internal audit process. Note the specific percentages applied to quantitative factors such as error impact and reliance on data.

Corporate controller Joseph Sclafani explains how a business unit could make significant improvements to its SVA through the management of operating risk by automating formerly manual processes:

> He [the manager] can change the risk profile. Maybe he's really manual-intensive. How do you make this [system] idiot-proof? Part of the problem is the number of manual handoffs. You look at re-designing your processes. The more you automate them, the more you can eliminate manual work. I also spend a lot of time pushing the architecture, the financial architecture. To me the three goals are to improve the control environment, streamline the process to save money, and provide information quickly to management. The real opportunity for cleanup here is looking at the opportunities for straight-through processing, automation end-to-end, eliminating hands.

One of the difficulties is the existence of legacy systems that originated in one of the three predecessor banks. Sclafani points out a typical problem area:

> Remember there are a lot of legacy systems out there. One of the challenges that you go through with the legacy systems is putting in subledger systems that do aging. We're looking at different technology now that does automatic matching. Let's say we have a receivable and things don't match: There's a receivable from you for $110.00 and you send us a check for $109.62. When you're dealing with small amounts, they can really get out of hand. Six months later we find out we've got hundreds of items like that. Well, we want to have technology that will automatically match up the receivables, where only exceptions pop out for manual investigation, rather than having a person sitting there comparing every receivable and check. We had one situation in our retail side, the deposit side, where losses were growing more than we wanted. We went in and put in a subledgering system. We did identifications and tracking, and the losses came down significantly. It's just a matter of people having the right information and having the systems to go out and chase the stuff down and deal with it.

Operating risk officer Aditya Mohan adds,

> What we're trying to do is reduce the severity of unexpected losses by changing behavior. And another thing that's influencing unexpected losses is the e-commerce business. It's changing the whole thing. So straight-through processing becomes more important because the customer wants the information Web-enabled. If you don't have straight-through processing, you won't be able to do that.

Sclafani comments wryly on the complexities caused by the legacy systems: "We're going to Web-enable everything the customer sees and then we're going to have a fleet of chipmunks in the back trying to get that stuff there so they can bring it up on the Web."

With technological change and constant evolution in the financial services industry, it is sometimes difficult for back-office staff to keep up. Systems were originally designed for doing business five or 10 years ago, yet routine tasks must be done timely and accurately regardless of the condition of the system. Sclafani explains,

Our biggest risk every day on the operating risk side is people not doing the basics. It's the basic fundamentals—when they aren't done, that's what costs us a fortune. If I look at where we run a lot of risks and where we have write-offs, it's for people not performing the basics. The biggest challenge you have in an organization is [getting] somebody to say, "We need help." Because what will happen is, they think it's a personal reflection on their ability to do their job. So they think, "I'll catch up, I can get it done," and you find out that they haven't caught up and they haven't been able to get it done, and then you've got a project that you've got to clean up.

Scenarios such as this demonstrate the importance of having business units continually update their systems to accommodate change; the SVA approach to operating risk is designed to provide direct incentives to do that.

## Operating Risk Self-Assessment

We use the COSO [Committee of Sponsoring Organizations of the Treadway Commission] document, but then we specifically tailor it to our businesses. We've taken the COSO document and we've taken the risk assessment documents that the controllers and internal auditors have done for a particular business and we've embedded those within the COSO document to identify what the risks are. On an annual basis, those self-assessments are completed by all the business areas and if there are weaknesses identified, the units also have to submit both plans and time frames for improving those weaknesses.

We've tailored it so that people *have* to give you responses, not just check off boxes. So we've tried to make it more interactive and then we've also embodied these risk assessments that we have.

Joseph Sclafani

One-third of the operating risk adjustment to capital under SVA is based on the business unit's risk assessment done by senior management, and one-third is based on the internal audit grade. A risk self-assessment is an important part of both. Originally motivated by a Federal Deposit Insurance Corporation (FDIC) regulatory requirement, the self-assessment has evolved into an important piece of Chase's operating risk management structure.

The complicated risk self-assessment is completed annually and is built on a COSO foundation, with modifications appropriate for Chase's needs. Appendix 3.3 contains an excerpt from the risk self-assessment instrument. This sample pertains to the Global Bank's accounting, control, and operations function. The appendix retains the organization and section headings of the original instrument, but includes only a sample of the questions under each of the five internal control sections. Note the Corrective Action Plan displayed early in the document and the Overall Self-Assessment Scorecard at the end.

Even with the best of controls, it is a daunting and never-ending task to manage operating risk for a large company in the financial services industry. Sclafani comments,

> I kid around with our general auditor—he said he has visions of an environment where you'll never have to bring anything to the audit committee, and then he'll be able to retire. I said, "I guess you're going to be here forever because of the nature of the beast." Things are going to change and we're going to have issues. Our goal has to be how quickly can we identify and resolve those issues—because they're going to happen. It's a part of business.

## Case Summary

Chase Manhattan traces its roots to a water company founded in 1799 in New York City. Over the decades, through mergers and internal growth, Chase has become the third-largest bank in the United States and recently, the most profitable. Outside observers have identified Chase's risk management system as one of its particular strengths.[17]

Chase's management of market risk and credit risk is particularly strong and innovative and incorporates the latest technology in sophisticated VAR (for market risk) and stress test analyses. But it was the introduction of shareholder value-added in 1998 that seemed to launch Chase into the small echelon of companies that have successfully implemented true enterprise-wide risk management. The SVA methodologies, although simple and straightforward, provide incentives for decision makers to incorporate risk considerations automatically into their day-to-day decisions. These individual decisions can easily involve tens of millions of dollars and, with the volatilities of today's financial marketplaces, can make or break quarterly earnings in a flash. Chase firmly believes SVA is an effective way to align the incentives of management with the interests of the shareholders.

Success in banking is a delicate balance of risk and reward. Chase is very careful about the risks it takes and the condition of its balance sheet. It wants to be paid for the risks; it wants managers to consider risks routinely. Chase does not want to eliminate risk, it wants to use it effectively. In the words of Shapiro, "We're in the business of risk management, not risk avoidance. We have to take risks to make money."[18]

# People Interviewed

Marc Shapiro, vice chairman, Finance, Risk Management and Administration

## Market Risk

Lesley Daniels Webster, executive vice president, Market Risk Management

## Credit Risk

Robert S. Strong, chief credit officer

David L. Pflug, Jr., managing director, Global Bank Credit

## Operating Risk

Joseph L. Sclafani, corporate controller

Aditya Mohan, operating risk officer

## References

Archival Material of the Chase Manhattan Corporation, accessed at www.chase.com.

Fay, Stephen. *The Collapse of Barings* (New York: W. W. Norton & Company, 1996).

"Forbes 500s Annual Directory," *Forbes* (April 17, 2000).

Leeson, Nicholas. *Rogue Trader: How I Brought Down Barings Bank and Shook the Financial World* (New York: Little, Brown and Company, 1996).

Lenzner, Robert. "Meet the New Michael Milken," *Forbes* (April 17, 2000): 198–205.

## Endnotes

1. However, Citigroup includes Citibank, Travelers Insurance, and Salomon Smith Barney. Citigroup is unequivocally the largest U.S. financial services company, with total assets of $740 billion and a market capitalization of $220 billion. According to the *Forbes* 500 list, Bank of America is the largest U.S. *bank*, with total assets of $630 billion and a market capitalization of $70 billion. *Forbes* assigns Citigroup an industry classification of *Insurance.*

2. Statistics from Chase's 1999 10-K filing with the Securities and Exchange Commission, and Robert Lenzner, "Meet the New Michael Milken," *Forbes* (April 17, 2000).

3. Hamilton, one of the Founding Fathers, had been a member of the Continental Congress and Treasury secretary under

George Washington. His portrait appears on the U.S. $10 bill. Burr had been a U.S. senator, and from 1801 to 1805, he was vice president under Thomas Jefferson.

4. There has been speculation that Burr deliberately inserted the enabling provision in the bill to create a bank that would compete with Hamilton's Bank of the United States, formed eight years earlier. There is no doubt that considerable animosity over a variety of matters existed between Hamilton and Burr, culminating in their celebrated duel in 1804, which left Hamilton dead.

5. Salmon P. Chase had been instrumental in the establishment of the early national banking system while Treasury Secretary.

6. Chemical Bank did even better—during the Great Depression, deposits actually grew by 40 percent.

7. Marc Shapiro, interview by Mark Haines and Jim Awad, *Squawk Box,* CNBC/Dow Jones Business Video (Interactive Desktop Video, Inc.), October 20, 1999.

8. New Economy companies are leaders in innovations (Internet, microprocessors, etc.) and include technology, information services, media, telecommunications, and life science companies.

9. Loan syndication is raising debt capital from a group of different financial intermediaries under the same financial structure and collateral for the same borrower.

10. "Unfavorable" means the price change goes against the company's position. A short position is a bet that the price of the underlying (here, the franc) will go down. If the price of the underlying increases, the holder of the position loses money upon settlement of the position. Conversely, a long position is a bet that the price of the underlying will go up.

11. Chase Manhattan 2000 10-K, 89.

12. Patrick McGeehan, "Chase Manhattan Must Cut Its Revenue After Discovering Some Nonexistent Trading Profits," *New York Times* (November 2, 1999): C8.

13. Several books have been written about this episode (see Leeson, 1996, and Fay, 1996, for example) and a feature film about it, *Rogue Trader,* starring Ewan McGregor, was produced.

14. In fact, General Motors used residual income in the 1920s. Residual income is actually a very broad concept. It requires only that a charge for invested capital be deducted from some measure of earnings. The definition of earnings and capital, and the procedure for calculating the capital charge, are left to the user's own devices.

    The popular measure economic value-added (EVA) was developed and trademarked by consulting firm Stern Stewart & Co. It, too, is a variation on residual income incorporating Stern Stewart's proprietary methodologies for figuring the various dollar amounts.

15. *Mark-to-market* means adjusting portfolio values to current market prices.

16. This means that the interest rate on the loan was the London Interbank Offered Rate (LIBOR) plus 10 percentage points. When the LIBOR is 9 percent, for example, the interest rate on the loan is 19 percent. The LIBOR is the rate at which the highest rated banks offer to lend to one another. It is compiled by the British Bankers Association.

17. See particularly Timothy L. O'Brien, "How Chase Manhattan Took Danger Out of Risk," *New York Times* (January 20, 1999): C1, C9.

18. O'Brien, "How Chase Manhattan Took Danger Out of Risk."

## Appendix 3.1
### Company Description of Market Risk and Its Measurement

Chase has developed comprehensive market risk management practices that incorporate and, in many instances, set the standard for best practices in risk management techniques and risk management execution.

Chase's Market Risk Management Group consists of approximately 60 professionals located in New York, London, Hong Kong, Tokyo and Brazil and functions independently from Chase's business units.

Chase is exposed to market risk in its trading portfolios because the value of its trading positions are sensitive to changes in market prices and rates. Market risks generally are categorized as interest rate, foreign exchange, equity and commodity risks.

Chase also is exposed to market risk in its investment portfolio and commercial banking activities (Asset/Liability ("A/L") because the revenues Chase derives from these activities, such as net interest income and securities gains and losses, are sensitive to changes in interest rates. Interest rate risk arises from a variety of factors, including differences in timing between the maturity or repricing of assets, liabilities and derivatives. For example, the repricing characteristics of loans and other interest-earning assets do not necessarily match those of deposits, borrowings or other liabilities.

In trading, investment and A/L activities, Chase also is exposed to basis risk, which is the difference in the pricing characteristics of two instruments. Basis risk occurs when the market rates or pricing indices for different financial instruments change at different times or by different amounts. For example, when Chase's Prime-priced commercial loans are funded with LIBOR-indexed liabilities, Chase is exposed to the difference between changes in Prime and LIBOR rates.

In 1999, Chase extended the market risk measurement and control disciplines used in its trading and investment portfolios to its A/L activities. The result of this effort has been an enhanced management of the market risk in its A/L activities and an improved picture of market risk across Chase as a whole.

### RISK MEASUREMENT

Because no single risk statistic can reflect all aspects of market risk, Chase utilizes several risk measures. These measures are Value-at-Risk ("VAR"), stress testing and other nonstatistical risk measures. Their use in combination is key to enhancing the stability of revenues from market risk activities because, taken together, these risk measures provide a more comprehensive view of market risk exposure than any of them taken individually.

#### Value-at-Risk

VAR is a measure of the dollar amount of potential loss from adverse market moves in an everyday market environment. The VAR looks forward one trading day and is the loss expected to be exceeded with a 1 in a 100 chance.

## Appendix 3.1
### Company Description of Market Risk and Its Measurement (Continued)

The VAR methodology used at Chase is historical simulations, which assumes that actual observed historical changes in market indices, such as interest rates, foreign exchange rates, and equity and commodity prices, reflect future possible changes. In its daily VAR calculations, Chase uses the most recent one-year historical changes in market prices and rates. Chase's historical simulation is applied to end-of-day positions, and it is shown by individual position and by aggregated positions by business, geography, currency and type of risk.

Statistical models of risk measurement, such as VAR, provide an objective, independent assessment of how much risk is being taken. Chase's historical simulation methodology permits consistent and comparable measurement of risk across instruments and portfolios. Historical simulation also makes it easy to examine the VAR for any desired segment of the total portfolio and to examine that segment's contribution to total risk. The VAR calculations are performed for all material trading and investment portfolios and for all material market risk-related A/L activities.

All statistical models have a degree of uncertainty associated with the assumptions employed. Chase believes its use of historical simulation for its VAR calculations is not as dependent on assumptions about the distribution of portfolio losses as other VAR methodologies that are parameter-based. The Chase VAR methodology assumes that the relationships among market rates and prices that have been observed over the last year are valid for estimating risk over the next trading day. In addition, Chase's VAR estimate, as with all VAR methodologies, is dependent on the quality of available market data. Recognizing these shortcomings, Chase uses diagnostic information to evaluate continually the reasonableness of its VAR model. This information includes the calculation of statistical confidence intervals around the daily VAR estimate and daily "back testing" of VAR against actual financial results.

### Stress Testing

Whereas VAR captures Chase's exposure to unlikely events in normal markets, stress testing discloses the risk under plausible events in abnormal markets. Portfolio stress testing is integral to the market risk management process and is co-equal with, and complementary to, VAR as a risk measurement and control tool. Giving equal weight to each produces a risk profile that is diverse, disciplined and flexible enough to capture revenue-generating opportunities during times of normal market moves but that also is prepared for periods of market turmoil.

Chase's corporate stress tests are built around changes in market rates and prices that result from pre-specified economic scenarios, including both historical and hypothetical market events. Using economic events (actual and hypothetical) as a basis for stress testing allows easier interpretation of stress results than scenarios based on arbitrarily specified shocks to market rates, volatilities or correlations. As with VAR, stress test calculations are performed for all material trading, investment

*Appendix 3.1*
*Company Description of Market Risk and Its Measurement (Continued)*

and A/L portfolios. Stress test scenarios are chosen so they test "conventional wisdom" and focus on risks relevant to the positions taken in Chase's portfolios.

Chase's stress test methodology assumes no actions are taken during a stress event to change the risk profile of its portfolios. This captures the decreased liquidity that frequently accompanies abnormal markets and results in conservative stress loss estimate.

Stress scenarios are built using a very detailed view of markets. For each corporate stress scenario, more than 11,000 individual shocks to market rates and prices are specified. These include, for example, highly detailed yield curve and credit spread shocks involving more than 60 countries, maturity-specific shocks to market volatilities and shocks to individual foreign exchange cross-rates. By minimizing the use of approximations and proxies in the construction of stress scenarios, the stress results are enhanced at the aggregate level and can be disaggregated to examine meaningfully the exposures arising from smaller portfolios or individual positions.

A key to the success of stress testing at Chase is continuous review and updating of stress scenarios. This is a dynamic process that is responsive to changes in positions and economic events and looks to prior stress tests to identify areas where scenario refinements can be made. During 1999, Chase implemented or substantially modified six corporate stress test scenarios.

Corporate stress tests are performed approximately monthly on randomly selected dates. As of December 31, 1999, Chase's corporate stress tests consisted of six historical and five hypothetical scenarios. The historical scenarios included in the 1994 bond market sell-off, the 1994 Mexican peso crisis and the 1998 Russian crisis. The hypothetical scenarios included examinations of potential market crises originating in the United States, Japan and the Euro bloc. For example, in Chase's hypothetical "flight to quality" scenario, political instability in certain emerging markets causes a general sell-off in emerging markets assets and an investment "flight" to U.S. and selected other "safe haven" countries.

Stress testing also is utilized at the trading desk level, thereby permitting traders and their management to explore in detail the impact of those economic scenarios that most stress the factors unique to the individual business activity. Desk-level stress tests are performed weekly.

Chase also performs NII (net interest income) stress tests that highlight exposures from factors such as administered rates (e.g., prime lending rate), pricing strategies on consumer and business deposits, changes in balance sheet mix and the effect of various options embedded in the balance sheet. NII stress tests take into account forecasted balance sheet changes (such as asset sales and securitizations, as well as prepayment and reinvestment behavior).

At year-end 1999, Chase's corporate NII stress tests consisted of one historical and four hypothetical scenarios.

*Appendix 3.1*
*Company Description of Market Risk and Its Measurement (Continued)*

### Nonstatistical Risk Measures

Nonstatistical risk measures include net open positions, basis point values, option sensitivities, position concentrations and position turnover. These risk measures provide additional information on an exposure's "size" and "direction." For example, a basis point value for a portfolio shows whether a one one-hundredth percentage point (or one "basis point") increase in a market rate will give rise to a profit or loss and of what magnitude.

During the first quarter of 1999, Chase extended the use of basis point value ("BPV"), previously used only for its trading portfolios, to supplement other measures of interest rate and basis risk in Chase's A/L activities.

### RISK MANAGEMENT

Chase has evolved a multi-tiered, many faceted approach to market risk control, combining several quantitative risk measurement tools.

Included among the controls instituted at Chase are Board of Directors-approved VAR limits and stress-loss advisory limits and the incorporation of stress test exposures into Chase's internal capital allocation methodology. When a Board-approved VAR or stress-loss advisory is exceeded, a review of the portfolio is automatically triggered.

Primary control of risk is established through limits. Chase's limit structure extends to desk-level activities and includes a listing of authorized instruments, maximum tenors, statistical and nonstatistical limits and loss advisories. The limit structure promotes the alignment of corporate risk appetite with trading investment and A/L risk-taking activities.

VAR limits on market risk activities exist at the aggregate and business unit levels. In addition, Chase maintains nonstatistical risk limits to control risk in those instances where statistical assumptions break down. Criteria for risk limits include, among other factors, relevant market analysis, market liquidity, prior track record, business strategy, and management experience and depth. Risk limits are reviewed regularly to maintain consistency with trading strategies and material developments in market conditions, and are updated at least twice a year. Chase also uses stop-loss advisories to inform line management when losses are sustained from a trading activity. Chase believes the use of nonstatistical measures and stop-loss advisories in tandem with VAR limits reduces the likelihood that potential trading losses will reach the daily VAR limit under normal market conditions.

Source: Adapted from 1999 Chase Manhattan 10-K Filing.

*Appendix 3.2*
*Operating Risk Guidelines*

## COMPLETION OF THE RISK MODEL

The Risk Model is included in the Audit Inventory in the General Auditing Department Business Plan database. The model has both quantitative and qualitative factors. Each factor is assigned a weighting according to its relative impact on the overall inherent risk, and a scoring level according to the particular characteristics of the unit being reviewed. The inherent risk is the sum of the products of each factor's weighting and scoring level. The maximum Inherent Risk Score is 5.

## QUANTITATIVE FACTORS

1.  Transactional Values/Volumes (15% of inherent risk)

    This considers indirect access to assets by initiating or modifying a transaction rather than direct physical contact. Automated systems create opportunities to appropriate assets without requiring physical access. This is also known as logical access to assets (i.e., electronic funds transfer). The amount of assets of this type is considered along with the ability to convert the asset into cash. This is measured by a liquidity factor. As an example, cash of $10,000 is more liquid than securities of $20,000 and is, therefore, considered more risky. In addition to liquidity factors, the daily volume of transactions that pass through the area is also considered.

2.  Error Impact (11% of inherent risk)

    Errors can affect the financial statements or management information systems. For example, errors on standing and transactional data, coupled with large transaction volumes, could seriously affect decisions based on incorrect data, with a consequential risk of bad publicity. A greater amount of risk is assigned if the data have bank-wide impact as opposed to data that affect only a department. Similarly, the sophistication of the customer also plays a role. A wholesale/professional customer would be more likely to identify an irregularity that some retail/private customers, especially in "hold mail" situations where a customer may not see a statement for an extended period.

*Appendix 3.2*
*Operating Risk Guidelines (Continued)*

3. Reliance on Data (8% of inherent risk)

   This category considers the reliance placed on the data by the bank and/or the customer. The level at which the error impacts the bank, as well as the sophistication of the customer, should be considered. Greater concern exists when there is no customer contact, as is the case in hold mail situations.

4. Nature of the Process (3% of inherent risk)

   When considering the processing environment, the type and level of automation used in the area, as well as the results of the last integrity control review are relevant. For example, automation together with good integrity controls to ensure consistent operation may serve to decrease the potential for error. Also, the lack of automation may affect the risk in the process.

5. Access to Physical Assets (3% of inherent risk)

   Assets in this category are those that can be obtained through direct physical contact. Examples include cash, negotiable checks, and securities. Liquidity factors are used to reflect the ease of convertibility into cash.

**QUALITATIVE FACTORS**

6. Quality of Management/Dept. Head (10% of inherent risk)

   This factor represents the management levels that are not exercising direct, hands-on supervision, but that set the overall tone and strategic direction of the group. This is usually at the senior vice president level, but may be higher or lower depending on the area's organization structure.

7. Degree of Management Judgment (10% of inherent risk)

   This factor relates specifically to the level of management discretion permitted for all or selected transactions. The concept is to distinguish between transactions that are routine in nature (branch deposit) and those that require a higher level of judgment and skill (trades). For example, trading in various instruments for profit by taking risk positions against trading based on customer instructions.

8. Degree/Quality of Supervision (10% of inherent risk)

   This factor represents the management level that is exercising the day-to-day supervision of the ongoing operations of the area being scored. This is usually the VP level, but may be higher or lower depending on the organization structure.

*Appendix 3.2*
*Operating Risk Guidelines (Continued)*

9. Assessment of Control Environment (11% of inherent risk)

   This factor evaluates the effectiveness of the control environment. Management self-assessment, regulatory report and the results of monitoring are all factors to consider in evaluating the control environment.

10. Product Characteristics (7% of inherent risk)

   This factor takes into account the risks inherent within the product itself. A new product would be considered more risky, due to the associated lack of experience. When assessing product maturity consideration should be given to its newness in relation to the market, the corporation and the individual department or branch. Also included in the assessment of product characteristics are its market and credit attributes. Market factors such as liquidity, price volatility and market maturity should be assessed along with consideration of credit exposure. Complexity in the areas of processing, accounting, and legal compliance should also be factored into the assessment of inherent product risk.

11. System Characteristics (6% of inherent risk)

   This factor considers the risk associated with the automated system that supports the operation. A new system would be considered more risky since it lacks any historical record of proper operation. Also the complexity of the system is affected by the mode of processing (on-line/Batch), the maturity of the technology employed and the number and types of interfaces, since a greater number of interfaces increases the effect upon other systems and may increase the risk. The method of access and processing may also affect the risk associated with the system.

12. Pressure to meet goals and objects (6% of inherent risk)

   This factor represents the pressure exerted on management and staff to meet goals and objectives. There is, and should be, a need to set realistic goals and objects for each area. This should not be excessive in nature, either through the setting of unrealistic goals (high overtime) or allowing an employee to significantly increase his compensation through incentive bonus and profit plan attainment at the expense of prudent business judgment (e.g., bonus based on loan originations regardless of credit quality and future performance). Also, unusually low pressure of work may lead to complacency and high error rates.

*Appendix 3.3*
*Example of COSO-Based Self-Assessment Program (excerpted)*

Note: This exhibit retains the structure and section headings of the original document but includes only a sampling of the questions.

**1999 Global Bank Self-Assessment Program**
**ACCOUNTING, CONTROL AND OPERATIONS (ACO)**

**Introduction**

Section 112 of the Federal Deposit Insurance Corporation Improvement Act (FDICIA) requires that we provide an annual statement as to the reliability of the financial statements, adequacy and effectiveness of our system of internal controls and compliance with laws and regulations. We support the conclusions reached in our year-end affirmation through reliance upon a number of control related programs. One such program is the annual FDICIA Self-Assessment exercise. As in past years, the Global Bank complies with this regulatory requirement through a series of questionnaires.

These questionnaires are designed to assist in evaluating the control environment against standards set forth in the *Federal Reserve Board Trading Activities Manual* and COSO Self-Assessment Guidelines. The questions have been formulated to apply to the various product support units and lines of business. In order to permit a meaningful comparison across all units, it is important that you stay within the standard format. When completing the questionnaire, please follow the instructions below:

An effective system of internal controls is equal with any other business objective at Chase. Management owns its control environment and is accountable for its adequacy and effectiveness. Effective internal controls help Chase:

- achieve its performance and profitability targets, and prevent loss of resources;

- provide reasonable assurances as to reliable financial reporting;

- provide reasonable assurances as to compliance with laws and regulations; and

- avoid damage to its reputation and other consequences.

The attached questionnaire is a tool to assist in evaluating the control environment of the Corporation. The questionnaire consists of five sections consistent with the

*Appendix 3.3*
*Example of COSO-Based Self-Assessment Program (excerpted) (Continued)*

five sections of internal control as defined by the Committee of Sponsoring Organizations of the Treadway Commission (COSO). These five sections are as follows:

### Section I.  Control Environment

The control environment sets the tone of an organization, thereby influencing the control consciousness of its people. It serves as the foundation for the other components of internal control, providing discipline and structure. Control environment factors include the integrity, ethical values, and competence of the entity's people; management's philosophy and operating style; the way management assigns authority and responsibility, and organizes and develops its people; and the attention and direction provided by the Board of Directors.

### Section II.  Risk Assessment

Every entity faces a variety of risks from external and internal sources that must be assessed. A precondition to risk assessment is the establishment of objectives, linked at different levels and internally consistent. Risk assessment is the identification and analysis of relevant risks to achievement of those objectives, forming a basis for determining how the risks should be managed. Because operating conditions continue to change, risk assessment is a continuous process.

### Section III. Control Activities (Please note, in the questionnaire this section is identified as Section V.)

Control activities are the policies and procedures that help ensure management directives are carried out. They help ensure that the necessary actions are taken to address risks to achievement of the entity's objectives. Control activities occur throughout the organization, at all levels and in all functions. They include a range of activities as diverse as approvals, authorizations, verifications, reconciliations, reviews of operating performance, security of assets, and segregation of duties.

*Appendix 3.3*
*Example of COSO-Based Self-Assessment Program (excerpted) (Continued)*

**Section IV.  Information and Communication (Please note, in the questionnaire this section is identified as Section III.)**

Pertinent information must be identified, captured, and communicated in a form and timeframe that enables people to carry out their responsibilities. Information systems produce reports, containing operational, financial, and compliance-related information that make it possible to run and control the business. They deal not only with internally generated data, but also information about external events, activities, and conditions necessary to informed business decision making and external reporting.

Effective communication also must occur in a broader sense, flowing down, across, and up the organization. All personnel must receive a clear message from senior management that control responsibilities must be taken seriously. They must understand their own role in the internal control system, as well as how individual activities relate to the work of others. They must have a means of communicating with external parties, such as customers, suppliers, regulators, and shareholders.

**Section V.  Monitoring (Please note, in the questionnaire this section is identified as Section IV.)**

Internal control systems need to be monitored—a process that assesses the quality of the system's performance over time. This is accomplished through ongoing monitoring activities, separate evaluations or a combination of the two. Ongoing monitoring occurs in the course of operations. It includes regular management and supervisory activities, and other actions personnel take in performing their duties. The scope and frequency of separate evaluations depends primarily on an assessment of risks and the effectiveness of ongoing monitoring procedures. Internal control deficiencies should be reported upstream, with serious matters reported to senior management and the Board.

**CORRECTIVE ACTION PLAN (CAP)**

| CAP No. | Self-Assessment Reference | Existing Deficiency | Corrective Action | Accountable Personnel | High/Low Risk | Targeted Deadline |
|---|---|---|---|---|---|---|
| | | | | | | |
| | | | | | | |

Total Number of Corrective Action Plans (CAPS):

Reporting Unit Name/Org. No.:     Submitted By:

Date:     Approved By:

*Appendix 3.3*
*Example of COSO-Based Self-Assessment Program (excerpted) (Continued)*

# I. Control Environment

## A. Commitment to Competence and Development of Individuals

| | | Yes | No | Part | Cross Reference* | | | |
|---|---|---|---|---|---|---|---|---|
| | | | | | FO | MO | ACO | Other |
| 1. | Is there evidence that staff members have the knowledge and skill requirements needed for their specific job functions?<br><br>Comments: | | | | | | | |
| 2. | Are employees sufficiently cross-trained to accommodate vacations, absences, and terminations?<br><br>Comments: | | | | | | | |
| 3. | Has the staff attended training programs?<br><br>Comments: | | | | | | | |
| 4. | Are there training programs to teach staff members their assigned business and control responsibility to perform their jobs as described?<br><br>Comments: | | | | | | | |

*Note: FO = front office; MO = middle office; ACO = accounting, control & operations; other = other units.

*Appendix 3.3*
*Example of COSO-Based Self-Assessment Program (excerpted) (Continued)*

**B.  Management's Philosophy and Operating Style**

| | | Yes | No | Part | FO | MO | ACO | Other |
|---|---|---|---|---|---|---|---|---|
| | | | | | Cross Reference* | | | |
| 1. | Is there a process in place to keep management abreast of new/changed accounting, operational, regulatory, law, and other relevant (e.g., trading, credit) policies that have a direct effect on any of the unit's operations? Comments: | | | | | | | |
| 2. | Is there a clear process of disseminating this information to the staff members that are affected and implementing the necessary changes to the business? Comments: | | | | | | | |
| 3. | Does management follow up on such changes in a timely manner? Comments: | | | | | | | |
| 4. | Is management's attitude toward controls consistent with that of the Corporation? Comments: | | | | | | | |

*Note: FO = front office; MO = middle office; ACO = accounting, control & operations; other = other units.

*Appendix 3.3*
*Example of COSO-Based Self-Assessment Program (excerpted) (Continued)*

## II. Risk Assessment

### A. Establishment and Dissemination of Operational and Financial Reporting Objectives

|   |   | Yes | No | Part | FO | MO | ACO | Other |
|---|---|-----|----|----|-----|-----|-----|-------|
|   |   |     |    |    | Cross Reference* | | | |
| 1. | Are business and control objectives, strategies, and operating plans for all identified businesses and activities, along with goals and deadlines clearly established, documented, and communicated to staff on a "need-to-know" basis?<br><br>a) Have they been properly approved by management?<br><br>Comments: |  |  |  |  |  |  |  |
| 2. | Does management have an adequate methodology for identifying and assessing risks (i.e., credit, market, systems, regulatory, operational) associated with each identified business activity?<br><br>a) Clearly documented?<br><br>b) Risk prioritized?<br><br>Comments: |  |  |  |  |  |  |  |
| 3. | Has a Control Designee/Control Officer been designated to assist management in identifying and monitoring the inherent business risks?<br><br>Comments: |  |  |  |  |  |  |  |

*Note: FO = front office; MO = middle office; ACO = accounting, control & operations; other = other units.

*Appendix 3.3*
*Example of COSO-Based Self-Assessment Program (excerpted) (Continued)*

| | | Yes | No | Part | \*Cross Reference\* FO | MO | ACO | Other |
|---|---|---|---|---|---|---|---|---|
| 4. | Are staffing requirements taken into account in developing business objectives, strategies, and operating plans to ensure the effective, efficient, and continuous performance of control procedures?<br><br>Comments: | | | | | | | |
| 5. | Is there a process to closely monitor business activity to ensure adherence to established objectives, operating plans, and mitigating control procedures?<br><br>Comments: | | | | | | | |
| 6. | Are changes to business objectives and operation plans clearly defined, documented (including accountabilities, time frames and targeted completion dates), and reviewed by the appropriate levels of management?<br><br>Comments: | | | | | | | |
| 7. | Are group management meetings held on a regular basis to ensure line management is aware of senior management's business objectives and goals?<br><br>Comments: | | | | | | | |
| 8. | Does management identify, monitor, and control regulatory and accounting risks with the assistance of the Divisional Compliance Officer and Divisional Controller, respectively?<br><br>Comments: | | | | | | | |

\*Note: FO = front office; MO = middle office; ACO = accounting, control & operations; other = other units.

*Appendix 3.3*
*Example of COSO-Based Self-Assessment Program (excerpted) (Continued)*

# III. Information and Communications

## A. Overall Communications Process

| | | Yes | No | Part | Cross Reference* | | | |
|---|---|---|---|---|---|---|---|---|
| | | | | | FO | MO | ACO | Other |
| 1. | Are there clear communication lines established to ensure line management and staff are promptly notified of critical information and decisions affecting their job functions?<br><br>Comments: | | | | | | | |
| 2. | Is there effective communication up, down and across the organization/ business lines and with external parties, such as customers, suppliers, regulators and shareholders?<br><br>Comments: | | | | | | | |

## B. Communication Mechanism

| | | Yes | No | Part | Cross Reference* | | | |
|---|---|---|---|---|---|---|---|---|
| | | | | | FO | MO | ACO | Other |
| 1. | Is there a mechanism in place to communicate significant issues including changes in business risks, identifying and reporting material losses, errors, and/or irregularities to senior management?<br><br>Comments: | | | | | | | |
| 2. | Are communication lines established to enable staff levels to report suspected internal and external improprieties/violations to senior management bypassing the normal chain of command?<br><br>Comments: | | | | | | | |

*Note: FO = front office; MO = middle office; ACO = accounting, control & operations; other = other units.

*Appendix 3.3*
**Example of COSO-Based Self-Assessment Program (excerpted) (Continued)**

| | | | | | Cross Reference* | | | |
|---|---|---|---|---|---|---|---|---|
| | | Yes | No | Part | FO | MO | ACO | Other |
| 3. | Is there a realistic mechanism in place to enable staff levels to provide recommendations regarding productivity, quality, etc.?<br><br>Comments: | | | | | | | |
| 4. | Is there a particular person/section designated to record, monitor, investigate and resolve customer and/or staff complaints, errors in processing, etc.?<br><br>a) Are customer inquiries accurately recorded/documented, acknowledged promptly, and properly followed up?<br><br>b) Are open, as well as closed files in proper order to facilitate disposition and/or for prompt follow-up?<br><br>Comments: | | | | | | | |

## IV. Monitoring–Requirements

### A. Overall Strength of Monitoring Activities

| | | | | | Cross Reference* | | | |
|---|---|---|---|---|---|---|---|---|
| | | Yes | No | Part | FO | MO | ACO | Other |
| 1. | Is actual operating performance compared to established performance measurements on a regular basis?<br><br>Comments: | | | | | | | |
| 2. | Is there a mechanism in place to investigate and address below-standard operating performance?<br><br>Comments: | | | | | | | |

*Note: FO = front office; MO = middle office; ACO = accounting, control & operations; other = other units.

## Appendix 3.3
### Example of COSO-Based Self-Assessment Program (excerpted) (Continued)

# V. Control Activities

## A. Overall Strength of Control Activities

| | | Yes | No | Part | Cross Reference* | | | |
|---|---|---|---|---|---|---|---|---|
| | | | | | FO | MO | ACO | Other |
| 1. | Do policies and procedures exist for all major activities to ensure effectiveness and efficiency of operations, reliability of financial reporting, and compliance with applicable laws and regulations?  Comments: | | | | | | | |
| 2. | Have the existing control procedures for all major activities, including critical functions mentioned below, been evaluated and do they comply with documented procedures?  Comments: | | | | | | | |

## B. Authorization

| | | Yes | No | Part | Cross Reference* | | | |
|---|---|---|---|---|---|---|---|---|
| | | | | | FO | MO | ACO | Other |
| 1. | Are incoming documents/instructions received from other departments/areas reviewed for proper authorization (general or specific), where applicable?  a) Is a current list of authorized signatures and dollar limits maintained?  b) Is adherence to signature requirements and limits independently reviewed?  c) Is the review appropriately evidenced?  Comments: | | | | | | | |

*Note: FO = front office; MO = middle office; ACO = accounting, control & operations; other = other units.

## Appendix 3.3
### Example of COSO-Based Self-Assessment Program (excerpted) (Continued)

| | | Yes | No | Part | Cross Reference* | | | |
|---|---|---|---|---|---|---|---|---|
| | | | | | FO | MO | ACO | Other |
| 2. | Are accounting tickets/journal entries signed by a preparer and checked/approved by an officer or authorized non-official/supervisor?<br><br>Comments: | | | | | | | |
| 3. | Are specific procedures in place for the approval of large or unusual (e.g., "exception/special handling") transactions?<br><br>Comments: | | | | | | | |
| 4. | Is approval of an officer or supervisory employee obtained for all correcting and reversing entries, as well as, overrides of control procedures?<br><br>a) Is the documentation for the "correction/adjustment" retained on file for a prescribed period?<br><br>Comments: | | | | | | | |
| 5. | Are internally generated transfer instructions (e.g., wire transfer, official check, book transfer) prepared in written form, approved by two area officers and maintained on file?<br><br>Comments: | | | | | | | |
| 6. | When tickets are batched, do batches contain evidence of an officer's review and approval prior to submission to data entry?<br><br>a)Is a review of the data entries performed after processing?<br><br>Comments: | | | | | | | |

*Note: FO = front office; MO = middle office; ACO = accounting, control & operations; other = other units.

*Appendix 3.3*
## Example of COSO-Based Self-Assessment Program (excerpted) (Continued)

|  |  | Yes | No | Part | Cross Reference* | | | |
|---|---|---|---|---|---|---|---|---|
|  |  |  |  |  | FO | MO | ACO | Other |
| 7. | In the absence of any authorized signer, is there an alternative course of action?<br><br>Comments: |  |  |  |  |  |  |  |
| 8. | Are dollar thresholds/limits established which require two or more authorized signatures for certain types of transaction, i.e., funds transfer request approval?<br><br>a) If so, are affected transactions reviewed for adherence to established thresholds/limits?<br><br>Comments: |  |  |  |  |  |  |  |

*Note: FO = front office; MO = middle office; ACO = accounting, control & operations; other = other units.

*Appendix 3.3*
*Example of COSO-Based Self-Assessment Program (excerpted) (Continued)*

## Global Bank

Reporting Unit's Overall Self-Assessment Scorecard

**Instructions:** After completing the individual FDICIA questionnaire below, the reporting unit may wish to use the Scorecard as a tool to provide management with an overall summary assessment of the reporting unit's control procedures, environment and compliance to Bank policies. It is recommended that a narrative be provided as reinforcement for your rating.

| COSO/FDICIA Integrated Framework | Adequate | Enhancement Requirements | Inadequate | N/A |
|---|---|---|---|---|
| **I. Control Environment** | | | | |
| A. Commitment to Competence and Development of Individuals | | | | |
| B. Management's Philosophy and Operating Style | | | | |
| C. Organizational Structure/ Assignment of Authority and Responsibility | | | | |
| D. Commitment to Integrity and Ethical Values | | | | |
| E. Human Resources | | | | |
| F. Policies and Procedures | | | | |
| **II. Risk Assessment** | | | | |
| A. Establishing and Dissemination of Operational and Financial Reporting Objectives | | | | |
| B. Risk Assessment Matrix (RAM) | | | | |
| C. Corporate Risk Assessment and Acknowledgment Policy | | | | |
| D. Service Level Agreements (SLA) | | | | |
| **III. Information and Communications** | | | | |
| A. Overall Communications Process | | | | |
| B. Communication Mechanism | | | | |
| **IV. Control Monitoring Procedures** | | | | |
| A. Overall Strength of Monitoring Activities | | | | |
| B. Monitoring and Assessment of Control Activities | | | | |

*Appendix 3.3*
*Example of COSO-Based Self-Assessment Program (excerpted) (Continued)*

| COSO/FDICIA Integrated Framework | Adequate | Enhancement Requirements | Inadequate | N/A |
|---|---|---|---|---|
| **V. Control Procedures over Specific Activities** | | | | |
| A. Overall Strength of Control Activities | | | | |
| B. Authorization | | | | |
| C. Reconciliation's | | | | |
| D. Access to/Protection of Assets (including Data) and Records | | | | |
| E. Transaction Processing/Recording | | | | |
| F. Trading Activities | | | | |
| G. Hold Mail | | | | |
| H. Segregation of Duties | | | | |
| I. Record Retention | | | | |
| J. House Accounts | | | | |
| K. Business Recovery Planning and System Development | | | | |

_____ Date:_____    _____ Date:_____
*Responsible Department*                 *Business Unit Control Designee*

# E.I. du Pont de Nemours and Company

*Risk management is a strategic tool that can increase profitability and smooth earnings volatility.*

Susan Stalnecker, vice president and treasurer

## Company Background

A painting in the lobby of the Hotel DuPont in Wilmington, Delaware, depicts DuPont's origins: A wagon loaded with dynamite meanders down a road while the faces of onlookers reveal concern at the passing of such high-risk cargo. In successfully making dynamite, DuPont managed its risks. While DuPont's primary business is no longer manufacturing dynamite, managing risk is ingrained in the company's culture. From a sign in the stairwell that reads, "Use the handrail" to an operational safety sign in the offices of senior management that reads, "The goal is zero," DuPont's management is focused on managing risk.

DuPont was established in 1802 by French immigrant E.I. du Pont de Nemours. The company's first product, black powder, earned accolades for its quality from such early Americans as Thomas Jefferson, who used the powder to clear land at his home, Monticello. During the twentieth century, DuPont transformed itself numerous times and became a chemical and research company. DuPont invented nylon in 1938 and developed many more products, including well-known brands such as Teflon, Lycra, Stainmaster, and Dacron. In the latter part of the century, DuPont diversified and spent more than $10 billion on acquisitions and joint ventures, and it expanded internationally. Figure 4.1 gives a chronology of some significant events in the company's history.

*Figure 4.1*
*DuPont Company Timeline*

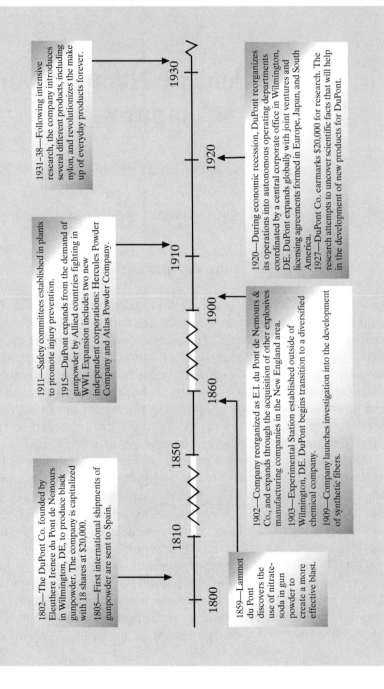

*Figure 4.1*
*DuPont Company Timeline (Continued)*

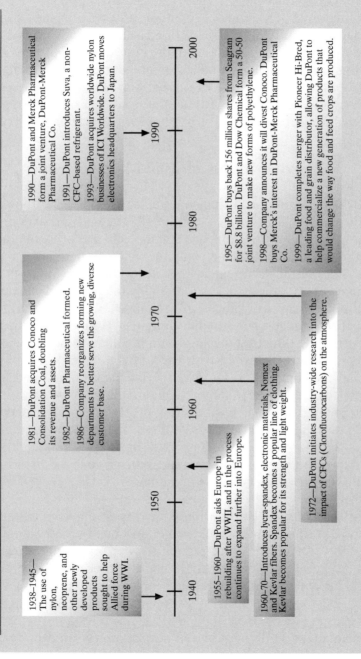

1938–1945—The use of nylon, neoprene, and other newly developed products sought to help Allied force during WWI.

1955–1960—DuPont aids Europe in rebuilding after WWII, and in the process continues to expand further into Europe.

1960–70—Introduces lycra-spandex, electronic materials, Nomex and Kevlar fibers. Spandex becomes a popular line of clothing. Kevlar becomes popular for its strength and light weight.

1972—DuPont initiates industry-wide research into the impact of CFCs (Clorofluorocarbons) on the atmosphere.

1981—DuPont acquires Conoco and Consolidation Coal, doubling its revenue and assets.

1982—DuPont Pharmaceutical formed.

1986—Company reorganizes forming new departments to better serve the growing, diverse customer base.

1990—DuPont and Merck Pharmaceutical form a joint venture, DuPont-Merck Pharmaceutical Co.

1991—DuPont introduces Suva, a non-CFC-based refrigerant.

1993—DuPont acquires worldwide nylon businesses of ICI Worldwide. DuPont moves electronics headquarters to Japan.

1995—DuPont buys back 156 million shares from Seagram for $8.8 billion. DuPont and Dow Chemical form a 50-50 joint venture to make new forms of polyethylene.

1998—Company announces it will divest Conoco. DuPont buys Merck's interest in DuPont-Merck Pharmaceutical Co.

1999—DuPont completes merger with Pioneer Hi-Bred, a leading food and grain distributor, allowing DuPont to help commercialize a new generation of products that would change the way food and feed crops are produced.

1940    1950    1960    1970    1980    1990    2000

Today, DuPont is the 16th largest U.S. industrial/service corporation, with 1999 revenues of almost $27 billion and net income of approximately $2.8 billion. Almost half of those sales come from outside the United States, making DuPont one of the largest U.S. exporters. DuPont operates in over 65 countries and has manufacturing, processing, and research laboratories around the world. DuPont's current strategy focuses on material and life sciences. Although it is not the same company as it was 200 years ago, risk management remains a critical part of its culture.

## Current Status of Risk Management

In the 1990s, DuPont faced challenges and risks different from its early black powder days. The business continually changes and so do the risks. For example, recently DuPont had a major change in its operations—the sale of Conoco, an energy company, and the purchase of Pioneer Hi-Bred International, an agriculture seed company—that altered its energy and commodities risks. Additionally, international expansion exposed the company to changes in exchange rates and interest rates. DuPont acknowledges in internal documents, "Business activities are, by their very nature, directly associated with the management of risk."

DuPont is never satisfied with the status quo, and in 1995 several factors led the company to improve its risk management and to adopt best practices for risk management. One major factor was a reorganization that created strategic business units (SBUs). Bruce Evancho, U.S. treasurer and global risk manager, notes, "It just made more sense to expect each of the SBUs, as independent businesses, to meet their own goals." However, senior management realized that the SBUs did not have the systems or the expertise to manage risk; they needed resources and assistance.

Another factor motivating the company to improve risk management was that financial risks in the general business community were getting more attention. Bank regulators were focusing more on this area, and several large derivative disasters had occurred at other companies. The combination of those problems and DuPont's creation of SBUs led management to question if they had the right level of risk mitigation and controls at each SBU. In studying best practices for risk management, DuPont gathered information from two areas. First, authoritative documents, in particular COSO's "Draft Derivative Guide"[1] and the Group of Thirty's global derivative study,[2] provided insights. Second, DuPont benchmarked its risk management practices with companies such as AT&T, Citicorp, Goldman Sachs, J.P. Morgan, Marsh McLennan, Merck, and Mobil.

## Risk Management Framework

As a result of the benchmarking effort, DuPont adopted a new risk framework with three key components:

- Corporate-wide policy

- Corporate-wide guidelines

- Line management strategies and procedures (see figure 4.2)

In designing the framework, the degree of flexibility was a topic of discussion. A framework that was too flexible would not provide much guidance, and a framework that was too rigid would not allow SBUs to manage risk and respond quickly to market changes.

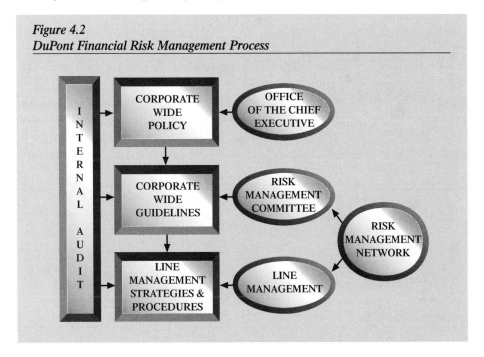

*Figure 4.2*
*DuPont Financial Risk Management Process*

## Corporate-wide Policy

Policies are critical to effective risk management. DuPont's policies are provided by the office of the chief executive and cover four aspects:

- Philosophy

- Risk objectives

- Authorized usage and limitations in managing a specific risk

- Risk committee

DuPont believes it is important to state its risk management philosophy clearly and up front. Its philosophy is captured in the following statement: "The company is expected to manage risk at a level consistent with business strategy and not engage in activities that are inconsistent with the Corporate Financial Risk Management Policy." One of the rudiments of the philosophy is that risk is managed not in silos but in the context of the business strategy. With respect to objectives and usage, DuPont's policy emphasizes that operating exposures must be understood and managed consistent with business strategy and risk objectives, again highlighting the importance of integration and linking risk management to the business. The goal is not risk management as an end but managing the business first.

DuPont's corporate policy also establishes the purpose and duties of the risk management committee. The committee is made up of high-level DuPont officers, including the CFO, treasurer, controller, and vice president of sourcing (see table 4.1). The committee assists the chief executive officer in setting policies and guidelines. Committee members also have the authority to execute any financial instruments necessary

*Table 4.1*
*Risk Management Committee*

| | |
|---|---|
| Gary Pfeiffer | senior vice president and CFO |
| Susan Stalnecker | vice president and treasurer |
| Henri Irrthum | vice president—sourcing |
| John Jessup | vice president and controller |
| Bruce Evancho, *now Webber Lee* | U.S. treasurer and global risk manager |

to manage risk. The committee is required to recognize DuPont's changing business needs and objectives, as well as any new trends in the risk management area. By maintaining close contact with the SBUs, the committee coordinates and integrates all risks and identifies any offsetting risk positions that may arise. Finally, the committee is charged with ensuring full compliance with accounting and disclosure requirements.

## Corporate-wide Guidelines

The second part of DuPont's framework identifies guidelines for risk management. DuPont's guidelines cover hedging versus speculation. Although speculation is not allowed, risk strategies that "intend limited management of positions over time to take advantage of market opportunities to reduce cost or risk" are permitted if a majority of the risk management committee members give prior written approval. In other words, DuPont does, at times, use its underlying business exposures to take a position on the market. Other specifics include identifying which derivative instruments are allowable and ensuring that certain instruments qualify for hedge accounting.

DuPont's guidelines also cover controls, valuation, and monitoring. DuPont requires line management to be responsible for controlling the risk management process. Controls include ensuring that the program is consistent with the policy and guidelines and segregating duties. The guidelines cover following limits, obtaining written authorization, complying with appropriate accounting requirements, and ensuring that adequate systems and processes are in place to support the risk program.

To DuPont, valuation means completing only transactions that can be reliably valued using internal models. Valuation also includes measurement of market and credit risk. For current exposures, DuPont adopted a mark-to-market approach, and for potential exposures, it adopted a value at risk (VAR) approach. DuPont also has procedures on using only authorized brokers and on managing counterparty risk. DuPont requires reviews of activities by its internal audit department, which issues a report to the risk management committee.

DuPont requires regular monitoring and reporting. This includes reporting all open positions, transactions during the most recent period, gains and losses on derivatives that were restructured or terminated, mark-to-market history or other analysis necessary to determine the effectiveness of any program, exposure by counterparty, and sensitivity analysis.

## Line Management Strategies and Procedures

Line management strategies and procedures are the final component of DuPont's framework. Line management is responsible for risk management. The policy states, "The need to assess financial exposures and formulate specific risk management strategies is an integral part of the business management process." How do line managers keep a corporate focus? The framework provides a response. Line managers must adhere to corporate policy and guidelines, including using central experts for executing risk management strategies, and they are responsible for assessing financial exposures as well as designing strategies for managing risk. They also work with the risk management committee and have access to the Risk Management Network (see table 4.2). The committee and network serve as consultants and resources to the SBUs.

DuPont recognizes that risk management is not an overnight fix and that although the company has not fully achieved the goal, it is on the way to better risk management. To get there and stay on the right path, DuPont needed a process and management's buy-in on the concept and process. It also needed to drill the process into the organization itself. That is, it needed the SBUs to accept the process and the risk framework. The framework provides several benefits. Evancho comments on

*Table 4.2*
*Risk Management Network*

| | |
|---|---|
| Bruce Evancho, *now Webber Lee* | Leader |
| Karen Meneely | Capital markets |
| Pat Whalen | Foreign currency |
| Steve Benson | Cash investment portfolio |
| Dave Maier | Commodities |
| Dan Montante | Risk management technology |
| Lloyd Adams | Counter party credit |
| Charles Clayton | Accounting policy |

its value, "The framework sits over this particular area to provide resources, structure, and provide the corporation with some continuity around the whole process." While the framework provides the structure, the SBUs have responsibility for managing the risk.

DuPont also recognized the need for a risk champion and team to get the new process implemented. It obtained the support of the CFO and the treasurer. Everyone wanted the best model and the greatest possible rigor to be incorporated into the process. The goal for the risk team was to implement the framework across all financial risks. Even with this approach, DuPont recognizes where risk management begins. As Evancho explains, "The ultimate risk manager of any company is the CEO. What we're in business to do is to take risk and get rewards. If you don't have any risks then you're probably not going to have any rewards."

## Risk Integration

A benefit of the framework was better integration of financial risks. Evancho notes, "Until we put this process in place, each group was a 'stovepipe' and did not look across the organization. There are certainly opportunities for integration we ought to be investigating." DuPont believes that financial risk management must be integrated and that risk management must be integrated into the business strategies and operations. An example of financial risk integration was a policy that mandated that all borrowings be in U.S. dollars. Now, however, by using the risk network, DuPont can see that some offsets naturally occur. Thus, having the framework and the risk network led the company to question the viability of the old policy. DuPont also attempted to integrate other risks. For example, the property and casualty insurance risk group now reports to the global risk manager of the risk management committee (see table 4.1). The insurance area covers many of DuPont's operational risks, as well as product liability risks.

Although not all risks can be fully integrated enterprise-wide, DuPont realizes that the process of examining risks is portable. Its experience with quantitative measures for financial risk, such as VAR, led it to examine property and casualty insurable risks with a process, examine those risks collectively, and attempt to apply more quantitative analysis to those risks. Evancho states the issues that occurred when DuPont began to look at risks across the organization: "We generally retain significant property and casualty risk but in the foreign currency area we may not choose to retain the same degree of risk. You begin to ask, 'Can you explain that?'"

DuPont explains it by factoring in the different approaches to risk management. The company is very good at managing property and casualty risks from its operations in preventive ways. Evancho explains,

> We always had a corporate policy of retaining significant exposure in this area because we control the risk. We spend a great deal of money controlling the risk in the safety and environmental areas. We pride ourselves in managing those risks. Our view is we ought to capitalize on that. It's been a tradition for many years and goes back to when the company was founded, and we were in the dynamite business. If you self-insure these risks you need to continue to monitor to be sure that you are investing in prevention because if you ever let down, you're setting yourself up for a problem.

DuPont also now tries to profile its major operational risks, because it seemed difficult to get an accurate measurement. Before setting up the risk framework, DuPont considered the accuracy of the overall risk profile as "high spot." As such, the company decided to examine the more strategic risks collectively (on an enterprise-wide basis) and tried to assess worst-case scenarios and probabilities of each event. Managers asked, "What, on an expected value basis, would these things look like on a risk profile?" This profiling was used to determine whether the right level of deductibles and self-insurance had been taken for the entire entity. One key factor in making that decision was DuPont's risk appetite. To DuPont, risk appetite is based on two factors: the company's ability to withstand a risk and the market's perception of the company's ability to withstand a risk.

Evancho explains further,

> People have done risk maps. They've got down to the umpteenth small item. Our concern (in how we manage risk) was more focused on staying away from measuring the high frequency-low severity risks because we think that is managed quite well. We wanted to focus on the low frequency-high severity risks because those are the

ones that perhaps have the potential to have a significant financial impact. We still need to refine that and start thinking more quantitatively. Although we're not going to run things by numbers, it allows us to analyze those numbers and think with a process.

Before the risk framework, DuPont's risk approach was less structured and sometimes inconsistent. DuPont believed implementing the risk framework was critical. Still, it recognized the limits. Evancho elaborates,

> We concluded that the important part of the process in the financial area is to identify the risk, quantify the risk, assess the company's risk appetite, and then optimize the risks using a robust quantitative process. But as we looked externally in 1995, there weren't any good analytical tools for corporations. They were becoming more available to banks with value-at-risk, but we are not a bank. The processes we saw were more for financial institutions. We did talk to one company that was plowing ahead, and we were surprised when that company said they spent $4 million in systems development and hired five MBAs. We didn't see the need for that kind of expenditure at that point. We decided to immediately implement the risk management framework and delay implementation of a comprehensive analytical process. My assessment was that it was an evolving technology and in three to five years the technology would evolve so that there would begin to be standardized tools readily available to corporations at a reasonable cost. We purposely made a decision to go with this (the framework), wait three to five years, and watch the market.

DuPont had taken the first steps to improve risk management. However, in the late 1990s, several events prompted it to upgrade and enhance its risk management. One was its participation in a benchmark study with 20 other large multinational companies. The study concluded that no company had yet incorporated state-of-the-art risk analytical tools across the whole spectrum of risk. It also noted that each company, like DuPont, believed the availability of these tools at reasonable costs was critical to the evolution of the corporate financial risk management process. At this time Susan Stalnecker had just become vice president and treasurer, and as she began to evaluate and restructure the global treasury function, one of the key principles she developed concerned risk management. The principle states, "Risk Management is a central organizing principle. (DuPont) Treasury will use state-of-the-art technology to comprehend and manage risk across complete spectrums of financial risk."

These events, as well as the split-off of its energy company (Conoco), DuPont's evolution to a material and life science company, the introduction of the euro, and new accounting requirements resulting from SFAS No. 133, led DuPont to conclude that it was time to develop its risk-based measures further and to better integrate all risks across the corporation.

## Focus on Earnings

DuPont positioned itself for the twenty-first century as a "science" company. However, a change in mission was not the only thing that raised risk awareness. Earnings growth was also important. DuPont desired sustainable earnings growth, quarter over quarter and year over year. DuPont, like many other public companies, recognized that negative earnings volatility is not received enthusiastically in the market and could result in a reduction in share price. In addition to investors, analysts, rating agencies, and regulatory agencies were all paying more attention to risk management. Because of such concerns (and sometimes overreactions), DuPont believed risk management strategies needed to be reevaluated and integrated even more.

The traditional way to view company performance was to focus on earnings. The problem with this approach is that earnings vary based on external market factors such as changes in interest rates, commodity prices, or foreign currency exchange rates. Becoming "world class" means recognizing this fact. DuPont wants to build sustainable earnings growth, and shareholders desire that growth. One way for investors to see that growth is for DuPont to remove (via better risk management) the influence of these external forces, so investors can see the real growth. This does not mean that cycles will not influence DuPont's earnings—its shareholders understand that cycles are a part of the company's business. With better risk management, however, shareholders should be able to see which parts of the cycles are business and management related and which are market factors that are out of the company's control. Thus, both management and shareholders can get a clearer picture of the company's performance and growth.

## A Common Language for Value Creation

One additional risk management enhancement DuPont desired was a common language, a common way to quantify and discuss risks. DuPont recognized its different approaches to managing operational risks (up front) and some financial risks (post hoc). It also recognized that it could manage some financial risks up front. It could get some SBUs to change their business models. For example, if an SBU had source income in a different currency, DuPont first held the SBU accountable on a dollar basis, which motivated the SBU's management to consider sourcing in the same currency. However, this approach did not completely mitigate the risk, and thus, a common language and a consistent approach were needed. Stalnecker notes, "What we have is a control process now. We don't have a value creation process. That's what we're trying to do."

## The Value of VAR

The question that DuPont's management addressed was how to get SBU managers to accept and integrate financial risk into their strategy and business decisions when some of them might not completely understand all of the complexities and concepts of financial risk. DuPont had used some traditional measures such as VAR and scenario analysis. DuPont's documents state that VAR is measured as "the maximum shortfall of value, regardless of how value is defined, that could be experienced due to the impact of market risk on a specific integrated set of exposures, for a period of time of a day or a month and confidence level (usually 95%)." Scenario analysis was simply analyzing "projected financial results with respect to selected market variables, with consideration for the potential diversification effects inherent in the company's overall portfolio of exposures and the probability of selected market moves occurring." While VAR is an accepted metric, it is not very useful to DuPont. Evancho comments, "Value at risk doesn't help us; it's too short term and narrow." DuPont's focus is not on the market value of a financial instrument portfolio but on earnings and cash flow. As a result, DuPont saw a gap in current metrics for risk management.

DuPont acknowledges that it always had state-of-the-art control practices but not state-of-the-art risk management practices—at least not until recent developments. Stalnecker discusses the new approach:

> What we've decided to do, in a fairly rigorous way, is to get a better feeling for those risk sources and their impact. What is the impact on earnings from a probabilistic standpoint? How are those risks interrelated? What is the correlation among those risks? What is our risk tolerance in terms of earnings per share volatility? Given that tolerance or lack thereof, how does that translate in terms of how we need to manage those individual elements in a correlated fashion?

## Becoming World Class in Financial Risk Management

To become world class in risk management, DuPont knew it needed to identify risk, quantify risk, and assess its risk appetite. The company needed a common language and a better view of how risk related to earnings in order to figure out how to add value creation through risk management. However, management did not believe it was fully up to speed on methods to quantify risk. In addition, software tools were needed to capture data and build models. As noted previously, DuPont did a best practices study and found that while a number of companies were making progress in managing risks, no company felt it had completely achieved the goal. For example, J.P. Morgan had a risk metric model, but it was based on VAR, and that was not suitable for DuPont.

### Seeking Additional Expertise

DuPont's managers recognized that they needed additional expertise and partners to enhance their risk management efforts. One step the company took was hiring a person with an MBA to assist with the process. A second step was partnering with another company, Measurisk.com,[3] whose employees have the statistical skills and databases DuPont needed to enhance its metrics and tools. Measurisk.com provides financial consultants and engineers and analytic tools, risk engines, and data feeds via the Internet. In essence, it is an application service provider in the risk management area. The company receives position information from DuPont electronically (via browser interface) and performs complex calculations to model potential market exposures. DuPont can view and receive the information over the Internet and enter it into its treasury systems. Companies like DuPont can access Measurisk.com's tools and receive interactive risk analysis as well as reporting capabilities. Measurisk.com provides the analysis via valuations and modeling techniques that are consistent with accounting standards and regulatory requirements. By leveraging Measurisk.com's systems, data, and expertise, DuPont will be able to keep its cost down while still having world-class tools. DuPont worked closely with Measurisk.com, and their partnership was announced in March 2000. The announcement highlighted the services the two had developed and the availability of the services to other companies. It was a major event for both DuPont and Measurisk.com.

The partnership gave DuPont two capabilities (or services) to help it become world class in risk management. First, it now has earnings at risk (EAR) capability using world-class methods, data, and models. Second, the partnership has developed services to assist companies in complying with the SFAS No. 133 reporting standard.

The SFAS No. 133 service will help DuPont in several ways. In addition to complying with this new SFAS, DuPont will be able to calculate and report fair values (required under SFAS No. 133) for derivative instruments and hedged exposures, measure hedge effectiveness, and develop scenarios to view alternative hedging programs.

## Earnings at Risk

In essence, earnings at risk calculates the maximum potential earnings loss (within a certain confidence interval) caused by the adverse movements of market factors. EAR allows DuPont to quantify the exposures it faces from risks such as changes in interest rates, currency, and commodity prices. This quantification assesses the effect of these exposures on DuPont's more traditional measures, such as profitability or operating cash flow. Evancho explains the benefit of EAR:

> We can quantify earnings at risk in any given quarter just from market movements. To do so, we first look at all cash flows with an identifiable market risk factor and then aggregate exposures to validate any natural offsets. Next, we run thousands of simulations

integrating market risk factors, volatilities, and correlations and how they could potentially impact earnings. For this exercise, we look at the extreme left tail of the potential earnings distribution. Let's say, for illustration purposes, that total earnings at risk for all of our market exposures is potentially $100 million. Now that we have it quantified, let's talk about what our appetite [for risk] is. It's similar to what we did with the insurance side—what do we think the company can live with? Is $100 million right or should we manage the risk in a way that brings it down to $50 million? We can then run all different kinds of scenarios and strategies to see what's the most effective way to manage the risk to bring it down to $50 million.

DuPont notes that the SBUs needed better communications on their risk. EAR enhances communication and provides the common language DuPont desired. Using EAR, the risk group can now discuss risk in a language the SBUs clearly understand. Evancho adds, "Earnings at risk is a language that most business people are concerned with." EAR enables the SBUs to understand their level of risk better and then make decisions to mitigate those risks. DuPont's risk group expects to work much more closely with the SBUs now that communication is clearer about the real level of risks. EAR also allows better communication with senior management. Stalnecker explains, "We do this work and identify earnings at risk and identify the earnings volatility. We can then use these data in a conversation with senior management as a way to determine the threshold limits for earnings volatility and therefore the desired parameters for risk management tactics like hedging."

## Earnings at Risk and Integration

Another benefit of using EAR is better integration. DuPont did not want risk to be managed only by an SBU, because on an enterprise-wide level the company can have natural offsets. Viewing risks on an enterprise-wide basis using a common metric (EAR) allows managers to see this offset better than they previously could. It also prevents over- or underhedging any single position.

Figure 4.3 illustrates this concept using simulated numbers. Integrating risk as much as possible allows DuPont to see the full exposure of risks as one number. In figure 4.3, the assumption is that DuPont faces $11.4 million in exposures. Note that this total exposure includes

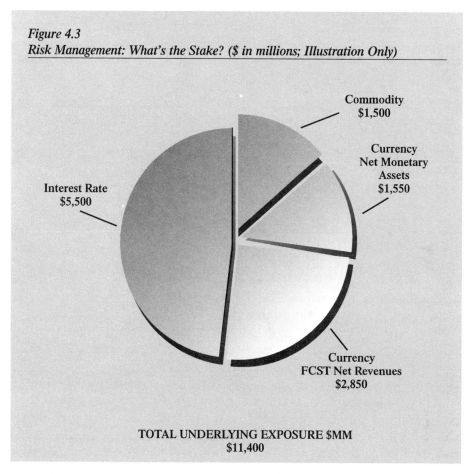

*Figure 4.3*
*Risk Management: What's the Stake? ($ in millions; Illustration Only)*

Commodity
$1,500

Currency
Net Monetary
Assets
$1,550

Interest Rate
$5,500

Currency
FCST Net Revenues
$2,850

TOTAL UNDERLYING EXPOSURE $MM
$11,400

forecasted revenue exposures (FCST). Other exposures come from changes in interest rate, commodity prices, and currencies.

While the knowledge of total risk exposure is valuable, how does a company manage this exposure and get the people responsible (SBU managers) not only to manage it well but to understand it in the first place? The answer again lies in using a common language. Table 4.3 demonstrates this next step. The risk exposures are converted into earnings numbers (in this case, earnings-per-share-at-risk). This view affords the opportunity to learn which exposure is affecting earnings the most or least. It also demonstrates the effect of any hedging on earnings. Note in this table that the total risk exposure is 50 cents per share

*Table 4.3*
*Underlying Exposures: Earnings at Risk (Illustration Only)*

| Underlying Exposures Type | $MM | Underlying | Earnings/Share at Risk Hedge | Net |
|---|---|---|---|---|
| Interest Rates | 5,500 | .03 | — | .03 |
| Commodity | 1,500 | .17 | (.07) | .10 |
| Currency Net Monetary Assets | 1,550 | .14 | (.14) | .00 |
| Currency FCST Net Revenues | 2,850 | .16 | — | .16 |
| Total | 11,400 | .50 | .21 | .29 |

without any risk mitigation. Management can relate this information to its own risk appetite to determine if this level is acceptable. If management chooses to hedge 21 cents per share, then the remaining exposure is 29 cents per share. The impact can be seen for each risk type. The exposure for commodities is 17 cents per share before any hedging and 10 cents per share after hedging.

Using this approach, DuPont can manage EAR to a specified level. Next, DuPont can look at the residual risk and decide if it is comfortable with the remaining EAR level. Managing risk to a specified level can start from the top or from the bottom. The top-down approach would set a certain dollar amount (limit) and then split that amount among all the risks DuPont faces. The bottom-up approach requires calculating the EAR for each specific risk and then summing them to see where DuPont stands and whether management will accept that level of risk. DuPont's risk management committee can use EAR to set strategies and approve programs, not on the basis of notional amounts but as determined by EAR levels.

DuPont recognized the need for new metrics because risk management focused on notional amounts had flaws. For example, if DuPont lets managers hedge 50 percent, what does that mean and how does the company measure real performance? Evancho explains, "When using a notional amount, people are going to second-guess what you did." If a manager chose to hedge 25 percent, then some will ask, "Why didn't you hedge 50 percent?" If you hedge 50 percent and the market moves the other way, then some will question why you hedged at all. EAR helps to eliminate this second-guessing and can clarify how effective a manager's strategies have been in meeting objectives.

Assume an EAR level is chosen as the target. The benefit of collecting and examining the data on an enterprise-wide basis is that it informs management of the risk sources. Figure 4.4 provides an example. In this case, assume DuPont is trying to manage to an EAR of $25 million. What areas and which SBUs are causing the EAR? Figure 4.4 shows that most of the risk is in SBU 2. Additionally, chemical prices are the source of most of the risk, and foreign exchange is the next-highest risk source. Figure 4.5 provides additional detail if management wanted to drill further to determine the specific source. For example, suppose management wanted to know which foreign currency is causing the risk. Figure 4.5 reveals that the euro is about 35 percent of the total exposure and the yen is another 15 percent.

Integrating the data allows management to see the big-picture relationship between earnings and expected earnings. The top panel in figure 4.6 shows the relationship between expected earnings and EAR by month. From this analysis, management can gain a sense of the actual earnings exposure over time. The figure shows how earnings and financial risk are related for every month of the year. Again, under this approach the company is not managing to a notional amount, which is an outdated method. Rather, it is managing to what all managers understand—earnings. The bottom panel of figure 4.6 shows this same information on an annual basis. Assume DuPont expected $670 million in earnings, but management wanted to know how financial risk would affect that amount. The figure reveals that DuPont is 95 percent confident that earnings will be at least $545 million. The difference is due to the EAR. Clearly, managers can use that information to determine how much risk they are willing to bear. A similar approach can be seen in figure 4.7, which shows that all enterprise-wide risks create a 30 percent chance that earnings will fall below the expected level of $640 million. This type of information can be invaluable in determining how to manage risk and how much to manage proactively via controls or retroactively via hedging, financing, or other techniques.

*Figure 4.4*
*Overall Earnings at Risk Analysis (Illustration Only)*

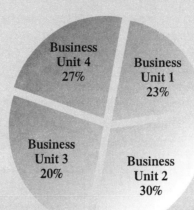

**Earnings at Risk Contribution by SBU**
*100% = $25 million EAR*

Business Unit 4 27%

Business Unit 1 23%

Business Unit 3 20%

Business Unit 2 30%

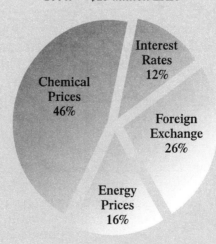

**Earnings at Risk Contribution by Risk Factor**
*100% = $25 million EAR*

Interest Rates 12%

Chemical Prices 46%

Foreign Exchange 26%

Energy Prices 16%

*Figure 4.5*
*Earnings at Risk by Risk Factor (Illustration Only)*

**Total EAR by Risk Category**

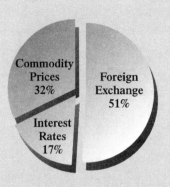

**Commodity Contribution to EAR by Major Commodity (100% = $16 million)**

**Foreign Exchange Contribution to EAR for Major Currency (100% = $26 million)**

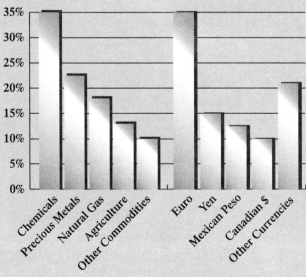

*Figure 4.6*
*Expected Earnings and EAR for Budget Year 2000 (Illustration Only)*

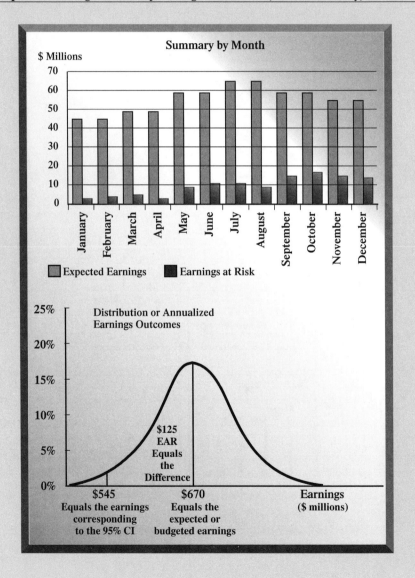

*Figure 4.7*
*Probability Assessment of Earnings Outcomes (Illustration Only)*

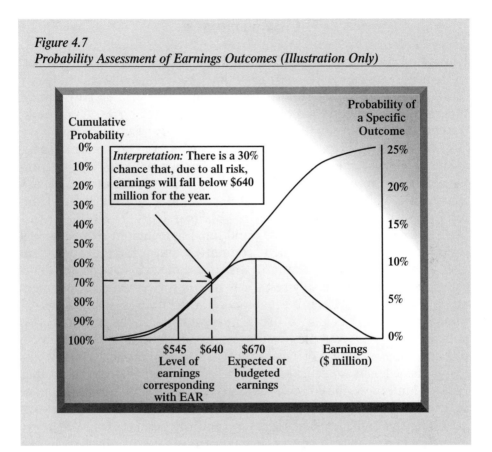

Collectively, the figures highlight the value of EAR as a process to quantify risk. DuPont can learn the effect of risks on earnings enterprise-wide, by SBU, by risk, and (by drilling down inside a risk) by each sub-component. DuPont can also look at other cross sections of how risk affects earnings. From this analysis, DuPont can see the maximum reduction in earnings within a given confidence interval. The earnings numbers can be converted to cash flow effects. Furthermore, this analysis can be subjected to stress testing. Stress testing is necessary because some statistical techniques are not relevant when considering low frequency–high impact events.

# 4

## Case Summary

DuPont began nearly 200 years ago as a black powder company that had to manage risk carefully just to survive. Risk management is deeply rooted in the corporate culture. Today, DuPont is a large corporation that produces a diverse set of products in many countries. As a result, the company faces a significant number of volatile risks. Such risks have led DuPont to expect more from risk management. DuPont's risk management enhancement evolved over a number of years and encompassed several major steps. The first step was to develop a new risk framework. This framework and its implementation took buy-in from top management and acceptance by SBU managers. The company established risk policies, guidelines, and line management strategies and procedures. A risk management committee and a risk network were also established. The committee and the network include top-level executives and serve as key resources in enterprise-wide risk management. The framework was a best practice at the time of its implementation. DuPont also began to use a more integrated approach to risk management. For example, insurance and operational-type risks were placed under the global risk manager. Using this approach, DuPont was able to transfer its analytical approach for financial risks to these other risks. Additionally, DuPont was able to determine whether its risk management approaches and strategies were consistent and whether it was assuming the right level of risks for each risk area. In spite of these gains, DuPont's overall approach was seen as a control process rather than a value-creating activity, and the company desired more from risk management.

In order to integrate risk further, DuPont needed a common language. Management found that not all managers understood or could readily use value at risk. This lack of understanding impeded their ability to manage risk, especially on an enterprise-wide basis. DuPont further believed that more sophisticated tools were required to manage risk in today's business environment. DuPont recently announced a partnership with Measurisk.com to codevelop EAR and SAFS No. 133 services. Measurisk.com provides these services to DuPont via the Internet. Measurisk.com also provides the market data, models, and risk engines used in the calculations.

EAR metrics allow DuPont to develop a common language. Managers and investors understand earnings more easily than other risk measures. The new metrics also facilitate better risk integration than had been possible previously. Using EAR enables DuPont to examine risks across all classes of exposures and to see how those risks affect earnings (or cash flows). This approach is dramatically different from managing risk on a notional basis. DuPont's management can analyze risks by strategic business unit or by each subcomponent of risk. It enables DuPont to see natural risk offsets, to decide whether hedging is really necessary, and to evaluate the effectiveness of hedge strategies. In addition, it enables DuPont to see the likelihood of achieving certain earnings levels for the entire enterprise and informs management of the level of earnings that are at risk by month, quarter, or for the entire year.

Previously, DuPont was taking a "stovepipe" approach to managing risk. Under the new approach, management can take an enterprise-wide perspective and analyze which risks are present and which risks offset each other. Previously, conflict among managers was inevitable because they each wanted to manage their own risk instead of taking an enterprise-wide view. The new approach allows DuPont to see its enterprise-wide risks more clearly and then convey that information both across and outside the organization. The new tools will also allow DuPont to better manage earnings volatility and preserve margins. DuPont can also look at decision making on a risk-return basis because it has elucidated the risks it faces.

# People Interviewed

Susan M. Stalnecker, vice president and treasurer

Bruce R. Evancho, U.S. treasurer and global risk manager
  *Now global e-business financial manager*

Daniel T. Montante, risk management technology analyst
  *Now senior risk analyst, treasury-global risk management*

# Endnotes

1. The "Draft Derivatives Guide" was published as a final document in 1996. See Committee of Sponsoring Organizations of the Treadway Commission, *Internal Control Issues in Derivatives Usage* (Jersey City, NJ: AICPA, 1996).

2. Group of Thirty, *Derivatives: Practices and Principles* (New York: Group of Thirty, 1993).

3. The Web site for this company provides this description: "Measurisk.com (www.measurisk.com) is a business-to-business (B2B) provider of Internet-based risk analysis for institutional investors, securities dealers and corporations. Measurisk receives position information from its clients electronically and performs complex calculations to model potential market exposures. Measurisk's service offers clients sophisticated analytical tools such as Value-at-Risk (VAR) and stress-testing to manage trading positions, monitor investment portfolios and model corporate exposures. Clients interact over the Internet to perform stress tests and scenario analyses of their positions or exposures using historic or hypothetical market conditions."

# Microsoft Corporation

*To win big, sometimes you have to take big risks.*[1]

Bill Gates

*At the end of the day, the chief risk officer is Bill Gates. He is the one who ultimately takes the risk of do we develop this product or go into this market.*

Brent Callinicos, treasurer

## Company Background

Microsoft is the world's leader in software for personal computers. More than 90 percent of the personal computers and workstations shipped in 1999 had a Microsoft product as their primary operating system.[2] Founded as a partnership between Bill Gates and Paul Allen in 1975, the company was incorporated in 1981 and went public in 1986. Figure 5.1 gives a chronology of significant events for Microsoft during the past 25 years.

On February 17, 2000, Microsoft officially launched Windows 2000, whose development involved as many as 4,000 programmers and required over 30 million lines of code. The company expects Windows 2000 to become the core of Windows DNA (Distributed interNet Architecture) 2000, which supports what the company is calling Next Generation Windows Services.[3]

In 1999, Microsoft was restructured into four divisions corresponding to its major customer groups: the Business Applications Group, Consumer Group, Developers Group, and Platforms Group. Figure 5.2 gives an overview of the major products for each of these divisions, and table 5.1 shows the company's growth in employees, revenue, and earnings over the past 10 years.

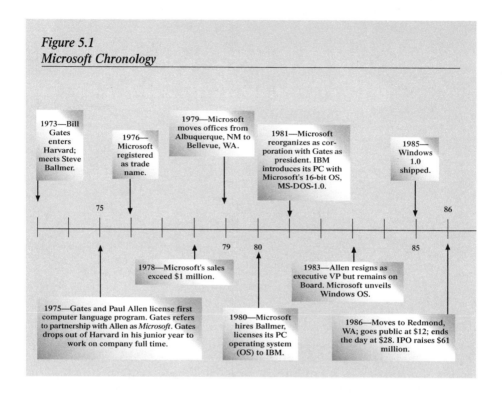

Figure 5.1
Microsoft Chronology

With the rapid growth of the Internet, the technological landscape for the computer software industry is undergoing tectonic change. Microsoft has moved from its original business model of selling discrete packaged software and operating systems for a single computer to a position of leadership in software, services, and Internet technologies that are designed to empower people any time, any place, and on any device. In Microsoft's 1999 annual report, the first item discussed under "issues and uncertainties" is "rapid technological change and competition":

> Rapid change, uncertainty due to new and emerging technologies, and fierce competition characterize the PC software industry. The pace of change continues to accelerate, including "open source" software, new computing devices, new microprocessor architectures, the Internet, and Web-based computing models.[4]

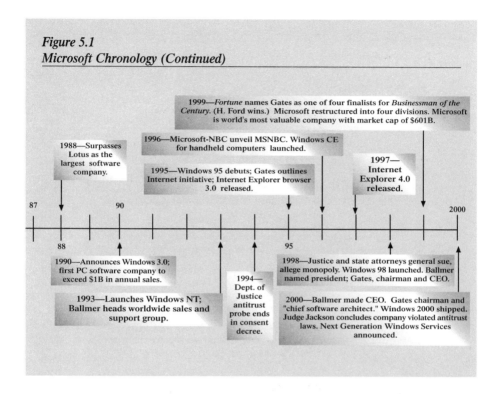

*Figure 5.1*
*Microsoft Chronology (Continued)*

In discussing the industry in which Microsoft competes, Steve Ballmer, president and CEO, stated in a 1999 interview on *Nightly Business Report:*

> Our industry is very dynamic. And if you're not preparing to replace yourself, someone else is preparing to replace you. And we've got to be girding up for the next sort of generation of things we need to do customer-wise, as well as technology-wise.[5]

Microsoft operates in a competitive, high-risk business, with rapidly advancing technology and ever-shortening product life cycles. In that context, Microsoft's risk management group seeks to construct and implement an enterprise-wide risk management system.

*Figure 5.2*
*Microsoft's Divisions*

**BUSINESS APPLICATIONS GROUP**

Microsoft Office, including its components Word, Excel, and PowerPoint, as well as BackOffice server software products.

**CONSUMER GROUP**

Microsoft Network, plus other consumer properties, including Expedia, Carpoint, Web TV, and MSNBC (50% ownership).

**DEVELOPER GROUP**

Products and services for programmers, including development tools and SQL server database products.

**PLATFORMS GROUP**

All versions of Windows except Windows CE, including Windows 2000 and Windows 98, as well as software for delivering music and video online.

Source: David Kirkpatrick, "The New Face of Microsoft," *Fortune* (February 7, 2000): p. 90.

*Table 5.1*
*Microsoft Headcount, Revenue Growth, Income*

| Fiscal Year Ending | Employees | Net Revenue | Net Income |
|---|---|---|---|
| 6/30/90 | 5,635 | $1.18B* | $279M |
| 6/30/94 | 15,017 | $4.65B* | $1.15B |
| 6/30/99 | 31,575 | $19.75B | $7.79B |

* The company changed the way it reports revenue associated with product support, consulting, MSN Internet access, and training and certification of system integrators. Net revenue prior to FY97 has not been reclassified at this time to reflect this change.

Source: *Microsoft Fast Facts,* June 30, 1999.

# Risk Management Group

Microsoft's risk management within the treasury function developed during the 1990s. The company established its risk management group in 1997. The group's leader, treasurer Brent Callinicos, reports to John Connors, CFO. Figure 5.3 presents the organization chart for the risk management group. The company does not have a chief risk officer position, and according to Callinicos, "Microsoft does not see the need for such a position." At one time, Microsoft did consider a risk management committee composed of top executives but decided that it would not be practical.

Under Callinicos, the group has focused on developing a comprehensive and integrated approach to risk identification, measurement, and management. The group's goal is to bring to the business risk area (i.e., nonfinancial risk) a level of measurement and management similar to that in the financial risk area.

# Financial Risk Management[6]

Financial risk management at Microsoft has been evolving since 1994, when the company began its foreign exchange hedging program. In about 1995, the company began to calculate VAR for its foreign exchange risk. According to author Philippe Jorion, "VAR measures the worst expected loss over a given time interval under normal market conditions at a given confidence level."[7] In 1996, the company fine-tuned VAR and became more analytically intense. In 1997, the risk management group began to think about using VAR in other areas such as the equity and fixed income investment areas, and in 1998 the group embarked on a project to correlate financial risks from a systems standpoint.

In 1996, Microsoft's treasury presented to the finance committee of the board of directors a white paper analyzing the factors that had contributed to the publicized derivative losses that several major companies had reported. As a result of this report, Microsoft created a comprehensive and integrated approach to financial risk measurement and management within the treasury function. As Callinicos describes it, the financial risk reporting structure "loosely resembles an enormous tree." The tree of risks includes foreign exchange, interest rate, strategic

*Figure 5.3*
*Microsoft Risk Management Group*

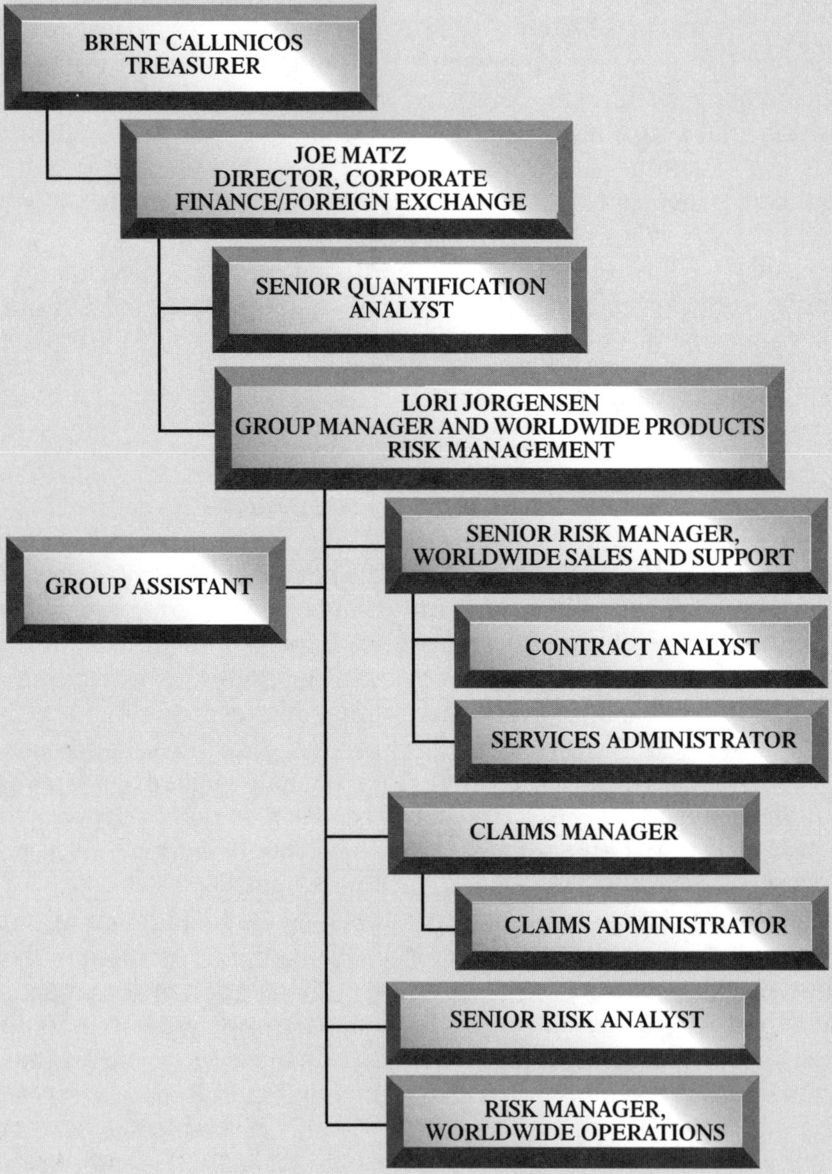

- BRENT CALLINICOS
  TREASURER
- JOE MATZ
  DIRECTOR, CORPORATE
  FINANCE/FOREIGN EXCHANGE
- SENIOR QUANTIFICATION
  ANALYST
- LORI JORGENSEN
  GROUP MANAGER AND WORLDWIDE PRODUCTS
  RISK MANAGEMENT
- GROUP ASSISTANT
- SENIOR RISK MANAGER,
  WORLDWIDE SALES AND SUPPORT
- CONTRACT ANALYST
- SERVICES ADMINISTRATOR
- CLAIMS MANAGER
- CLAIMS ADMINISTRATOR
- SENIOR RISK ANALYST
- RISK MANAGER,
  WORLDWIDE OPERATIONS

equity, and employee stock option program risks. Callinicos elaborates on the effort:

This 1996 initiative improved upon several preexisting efforts at Microsoft to manage financial risks, including efforts to manage the dilutionary effects of its employee stock option program through stock repurchases and a put warrant issuance program and efforts to manage foreign exchange risk associated with the company's global business activities. It also created company interest and support in developing specific portfolio guidelines for Microsoft's US$35 billion investment portfolio (which comprised eight interrelated, but distinct, investment funds, including both internally managed funds and strategic equity investments) and an initiative to develop a plan to manage both high-frequency, low-cost risks and low-frequency, but potentially catastrophic risks within its investment and strategic equities portfolios.[8]

This effort also led to the creation of Gibraltar, the company's treasury information system. Gibraltar allows Microsoft to view all of its risks holistically rather than on a silo basis. As Callinicos explains,

Gibraltar…is in effect a treasury systems reengineering effort designed to systematically integrate Microsoft's treasury function, resulting in what Microsoft refers to as a "digital nervous system" (DNS). DNS components include a data warehouse with on-line viewing capabilities, an associated performance measurement module, a treasury transaction system and a financial risk analysis/reporting system.[9]

With Gibraltar, Microsoft's treasury can give senior management an aggregated view of the market risks assumed by its capital markets group.

Gibraltar also performs VAR analysis on the company's holdings. Microsoft's 1999 annual report notes that VAR is used to estimate and quantify market risks, which include foreign currency, interest rate, and equity price risks. The company measures VAR at each node of the tree's branches and reports "to the individuals within Microsoft responsible for the exposures and assets represented by each node."[10] Microsoft's 1999 annual report explains the aggregated VAR as follows:

Assumptions applied to the VAR model at June 30, 1999 include the following: normal market conditions; Monte Carlo modeling with 10,000 simulated market price paths; a 97.5% confidence interval; and a 20-day estimated loss in fair value for each market risk category. Accordingly, 97.5% of the time the estimated 20-day loss in fair value would be nominal for foreign currency denominated investments and accounts receivable, and would not exceed $95 million for interest-sensitive investments or $1.38 billion on equity securities.[11]

To measure VAR, Microsoft developed its own system, known as IRMA (Internal Risk Management Application). The treasury function also uses two third-party packages, and all three systems are used to check the numbers that the others generate. Callinicos explains, "We use three systems to measure the risk because you never know what one system is going to give you versus another one. We want to make sure at least directionally the risk is the same and, hopefully, from an order-of-magnitude standpoint the risk is the same as well."

The VAR calculation provides a way to respond when someone asks, "How much risk is Microsoft taking?" Before Microsoft used VAR, to respond to that question, Callinicos states,

We would have to ask the questioners many questions in terms of what they really meant. Did they mean value at risk? Did they mean worst case? Did they mean specific scenarios? What time horizon? So instead of asking those questions, the risk management group went forward with an approach that we would tell anyone who asks what we mean when we say we have risk.

While the Microsoft board of directors had seen VAR for foreign exchange risk, the risk management group educated board members on VAR calculated to include interest rate and equity risks. The group also began to correlate the various financial risks robustly. Callinicos makes a presentation to the finance committee of the board of directors every quarter, and the CFO also has access on the intranet to a report on financial risk.

Microsoft does not rely solely on VAR to measure its financial risks. It also uses stress testing through scenario analysis to consider the impact of political, geographic, and economic circumstances. Stress testing through scenario analysis can determine how sensitive Microsoft might be to the 2.5 percent outlier events. Outlier events that might be considered are an earthquake on the West Coast or a currency devaluation like those that occurred in Russia and some Latin American countries. Scenario analysis around an earthquake is relevant to Microsoft's financial risk because it has $18 billion worth of investments in high-technology companies, most of which are on the West Coast. Rather than just consider the impact of an earthquake in the abstract, the risk management group analyzed what happened at Kobe Steel in Japan when an earthquake occurred there. Callinicos emphasizes that "VAR is a slightly academic approach, while scenario analysis provides a way to bring to the board's attention events that are more easily identifiable, and thus it is a useful process, particularly if you extrapolate from a scenario that really happened. For that reason, scenario analysis is also being used on the business risk side." (The use of scenario analysis for identification of business risk is discussed later in this case study.)

Financial risk management is not just a way to protect the company's financial statements from shifts in interest rates or currency movements. It is also a form of business risk management. For example, Microsoft's foreign exchange program for soft currency offers price protection for areas with unstable currencies. Microsoft sells its products to distributors in dollars, but distributors sell products in local currencies and have risk from unstable currencies. Even if the risk of devaluation is fairly remote, if the distributors think otherwise, they will stop ordering products from Microsoft. Distributors operate on thin margins, and if they do not get price protection, a devaluation could wipe out their profits. For a minimum cost, Microsoft will provide price protection to the distributors to protect their margins. This is a case in which financial risk management has to wear a "business hat." As Callinicos explains, "In the overall corporate scheme of things, this situation is a small risk for Microsoft. However, from a customer goodwill and subsidiary standpoint, this price protection is invaluable."

## Business Risk Management

As noted in figure 5.3, the risk management group divides business risk management responsibilities into world-wide products, sales and support organizations, and operations. In explaining Microsoft's approach to business risk management, Callinicos states,

## 5

Microsoft is first run by the product group, then maybe by sales, and finance and risk management will come after that. The risk management group or treasury will not run the company.

The risk management group is here to bring to the attention of our vice presidents, senior vice presidents, or higher management some of the things they should think about on risk management and to share examples of risk management. The group supports and influences operating managers on risk management.

An ongoing activity of the risk management group is to work with the business unit managers. Lori Jorgensen, risk management group manager, notes, "The risk management group provides valuable insight to managers of the business units." She suggests that the risk management group adds value in two ways. First, the group may undertake risk financing. To do this, Jorgensen notes, "The risk management group needs to have a clear view of the company's current risk profile so that it can validate the risk financing plans." An essential question is "Do the plans accommodate the risk profile that exists?"

Second, the risk management group adds value through its "quantification resources, which include a senior risk analyst and senior quantitative analyst with a Ph.D. in mathematics. With these resources, the risk management group can help the business unit do modeling to look at risk and to validate conclusions managers may have already made." The risk management group can thus give different input to each operational unit, opening the door for each unit to "stay current on what is happening in the business."

Callinicos notes that risk management group members act as "evangelists on risk management" with the business unit managers. Jorgensen adds,

A lot of the success of the risk management group comes as a result of its evangelism. While in the final analysis Microsoft is probably more technology driven than most companies, it is still a people business. It is people behind the technology, and the right people have to think about the right things in order to use the technology for whatever purpose, including risk management.

Risk managers evangelize through the use of the company's intranet and through face-to-face time with the business unit managers.

## The Intranet

Every department has its own intranet site, and communication through the intranet is part of the firm's culture. Microsoft wants all managers to understand the risks embodied in the decisions they make. To assist them, the risk management group has developed Web-based knowledge tools. As new projects are launched, business managers are encouraged to consult risk management's intranet site. Risk checklists, anecdotes, and best practices on the intranet serve as a trigger for operating management to think about risks.

Promotion of intranet use and the extent to which data are shared and accessible across the company are unique aspects of Microsoft's culture. At their desktops, employees have access to virtually any financial data. In his recent book, Bill Gates expresses this philosophy about sharing information: "A company's middle managers and line employees, not just its high-level executives, need to see business data." [12] He further suggests that "employees shouldn't have to wait for upper management to bring information to them. Companies should spend less time protecting financial data from employees and more time teaching them to analyze and act on it." [13] Certainly, some information is password protected. However, new employees with experience in other companies are amazed at how much information Microsoft shares.

## Face-to-Face Time

In addition to the intranet, the risk management group relies on face-to-face time with the business unit managers. Jorgensen says she and other risk management group members are evaluated on how much time they spend with their client group. According to Jorgensen, "Spending time with a director or product unit manager is essential to having an enterprise-wide view of risk within our group." As she notes,

> People tend to work on a project and then move to another one. And as they work on the next project, they may recall that an issue came up on the previous project and a person from the risk management group was able to assist in understanding the risks involved. So they will call us or we will seek them out to understand their current project.

It is important to acknowledge a cultural truth about Microsoft, which is that we have very smart people embedded in all of the business units and all of the operating divisions. They are very focused on making their activities successful, however they define success, and that is an inherently "risk management" attitude. So when you have really smart people that are in place, close to the business and part of the business, the job of the risk management group is to learn from them and see how we can leverage the wisdom gained across the enterprise and share best practices. Further, perhaps we can add some incremental value by providing information they have not considered.

Working with a business unit helps the group find out what the managers are most concerned about. Given her knowledge and experience, Jorgensen focuses on what managers are perhaps not thinking about, or not thinking about as thoroughly as they should. With the business unit management, she asks "what the worst-case scenario would be for that particular business." She works with management to identify the "stresses that could bring about this worst-case scenario" and identify and aggregate various risks. A single worst-case scenario can trigger multiple events that signal problems. Jorgensen summarizes, "We must clearly define the worst-case scenario, what things have to happen and how likely are they to happen? How bad would it be, or what is a more likely scenario? That is the overall approach we try to follow."

When she is briefed on a product, Jorgensen uses the information gained "to reach out across the operations groups to trigger other resources that may be able to provide insights on managing the risk for that particular undertaking." The business units are focused on making their products a financial success and thus are receptive to working with the risk management group. The risk management group, in turn, seeks every opportunity to learn what is going on throughout the corporation. Group members seize the chance to speak to product and sales groups about risk management. By maintaining close contact with the numerous controllers and financial analysts in the product and sales units, they can leverage their contacts throughout the organization.

In addition, the legal department and the risk management group stay in close contact regarding developments within the product and sales units. Similarly, the internal audit department and the risk management group coordinate their efforts and partner whenever they can to be more efficient in working with their internal clients. The three risk managers (see figure 5.3) also work as a team because an event in one risk manager's client group may affect one of the other's client groups. As Jorgensen emphasizes, "It is very important for the three of them to work in collective fashion and coordinate with each other."

Callinicos adds, "The risk management group has ongoing meetings with new business groups, new areas of the company, and new product lines." As a further challenge to the risk management group, in many instances the company is launching a new business model rather than merely building on a previous model by announcing a new release of an existing product. For example, to support Expedia, Microsoft had to become a licensed travel agent, and for the Home Advisor product, it had to become a licensed mortgage broker. As new business models like these emerge, risk identification is not simply an incremental process but requires identifying a whole new list of risks.

Callinicos summarizes the importance of face-to-face, continuous contact:

> By having the business units educate us on intricate details of their business, the risk management group can be aware of perhaps 90 percent of the risks facing Microsoft. While the business units are focused on providing the best possible product or service to customers in a timely manner, the risk management group can partner with them to manage their risks. The risk management group is in place to create better awareness of possible risks to the business units, and operational risks are the first to be considered. Is there something the company can change about the very nature of how it does business that eliminates the risk?

Through all the avenues described, the risk management group helps the operations group identify the "material risks" related to a product or sales activity. After identifying the material risks, the risk management group works with the parties involved to rank them. The next step is to address a particular risk high on the list. As Jorgensen explains,

> What is the number one risk? Is there anything that we can do about it from a financing perspective? From a risk mitigation perspective by aligning with the legal department or other operation groups to

moderate the risk? If we cannot do anything because it is a behavior embedded within the product, then we need to quantify for the business unit the value of the risk so they can include that in their decision.

An example of how risk analysis can affect a business decision is the revision of the pricing of an innovative PC keyboard. Risk analysts included in the price the cost of defending potential litigation concerning repetitive strain that leads to crippling wrist injuries. As a result, the royalty was increased by $2.82 per unit.[14] Although risk managers had considerable empirical data about litigation arising from keyboard injuries and could therefore quantify the risk, most of the products at Microsoft do not lend themselves to this specific kind of analysis. Jorgensen notes, "It is important for the organization to have an awareness of risks and to consider how they might impact the sales price of a product."

## Identifying Business Risks Through Scenario Analysis

In addition to the ongoing effort to identify risks related to new products, the risk management group is working on a white paper that will take a strategic approach to material business risks. The completed paper will be taken to the finance committee of the board of directors.

The risk management group is using scenario analysis to identify Microsoft's material business risks. For example, because Microsoft has a campus of more than 50 buildings in the Seattle area, earthquakes are a risk. As Callinicos states, "In the past, we have looked at silos of risk. For example, we may have looked at property insurance when we considered the risks of an earthquake and thought about protecting equipment, damage to buildings, and that type of thing."

To take a holistic perspective in considering the risk of an earthquake, Callinicos notes that management must ask,

What is most important to Microsoft? Is it really the property? And when you say most important, what you really mean is, what would the predicted reaction be and the potential impact on our stock price? That is what it comes down to, really, if a major earthquake occurred here. The real risk is not that buildings get damaged but that it causes business interruption in the product development cycle and that we cannot do business. The fact that we have substantial property insurance does not mean that we sleep well at night because we are covered for that risk.

By doing scenario analysis for the risks related to an earthquake, Callinicos states,

You conclude that property insurance does not really cover you for all the risks associated with an earthquake. You are covered for one outcome of the event but not for the real risk that you need to be worried about as a company. So that is why it is important to step back and ask strategically, "What are we trying to protect against?"

The risk management group has analyzed this disaster scenario with its advisors and has attempted to quantify its real cost, taking into account how risks are correlated. In the process, the group has identified risks in addition to property damage, such as the following:

- Director and officer liability if some people think management was not properly prepared

- Key personnel risk

- Capital market risk because of the firm's inability to trade

- Worker compensation or employee benefit risk

- Supplier risks for those in the area of the earthquake

- Risk related to loss of market share because the business is interrupted

- Research and development risks because those activities are interrupted and product delays occur

- Product support risks because the company cannot respond to customer inquiries

This scenario involves a number of risks, and the total costs could be very large. Simply buying insurance or issuing catastrophic bonds does not manage all the risks. Rather, as Callinicos states, "The risk management group, once it has identified the risks, partners with other areas of the company. We together look at the disaster recovery plan, think about the company's backup site, and think about what the impact would be on various groups in the company."

Scenario analysis is not just an academic exercise; it is possible to study what actually happened to other companies. The risk management group looked at what happened to Kobe Steel when the Kobe earthquake occurred. Callinicos suggests some relevant questions: "What happened to Kobe Steel's stock price? How did their stock do in relation to the appropriate stock market index? Did they get sued? How long did it take them to get up and running again?"

The risk management group is not basing the white paper on hypotheticals; once it has identified risks, it looks for similar events at other companies and their results. This approach will provide a basis for recommendations. The basic question, according to Callinicos, is, "What can we learn from them?" With the assistance of its outside advisors, the risk management group learned, to the extent that information was public, how the companies were affected, what they communicated, the reaction in the business community, and the effect on their stock price.

When it completes the scenario analysis, the risk management group will make recommendations from a strategic perspective. The group itself will likely be responsible for implementing some recommendations, while some will be directed to other areas of the company. A benefit of the scenario analysis is to instill a risk management mindset throughout Microsoft's operations. As Callinicos explains, "The first choice is operational. Is there something you can do by the very nature of how the company does business that eliminates or reduces the risk so that we do not have to deal with it later?"

Other scenarios included a stock market downturn or a bear market. Microsoft has financial exposures in such a situation because as of fiscal year-end 1999, it had over $17 billion in cash and short-term investments and over $14 billion in equity and other investments. When peeling back the layers of impact, the group had to consider the impact on:

- The company's investments
- Its stock option plan, since a primary source of compensation for Microsoft employees is stock options
- Employees' incentives if more cash compensation is required
- Suppliers and customers whose growth depends on their stock price

- The company's research and development to the extent that it has lower sales and thus less money for investing in that effort
- Director and officer liability should the stock price decrease more than that of other companies
- The company's operations outside the United States should the downturn be worldwide

As Callinicos states, "The role of the risk management group is to initiate the thinking about these issues and to get people to consider what the company would do under this scenario. What would we be doing about it? What would we be forced to do? What would be good and what would be bad?"

The risk management group has defined five or six scenarios such as the two described above, and identified the material risks for each. Callinicos emphasizes, "The scenarios are really what we are trying to protect against."

## Measuring and Prioritizing Business Risk

An important result of scenario analysis is to put a dollar amount on the risks. The natural question in the earthquake disaster scenario is "What will it cost the company?" While the quantification of business risks is not exact, the risk management group believes that it is essential. George Zinn, director of corporate finance, who has direct line responsibility for financial risk management, observes, "The approach we have taken in financial risk and business risk is to try to quantify what we can and not necessarily worry that we are unable to capture everything in our measurement." The risk management group has staff who are very good at analyzing a situation in terms of "what is this like?" In many cases, Jorgensen states,

> Quantification is really an intuitive process. What do we know that is like the situation we are now analyzing? Then we get data on some kind of proxy basis, run the models, and go back to the business unit we are dealing with and ask "Does this feel about right for this risk?" It is really an iterative process until at the end of the day you come up with an order of magnitude as opposed to precision.

"Unfortunately," Callinicos emphasizes, "the areas where you have a lot of data tend to be the high-frequency events, and those events tend to be the small-magnitude events."

In the quantification effort, the risk management group has used its advisors, Aon, and Goldman Sachs. The latter has a group that focuses on capital market solutions to risk management. The risk management group has used consultants in two areas: providing data on incidents for the risk management group to analyze and supplying the group with information, either on a name basis if that is approved, or on a no-name basis, on how other companies are dealing with specific risks. "The approach the group takes to its consultants," Zinn explains, "is to make sure we are being smart about things and approaching an issue in a manner where we do not find we are so far down the road that we have not considered something. They are ultimately a fresh set of eyes."

After the group has identified and quantified business risks, it uses risk mapping to prioritize the risks as to their severity and frequency. Figure 5.4 presents a risk map.[15] The earthquake disaster scenario would probably be mapped in the second quadrant, very high on the vertical axis, meaning that it has high severity and low frequency. A risk map does not indicate correlations between risks but rather shows, on a silo basis, the severity and frequency of a particular risk. It does not define a solution, but it does provide a ranking of the risks. As Callinicos observes, "A risk map kind of gives you the 80/20 rule (i.e., you should spend 80 percent of your effort in risk management on 20 percent of the risk)."

The risk map provides an opportunity to look at risks strategically and tactically. In business risk management, both views must be considered. Jorgensen explains,

> We could establish risk-financing programs at a strategic level that may not be sufficient to meet the needs of an international subsidiary and other business unit profit and loss statements. So one of the things we test continually is "What is that line between tactical and strategic?" That line should be consistent between financial and business risk management. Below that line in the tactical area, we make certain financing decisions that may include risk transfer insurance, using a captive, and a variety of more traditional approaches. Above the line in the strategic area, we would make different financing decisions.

*Figure 5.4*
*Risk Map*

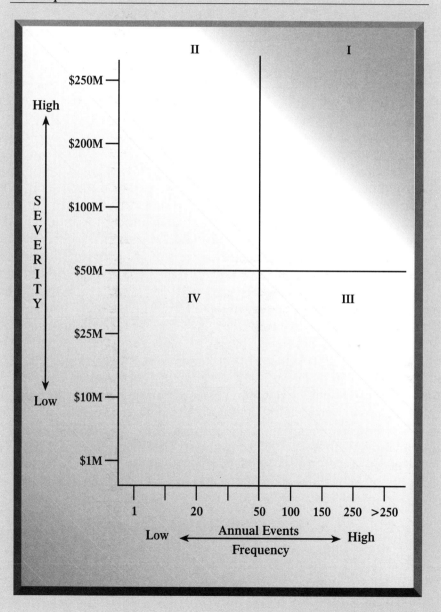

The risk map for Microsoft is confidential, but it does include both financial and business risk. Also, some of the risks on the map have more quantitative backing than others, where severity and frequency are determined by "What do we think that risk could look like?" In placing a risk on the map, the group considers Microsoft's three-year plan. The group does not want a snapshot of the business today; that could lead to solutions that would soon be out-of-date. The group also goes back to the business units to confirm the placement of a risk on the map. If they do not, Callinicos says, "the effort is just an ivory tower exercise." Also, in presenting the map to top executives, the group can better defend the placement of a risk if it has received confirmation from the business units.

With an understanding of risks, their severity, and their frequency, the group next turns to solutions. Microsoft's decisions to retain, transfer, share, or avoid a particular risk are confidential, so we can present only a general observation. A relevant question at this point in the process is "What do Microsoft's shareholders and Wall Street really expect from the company in terms of risk management?" As Callinicos explains, "A dollar of risk in capital markets may be perceived differently than a dollar of risk somewhere else, because of the message that that particular dollar of risk sends when you lose the dollar. What we have been trying to do is to think about what our shareholders and Wall Street really expect of us in terms of risk management."

As mentioned previously, the risk management group is working on a white paper on business risk management. The recommendations in the white paper "will be a combination of communication strategies to other areas of the organization and a strategic approach to managing risk, which would be a quantum leap from where Microsoft is currently in managing business risk," according to Callinicos. The risk management group hopes to get answers to such questions as "What do we want to do? Why do we want to do it? How do we plan to do it?"

## Awards for Risk Management

Microsoft's risk management efforts have been recognized outside the company. In 1999, Gregory Maffei, then senior vice president and CFO, received the CFO Excellence Award for risk management, sponsored by *CFO* magazine and Arthur Andersen. The award cited Microsoft as a "pioneer of the enterprise approach to risk management."[16]

At the 1999 Alexander Hamilton Awards for Excellence in Treasury Management, Microsoft received a gold award for financial risk management. The award, sponsored by *Treasury and Risk Management* magazine, noted that Microsoft had turned the "financial crisis of Asia and Brazil into significant gain for the company."[17] In 1998, Microsoft received an Alexander Hamilton Award for Overall Treasury Excellence. It called attention to the Microsoft treasury's use of technology to design a Web-based tool to share risk information through the company's intranet.[18] Also in 1998, Callinicos received the Ernst & Young Global Risk Manager of the Year Award, and in 1999 Microsoft received the Corporate Award for Risk Management Solutions from Treasury Management International.

## Case Summary

Microsoft's risk management group emphasizes financial and business risk. Financial risk management focuses on market risks, which include foreign currency, interest rate, and equity price risks. The group has made more progress in the financial risk area than in the business risk area in terms of risk identification and measurement. It uses VAR to quantify financial risk and subjects the resulting number to stress tests through scenario analysis. The CFO receives a weekly report on financial risk.

In the business risk area, the group is also using scenario analysis. By using broad, far-reaching scenarios, the group has identified numerous risks and has attempted to measure, quantify, and prioritize them. The group is preparing a white paper on business risk, which it will present to the finance committee of the board of directors.

One role of the risk management group is to engage in evangelism regarding risk management. To this end, the group has developed an intranet site that focuses on risk management, and the group maintains face-to-face contact with business unit managers. The goal is for operations people to consider risk in their everyday decision making.

# People Interviewed

Brent Callinicos, treasurer

Lori Jorgensen, risk management group manager

George H. Zinn, director, corporate finance

# Endnotes

1. Bill Gates, *Business @ the Speed of Thought* (New York: Warner Books, 1999): 262.

2. Adam Cohen, "Microsoft Enjoys Monopoly Power...," *Time* (November 15, 1999): 69.

3. "Microsoft—Togetherness," *The Economist* (January 22, 2000): 65–66.

4. *Microsoft 1999 Annual Report,* 23.

5. *Nightly Business Report,* National Public Radio broadcast (June 8, 1999), Transcript # 99060801-118.

6. Most of this section is based on Brent Callinicos, "Trimming Risk From Microsoft's Corporate Tree," in *Case Studies in Corporate Risk Management,* edited by Gregory W. Brown and Donald H. Chew (London: Risk Books, 1999): 349–366.

7. Philippe Jorion, *Value at Risk: The New Benchmark for Controlling Market Risk* (New York: McGraw-Hill, 1997): xiii.

8. Callinicos, "Trimming Risk," 350.

9. Ibid., 352.

10. Ibid., 349.

11. *Microsoft 1999 Annual Report,* 25.

12. Gates, *Business @ the Speed of Thought,* 18.

13. Ibid.

14. Edward Teach, "Microsoft's Universe of Risk," *CFO* (March 1997): 69.

15. A risk map for Microsoft was published in 1997. [See Lucy Nottingham, *A Conceptual Framework for Integrated Risk Management* (Ottawa, Ontario: The Conference Board of Canada, 1977): 8.] We were advised that the risk map was very out-of-date. Microsoft management stated that the current risk map was confidential. We decided not to include the obsolete risk map in this study.

16. Edward Teach, "The Finest in Finance: Gregory B. Maffei," *CFO* (October 1999): 48. Mr. Maffei left Microsoft in January 2000 to become CEO of Fiber Inc.

17. Jonathan Moules and Jed Horowitz, "Guts and Glitter," *Treasury and Risk Management* (November 1999): 29–20.

18. Margaret Price, "The Valedictorians: Part 1 of 2," *Treasury and Risk Management* (November 1998): 30.

# United Grain Growers Limited

*I think the point to risk management is not to try and operate your business in a risk-free environment. It's to tip the scale to your advantage. So it becomes strategic rather than just defensive.*

Peter G. M. Cox, CFO

## Company Background

United Grain Growers Limited (UGG) is the third-largest grain handler and distributor of crop inputs (seed, fertilizers, herbicides, and pesticides) in Canada. UGG was formed in 1906 and, until 1993, operated as a farmer-owned cooperative whose primary business and income came from grain handling in western Canada. Western Canada has more than 100,000 farms, and in 1997, farm expenditures on crop inputs and feed totaled approximately C$4 billion. In the late 1990s, Canada's share of world wheat trade was 22 percent, virtually all produced in western Canada.

UGG fulfills a key role in the "seed-to-supermarket" food system. It provides a reliable supply channel, with on-time delivery to exacting specifications. Canadian law requires that all wheat and barley destined for human consumption be sold through the Canadian Wheat Board (CWB). These are known as "Board grains," for which UGG is paid a preestablished handling tariff per tonne. UGG also buys "non-Board grains" (e.g., canola, flax, linola, peas, feed barley, and other grains not subject to the CWB monopoly) and markets them domestically and internationally. UGG earns a margin on non-Board grains based on the efficiency with which it markets and manages inventory and hedges its positions on world futures markets. UGG serves as the link between the

CWB and the farmer for handling Board grains, and between the farmer and the market for non-Board grains. UGG delivers Board grains, purchased on behalf of the CWB, to meet CWB sales contracted on domestic and international wheat and barley markets. UGG sells non-Board grains, purchased directly from farmers, on its own account in domestic and international markets.

Either farmers deliver grain to the company's temporary storage elevators, located at strategic points across the prairie growing area, or UGG picks it up from the farms. UGG then weighs and grades the grain and decides whether to clean it (remove any foreign material) at the elevator or at port terminals—a later stage in the handling process for export sales. UGG also gathers production information, sources further grain supplies, and markets crop input products at the elevators.

## A New Business Environment

Although grain handling may appear to be a relatively stable business, the last decade of the twentieth century brought dramatic changes to UGG's business environment and the company itself. For most of UGG's history, Board grains represented 80 percent or more of Canadian production, providing relative stability in the grain-handling companies' profit margins (from the preestablished handling tariffs paid by the CWB). In the early 1990s, Canadian production of non-Board grains increased substantially in response to international demand, primarily for oilseeds, reducing Board grains to approximately 60 percent of total throughput. This situation exposed Canadian grain handlers to the greater risk of marketing significantly more grain directly on international commodity markets.

At the same time, pressure was building for world trade reform on export subsidies, tariffs, and other barriers to international trade in agricultural products (such as had already occurred with manufactured goods). Also, grain transportation by rail (the principal means of shipment) in Canada had been subject to extensive government intervention for almost a century. But over the past 10 years, progressive reforms to the government regulations have provided a powerful incentive to grain handlers to invest heavily in modern, high-throughput elevators to take advantage of the increasing opportunity to load rail cars more cost-efficiently in large blocks. Always subject to the vagaries of the weather and the international market for agricultural products, the Canadian industry was also buffeted during the late 1990s by a decline in grain shipments (from a long-term growth trend), and during the past two years, commodity prices have been depressed, causing farmers to cut back purchases of crop inputs.

UGG survived successfully as a cooperative into the mid-1980s, missing dividend payments in only three years during the 1930s as a result of a prolonged prairie-wide drought. However, from a peak in 1984, earnings declined steadily, culminating in a substantial loss in 1989.

This array of challenges and uncertainties acted as a catalyst for a number of major changes within UGG. The company acknowledged that it must respond to the prospect of increasing competition and the changing needs of a rapidly evolving customer. In 1991, UGG changed its by-laws to allow, for the first time in its history, the appointment of a non-farmer CEO, drawn from UGG's management. That year, the company also dramatically changed its strategic direction. In 1992, a special act of the Parliament of Canada allowed UGG to change its charter and become a public company, which it did in 1993 by issuing shares that trade on the Toronto and Winnipeg stock exchanges. During the same period and into the mid-1990s, the company went through a series of rapid changes, divesting noncore assets (such as its oilseed crushing and printing operations), initiating an elevator infrastructure rationalization and reinvestment plan, reorganizing and downsizing livestock feed manufacturing, and developing its crop inputs business.

The new company was facing a rapidly changing market with a new strategic plan. The changing economics of grain handling, with partial deregulation of rail transportation, demanded lower cost structures, particularly for a newly minted public company. In the five years leading up to 1999, UGG spent more than C$200 million (2.5 times depreciation) on infrastructure renewal (excluding acquisitions and other investments). See table 6.1 for UGG's financial highlights. The imperative of improving its return on equity spurred UGG to achieve higher throughput and install a more cost-efficient elevator system that can both handle more grain and provide crop input distribution facilities to farmers. UGG plans to make its grain-handling system the most efficient, low-cost network in Canada. This focus has already led to annual cost savings of more than 10 percent and, in a fully deregulated grain-handling industry, could provide the basis for increasing UGG's market share. The strategy of developing the company's crop inputs business has also been successful, increasing sales from C$75 million to C$300 million over 10 years. Rationalization of the livestock feed manufacturing division led to an increase in operating income from C$1 million to C$7.25 million over five years. Although these strategic developments have led to a string of progressively stronger earnings until the downturn in agricultural markets in 1999 (see table 6.1), they have also changed the face of UGG. Traditionally, the company generated most of its earnings from grain handling. In 1999, however, for the first time in UGG's almost 100-year history, grain handling did not produce the majority of its operating income (see figure 6.1). Moreover, as the agribusiness recession in 1999 demonstrated, the combination of external events and a rapidly changing business environment can create considerable fluctuations in revenues and earnings, which have been reflected in the stock price (see figure 6.2).

Only one thing seems certain—uncertainty and risk will not only continue but also will require new approaches to business. Risk and the opportunities it creates are not new to UGG and its farmer-customers. The company has always operated in an inherently risky environment. But how can UGG continue to fulfill its corporate mission of "meeting farmers' business needs" and improve shareholder value at the same time? UGG is seeking, as the CFO states, "to tip the scales" so that risk is turned into a competitive advantage rather than a threat. To do this, the company must continually improve management of all its risks, bringing ever-increasing discipline and rigor to the loss prevention and mitigation processes.

## The Road to Enterprise-wide Risk Management

To understand UGG's approach to extending the scope of its risk management activities, it is necessary to appreciate something of the culture it has developed during the past decade. UGG has become a company that responds positively to change. Senior management prides itself on adopting a flexible, pragmatic approach to doing business and on being open to new and innovative ideas. Brian Hayward, the company's (first nonfarmer) CEO, notes, "Every once in a while, for some reason, we

*Table 6.1*
*UGG's Financial Record as a Public Company (C$ in thousands)*

|  | Years ending July 31 | | | | | |
|  | 1994 | 1995 | 1996 | 1997 | 1998 | 1999 |
|---|---|---|---|---|---|---|
| Operating income |  |  |  |  |  |  |
| Grain handling | 13,561 | 14,906 | 28,612 | 27,242 | 29,810 | 14,218 |
| Crop production services | 7,990 | 11,206 | 5,717 | 18,918 | 20,540 | 16,646 |
| Livestock services | 2,054 | 3,292 | 4,730 | 5,266 | 7,247 | 5,076 |
| Farm business communications | 699 | 397 | 267 | 1,206 | 1,565 | 1,242 |
| Corporate and other | (11,692) | (14,650) | (15,236) | (14,180) | (15,827) | (15,546) |
|  | 12,612 | 15,151 | 24,090 | 38,452 | 43,335 | 21,636 |
| Interest and securitization expenses | (8,840) | (14,869) | (16,025) | (13,708) | (11,409) | ($13,569) |
| Earnings before income taxes | 3,772 | 282 | 8,065 | 24,744 | 31,926 | 8,067 |
| Unusual items | (2,022) | (12,527) |  | (4,521) |  |  |
| Provision for income taxes | (1,597) | 4,860 | (2,214) | (11,164) | (15,594) | (4,492) |
| Net earnings | 153 | (7,385) | 5,851 | 9,059 | 15,332 | 3,575 |
| Capital expenditures and acquisitions | 27,725 | 43,894 | 26,826 | 21,904 | 53,760 | 82,563 |
| Depreciation and amortization | 12,926 | 15,422 | 16,108 | 16,336 | 17,242 | 20,787 |

seem to end up looking at an issue purely pragmatically but in a way that, for some bizarre reason, nobody else has done."

One example occurred in 1992 when UGG upgraded its computer platform. Instead of adopting the then-conventional approach of migrating to a larger mainframe computer, UGG decided to build a complete client-server system from scratch (and make it year 2000 compliant—years before most organizations had recognized the issue). At that time, few companies had considered a client-server setup. As a direct result of this initiative, UGG was nominated for the Smithsonian award for the innovative use of client-server technology in 1995.

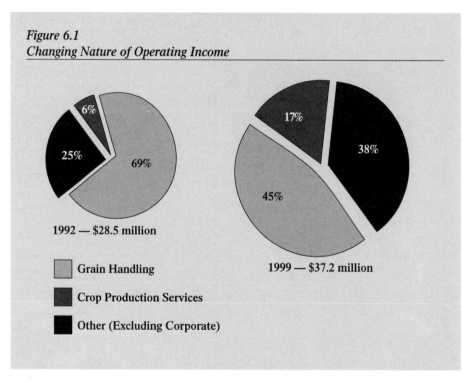

Figure 6.1
*Changing Nature of Operating Income*

1992 — $28.5 million

1999 — $37.2 million

- Grain Handling
- Crop Production Services
- Other (Excluding Corporate)

Other events converged to start UGG on the road to enterprise-wide risk management. UGG noted that the mid-1990s seemed to be the "age of corporate governance." External events such as the Barings Bank and Orange County financial disasters attracted the company's attention, as did key documents such as guidelines from the Canadian Institute of Chartered Accountants Criteria of Control Board (the Canadian version of COSO) and the Toronto Stock Exchange's Dey Report, "Where Were the Directors?" According to Brian Brown, manager of corporate audit services,

> There was a growing consensus that boards of directors and senior management should become more fully aware of the key components of good corporate governance, one of them being risk management. Do the board and management have a comprehensive understanding of the risks the company faces? And do they understand the full implications of adverse experience with those risks?

*Figure 6.2*
*UGG Stock Price: July 1993 to June 1999*

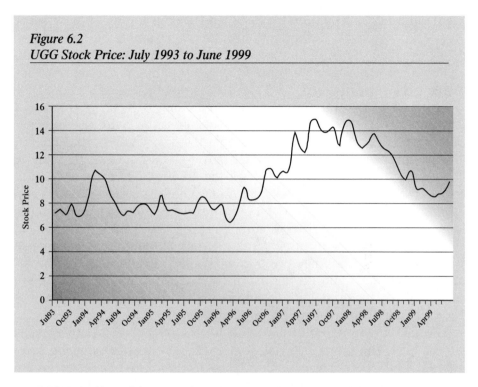

UGG believed it was already managing most of its business risks effectively. However, some of its risk management was explicit and some was implicit, with different tolerance levels in different areas of the business. For example, UGG already had a treasury group managing foreign exchange and interest rate exposures and a grain marketing group managing commodity price and basis risk. However, because the two groups report to different senior managers, they were not using a common methodology to develop position limits. In addition, UGG's risk and insurance management group was already conducting "exposure reviews and analyses" for each business sector. This process, however, had a traditional insurance (property and casualty risk) focus rather than a holistic scope that incorporated exposure to business risks. It nevertheless provided a useful framework within which to assess exposures in each business segment and discuss loss control issues with divisional business managers. Although UGG believed it already had good risk policies, risk control practices, and formal reporting, it sought to improve internal communication, accountability, focus, and understanding of the costs of its principal risks (including non-traditionally insurable business risks). It also wanted a risk management system that enabled it to respond more effectively to risks that posed the greatest threat in terms of either frequency or severity.

An early step toward improved understanding of business risks was a 1995 audit of UGG's treasury department conducted by treasury specialists as part of an international benchmark study. UGG participated in the study because it wanted to verify that it had a full understanding of its exposures and was using state-of-the-art methods to quantify and monitor how well it was managing them. UGG learned several things from this review. Although its overall control structure was judged superior, the treasury specialists identified aspects that could be improved. They recommended the use of value-at-risk methodology to enhance quantification and validate position limits, the creation of more formalized policies and exposure limits, the active involvement of executives and the board in approving risk policies and monitoring compliance, and the creation of a risk management committee.

As UGG considered its approach to risk management, other issues arose. First, there was growing awareness at the policy-making level that UGG needed a more comprehensive view of its risk management practices. Second, the company knew that increasingly sophisticated tools were becoming available to measure the probable cost of risks being assumed daily. Without this increased precision, UGG believed intuition was playing too great a role in decision making. Making less than fully informed decisions led to several questions. How could UGG allocate capital as efficiently as possible if it did not know the true cost of risk? How could the board of directors fully evaluate management's performance if it was not equipped to evaluate the impact of controllable risks compared to uncontrollable risks on the company's performance? According to CFO Peter Cox, "Truly effective management assessment should factor in and recognize performance in relation to manageable risks and discount the effects of unmanageable risks."

A third issue was that UGG saw inconsistencies in its approach to different risks—that is, as the company examined its approach to enterprise-wide risk management, it became apparent that it was not consistently adopting the same level of risk tolerance throughout the company. This led to a fourth issue: insufficient articulation of a clear risk tolerance or acceptance level established and communicated enterprise-wide. Finally, UGG recognized that in setting standards of enterprise-wide risk tolerance, it needed to consider the risk tolerance of its stakeholders—specifically, that although a farmer-owned cooperative might be expected to be conditioned to the effects of drought or commodity price fluctuations, public shareholders might not be as forbearing.

The combined effect of these influences led UGG to consider infrastructure issues. The company had determined that it needed enterprise-wide risk management policies and so formed a risk management committee that included the CEO, CFO, corporate risk manager, treasurer, manager of corporate audit, compliance manager, and divisional managing directors (as required). In addition to recommending policy and process, this committee was responsible for formal reporting to the audit committee of the board of directors on risk management performance—which was expanded to include more comprehensive information on performance in relation to the full range of risk exposures, not simply the previous practice of reporting adverse experience with insured risks, treasury, and derivatives trading exposures.

## Strategic Risk Management Project

The board of directors mandated that the risk management committee assume responsibility for the Strategic Risk Management Project, with the stated objectives of identifying the principal risks and developing appropriate solutions to manage them as effectively as possible. Committee members identified three key components in the risk management process:

1. Risks must be identified.

2. Risks must be evaluated, including analysis and quantification of the impact of the risks on UGG's financial performance, which UGG acknowledges is an ongoing process.

3. The optimum mix of risk management strategies must be determined. That is, UGG must balance loss control (investing in processes and systems to reduce, prevent, or avoid risks), risk transfer (paying a third party to assume the risks or

transferring the financial responsibility by contract), and risk retention (financing the losses either through internal preloss funding or postloss absorption).

The committee's overall goals were to lower the long-term cost of risk, protect UGG from excessive downside risk, and, if possible, reduce potential earnings volatility.

## Hiring Consultants

UGG believed it needed a more comprehensive process to achieve these objectives and recognized its need for consulting advice. The company used several criteria to select consultants:

- They should understand UGG's business.

- They should have leading-edge risk management expertise.

- They should be capable of providing whatever support UGG required to reach solutions that could be implemented practically given UGG's financial resources.

- They should have the quantitative skills required to provide the best possible measures of the risks the company faced.

- They should have the tools (e.g., software, models) to help analyze risks on both an individual and consolidated basis.

UGG chose Willis Risk Solutions as its consultants.

## Risk Identification

The next step in the process was to identify UGG's risks. Considering the enterprise-wide approach UGG sought, this step was designed to ensure that UGG covered all its risks. Furthermore, the company needed to assess the significance of each risk. To do this, UGG assembled a team of 20 people from across the company. This team worked with the consultants in a day-long brainstorming risk identification session. Brown comments on the selection of the team: "People were selected who had some visibility and global perspective or understanding of the company and who represented a broad range of the company's operations."

The team comprised most of the executive group, including the CEO and CFO, as well as employees selected for their understanding of different aspects of the company's operations. The objective was to identify every risk UGG faced—business by business—including but not confined to financial, property, and casualty risks. The result of the session was a list of 47 key business risks (including those currently insured).

The list was noteworthy for a number of reasons:

- It included the obvious risks (to an agribusiness), such as weather, commodity price/basis risk, inventory spoilage, and livestock disease.

- It included financial risks such as foreign exchange, leverage, and interest rate risk.

- It included less usually recognized risks such as strategic planning, data accuracy, loss of key personnel, technology, intellectual property rights, and even the possibility of the province of Quebec separating from Canada.

The team also ranked the risks on a scale from 1 to 3:

1. Highly critical

2. Moderately important

3. Least important

For some risks there was considerable variability in the rankings within the team. For example, most of the team believed that regulatory risk was critical, but some believed it was less important and one believed it was unimportant. Although it is unlikely that complete agreement can be reached on ranking risks, ranking patterns did emerge across the group.

The team then focused on a narrower group of risks. The list of 47 was pared down to 24, and 18 were further segregated into three groups of six. Of these 18, UGG prioritized six on which to concentrate the initial round of in-depth analysis based on their perceived priorities for further evaluation and quantification. Not all the 18 risks initially "short listed," and more particularly, the six that UGG selected to study first, were necessarily those ranked as most important in the brainstorming process, a fact that highlights another aspect of UGG's focusing process:

Because the company believed it was already managing many of its risks well, the risks prioritized initially were those that UGG believed most lent themselves to being better managed with the insights gained through more intensive quantification.

One of the criteria UGG used to choose the first six risks was that they represented core business risks. Another was that they were either currently uninsurable or the availability of insurance was limited. Two risks, because they related to events beyond the company's control, did not lend themselves to being managed proactively within the company.

## Risk Quantification and Validation

The next step was to validate the company's perceptions of the significance of the six risks. For example, UGG knew that its receivables portfolio and credit risk represented an important exposure. UGG also knew (from its experience in securitizing them) that farm receivables generally represent a superior credit risk. However, the company did not have solid empirical evidence of the variability of this risk—that is, the extent to which UGG's exposure to losses might increase during farm income crises (resulting from such events as drought or depressed commodity prices). As a UGG document at the time stated, "The essential question is whether we know enough about the principal risks to begin developing solutions." The significance of this question lies in the resulting step in the process. Although team members can rank a risk as important and may believe it can be better managed, how do they know whether it actually has as much effect as they think it does? This question is critical to formulating an appropriate management response—to avoid over- or underreaction. Of course, until the level of risk is validated by quantitative analysis, it is difficult to be sure that a truly effective solution has been adopted. Michael J. McAndless, corporate risk manager, comments on knowing this "real" level of risk:

> Whether you ultimately act or not on a specific risk, the important thing is to know exactly what it is so that the action or inaction is a well-informed response. We now know a whole lot more about our exposures, and, I think, this knowledge may actually allow us to take a bit more risk.

Knowing its dollar exposures to risks and, most important, its frequency distributions was key to improving UGG's risk management practices. The approach UGG and its consultants took and the results they obtained depended on the nature of the risks and the amount and quality of data available. Initially there were some concerns. Treasurer George Prosk notes,

> One of the issues we faced was, of course, that it was easy to say we needed a more comprehensive enterprise risk management approach, one that incorporated value at risk—and it's relatively easy for a guy in financial markets to do this. But it's much harder to try to get a handle on the less easily measurable business risks. How do you identify a value at risk model for those kinds of situations?

The quantitative skills of the consultants were critical to overcoming this problem. Even then, to compile a sufficient profile of some risks, it was necessary to gather data going back as far as 30 years. The result, however, was a much better understanding of the potential effects of the risks analyzed.

The quantitative methods used enabled UGG to establish VAR for each exposure. Figures 6.3 and 6.4 illustrate the type of results UGG obtained from the quantitative analysis. Figure 6.3 shows the probability and expected amount of losses for a sample risk. The vertical axis represents the probability of annual losses exceeding the amounts shown on the horizontal axis. Figure 6.3 also shows that the total VAR (at the 95th percentile) is approximately $6.2 million—that is, 5 percent of the time, UGG can expect to incur losses of $6.2 million or more from this risk over the measured period of time. This is a relatively high-impact risk to UGG, but of course, the probability (or frequency) of losses equaling or exceeding this amount is relatively low. Conversely, UGG can expect to incur losses in excess of $300,000 in nine years out of ten from this risk. Average exposure (at the 50th percentile) is about $1.15 million per year.

Quantifying the severity and frequency of losses in this manner can be revealing. Using this analysis, UGG determined that some risks were not as significant as it had estimated using less sophisticated techniques. In one instance, in which UGG had previously judged that it usually incurred losses, the analysis revealed that the company frequently incurred gains.

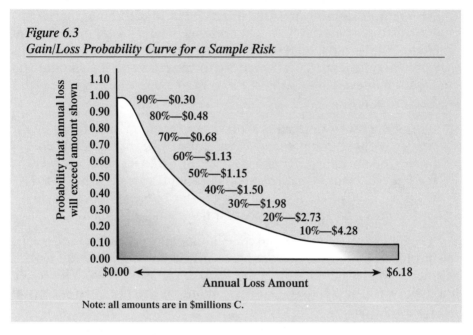

*Figure 6.3*
*Gain/Loss Probability Curve for a Sample Risk*

Note: all amounts are in $millions C.

Figure 6.4 shows another means of demonstrating the impact of particular risks on the company: the effect on earnings per share (EPS) of eliminating a particular risk. By plotting EPS both with and without the impact of the losses from that risk, figure 6.4 reveals that, in this example, there is a 50 percent chance that EPS will be less than $2.40 and a 90 percent chance that EPS will be less than $3.20 (actual figures have been altered to preserve confidentiality). If that risk could be completely eliminated, the probability of EPS being less than $3.20 per share would be reduced from 90 percent to 80 percent, and the lowest probable limit on earnings might be increased from less than zero to $1.20. In practice, the cost of few, if any, risks can be reduced to zero, but this technique does demonstrate their relative impact—in terms of severity and frequency—on a company's financial performance.

Not surprisingly, the analysis and risk quantification process confirmed that UGG's major business risk was grain-handling volume. UGG had initially characterized its greatest risk as weather—specifically the effect of drought on the harvest. The analysis demonstrated, however, that the greatest risk was not the weather itself but a risk generally (but not always) correlated with the weather—grain-handling volume.

*Figure 6.4*
*Impact of a Sample Risk on Earnings per Share (EPS)*
*(actual figures have been altered to preserve confidentiality)*

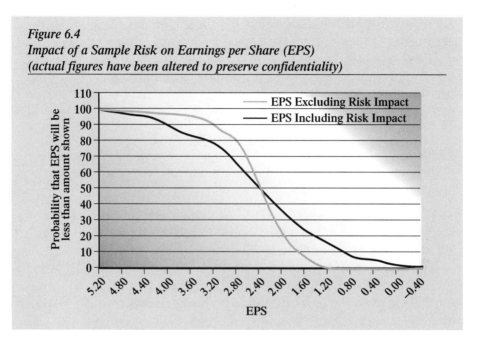

Coming to appreciate this subtle difference in the nature of the risk was an important step toward better risk management. Clearly, weather affects volume, but so do other factors. Also obvious is the fact that weather is out of UGG's control. However, although a suitable derivative to hedge the weather risk had proved elusive, UGG did find that, through transfer, it could manage the financial impact of the volume risk.

The quantitative analysis also provided information on the aggregate effect of the first group of six risks: They could contribute as much as 50 percent of the variance that occurred in the company's revenues. This can be seen in figure 6.5, which shows revenues for 1980 to 1994 (for confidentiality, amounts have been suppressed). The figure shows actual revenues compared with "risk-corrected" revenues, with actual revenues demonstrating the historical variability in UGG's revenues. Risk-corrected revenues indicate how much variability could be reduced if particular risks were eliminated.

Figure 6.5 reinforces the value not only of knowing what a company's risks are but also of systematically quantifying their severity and frequency. Until a company fully appreciates this overall effect, it is difficult to make sound decisions concerning risk acceptance, sharing, transfer, or financing.

Once a company knows its risk levels, it can make better informed decisions to reduce the degree of revenue volatility illustrated in figure 6.5. If cost-effective financing opportunities are available, they may be a desirable option. Alternatively, it may be possible to manage the risk by other methods. McAndless comments,

> You have choices. Do you look at a financing option, to possibly transfer the risk—which costs money, of course—or do you just manage the business within limits and apply strong risk-control techniques and discipline, retaining the financial impact of the risk on your own account?

The insights gained from rigorously analyzing and quantifying the principal risks can enable management to reconsider the levels of risk it takes and the degree of control it exercises. If the analysis and quantification process confirms management's previous rating of a risk, the related processes and controls should already be appropriate to the level of risk. However, if a risk is found to be lower than previously assumed, the processes and controls that have been established to manage that

*Figure 6.5*
*Actual Revenues Versus Risk-Corrected Revenues*

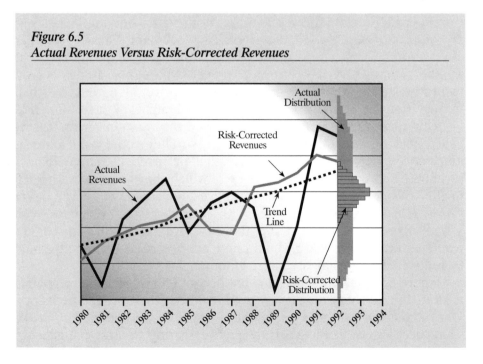

risk may be excessive (cost inefficient). Thus, a company can use the knowledge it gains to reallocate capital or resources.

Some risks, however, cannot be quantified. Two examples of non-quantifiable risks that UGG encountered were technology and regulatory risks. McAndless states, "We know that technology risk is there somewhere but we still don't know how to quantify it. There will always be risks that we don't know how to quantify."

As the process evolved, UGG also learned that a new approach to risk management would not come overnight. Figure 6.6 shows an approximate timeline of events related to the risk management project, demonstrating that the process can take considerable time.

However, UGG has also realized most of the benefits it expected from the process—some of which are significant. They include a risk management framework and reporting structure, better knowledge of its risks, and validation of risk tolerance levels—plus a risk financing solution that transfers a substantial part of UGG's earnings volatility to a third party.

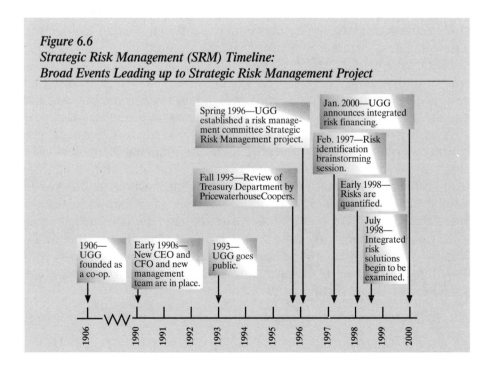

*Figure 6.6*
*Strategic Risk Management (SRM) Timeline:*
*Broad Events Leading up to Strategic Risk Management Project*

Spring 1996—UGG established a risk management committee Strategic Risk Management project.

Jan. 2000—UGG announces integrated risk financing.

Feb. 1997—Risk identification brainstorming session.

Fall 1995—Review of Treasury Department by PricewaterhouseCoopers.

Early 1998—Risks are quantified.

July 1998—Integrated risk solutions begin to be examined.

1906—UGG founded as a co-op.

Early 1990s—New CEO and CFO and new management team are in place.

1993—UGG goes public.

1906 | 1990 | 1991 | 1992 | 1993 | 1994 | 1995 | 1996 | 1997 | 1998 | 1999 | 2000

# Integrated Risk Financing

At the outset, Cox was particularly interested in reducing the company's cost of risk (premiums plus retained losses). Claims recovered on UGG's property and casualty insurance programs were averaging approximately 40 percent of total aggregate premium expense; so-called insurance friction costs were around 60 percent of premiums, even though UGG had significantly reduced insurance premiums over several years. The problem was not excessive premiums for the risks insured but the company's inability to use the benefit of very low loss ratios (in some cases, zero) on some lines of insurance to offset less favorable loss ratios on others. Willis Risk Solutions believed that some of these risks could be managed more efficiently by bundling them into a portfolio, rather than continuing to manage each separately because most of the exposures were uncorrelated. By integrating the risks into one "pool" of risks, UGG could use good loss experience on one line to offset poor loss experience on others, potentially reducing the company's long-term cost of risk.

Quantifying the first six business risks showed that five of them were sufficiently well managed by conventional internal control techniques. The remaining major business risk, which resulted in very substantial periodic losses (in the form of revenue reductions from normal levels), was grain-handling volume. The quantitative analysis indicated that prairie-wide droughts occur, on average, about once every 12 years and can reduce grain-handling volumes and revenues in the subsequent year by as much as 20 percent. It also showed that other less frequent, less severe external factors can affect the volume of grain handled. Obviously, this risk was beyond management's control. The quantitative analysis also showed that it was not correlated with the insured risks. Armed with sufficient data on grain-handling volumes to enable an insurer to price the risk, UGG's consultants suggested that the company seek an "insurance" solution to transfer this risk. By combining the grain-handling volume risk with the noncorrelated property and casualty risks that lent themselves to being insured within an integrated program, UGG might obtain further gains:

- Further reduce the long-term cost of risk (from the "portfolio effect").

- Reduce earnings volatility.

- Increase leverage capacity by transferring part of a previously retained risk to a third party.

Integrated risk financing programs were not entirely new at the time (mid-1999). Some had been in place for more than a year, but most of them integrated financial risks (previously hedged in derivatives markets) with traditionally insured property and casualty risks. UGG's mix integrated a previously uninsurable business risk with property and casualty risks. With this concept in mind, UGG agreed to have Willis market its program to a number of major international insurance companies.

Somewhat to UGG's surprise, several insurers expressed an appetite to underwrite the combination of risks that UGG was bringing to the market. As a result, UGG was able to announce in November 1999 that starting on December 31, 1999, it would establish an integrated risk-financing program with Swiss Re, combining property and casualty with grain-handling volume risk. This program was a key result of UGG's risk analysis process. In announcing it, Cox stated,

> With this program in place, UGG will be protected with what amounts to a floor on any substantial drop in grain-handling revenue, providing more stability in UGG's earnings growth going forward.

Moreover, the premium on the new program was only marginally higher than those on the previous policies for property and casualty risks—with the added protection on grain-handling volumes. This program is testament to the power of the portfolio effect. By bundling the risks into one program, UGG can offset poor loss experience on one risk against favorable experience on others and reduce the "friction costs" of multiple programs. Figure 6.7 illustrates how this might increase shareholder value. The graphs to the left indicate the effect on earnings volatility of reducing the long-term cost of risk and transferring part of the cost of a major business risk: Earnings distribution is reduced and the median increased. The graphs to the right show that share price is likely to follow a pattern similar to earnings, with one significant difference: The reduction in earnings volatility, because it is likely to reduce the company's beta, should not only reduce share price volatility but also increase the average price over time.

*Figure 6.7*
*Effect of Integrated Risk Management on*
*Earnings, Share Price, and Shareholder Value*

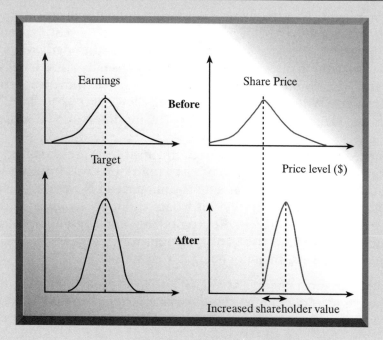

Another benefit UGG expects over time is a reduced cost of capital, resulting from the leverage effect referred to above. UGG would not disclose the precise calculation of the integrated program's effect on leverage because doing so would reveal details of premiums, deductibles, insurance limits, and so forth, which it wishes to keep confidential. As Cox puts it, however, "It is intuitively obvious that transferring a significant portion of a major potential business loss off-balance-sheet reduces the need for precautionary capital."

UGG estimates that the program has enabled it to increase leverage by approximately 2.5 percent—from 50 percent at July 31, 1999, to 52.5 percent—without increasing its overall level of risk. Table 6.2 illustrates how this will reduce the company's cost of capital. The higher debt levels, carrying a lower cost than equity and forming a greater proportion of total financing costs, reduce the overall cost of capital to the company.

*Table 6.2*
*The Effect of the Integrated Risk Financing Program on UGG's Cost of Capital*

| | Actual at July 31, 1999 | | | After Integrated Risk Financing Program | | |
|---|---|---|---|---|---|---|
| | Funds Invested | After-tax Cost of Funds | | Funds Invested | After-tax Cost of Funds | |
| | (C$ million) | (%) | (C$ million) | (C$ million) | (%) | (C$ million) |
| Short-term debt | 138.3 | 2.8% | 3.9 | 144.2 | 2.8% | 4.1 |
| Long-term debt | 150.3 | 4.5% | 6.7 | 156.7 | 4.5% | 7.0 |
| Total debt | 288.5 | 3.7% | 10.6 | 300.9 | 3.7% | 11.1 |
| Deferred taxes | 51.6 | | | 51.6 | | |
| Shareholders' equity | | | | | | |
| Preferred shares | 22.1 | 5.0% | 1.1 | 22.1 | 5.0% | 1.1 |
| Common shares | 211.1 | 13.0% | 27.4 | 198.7 | 13.0% | 25.8 |
| Total funds invested | 573.4 | 6.8% | 39.2 | 573.4 | 6.6% | 38.0 |
| Leverage | 50% | | | 52.5% | | |
| Reduction in cost of capital | | | | | 0.2% | 1.2 |

## Risk Management Infrastructure

A final outcome of UGG's risk management process was an improved risk management infrastructure. That infrastructure now includes new software tools that enable UGG to quantify its risks more accurately and prepare alternative scenario analyses. Another improvement to the infrastructure was a change in method. McAndless comments,

> A few years ago, in each of the operating divisions, we started to do a traditional exposure analysis: "OK, here's your business. This is your liability exposure, your property exposure, and environmental exposure." Then we went through all those things and ensured either management control systems or insurance were in place to respond. What we're now doing is extending that process to the nontraditional or enterprise risks.

Perhaps the most important infrastructure enhancement was the formation of the risk management committee. The committee was established early in the process and now meets to review risks and report to the audit committee quarterly. The committee issued the "Risk Management Philosophy, Policy, and Framework," a statement of UGG's approach to and tolerance for risk. It discusses UGG's plan to be proactive in assessing all material risks. It also provides guidance on UGG's level of materiality—if the VAR "meets or exceeds the threshold of materiality considered by the shareholders' auditors." The document indicates that the purpose of the risk management committee is to "assess the risk profile" of the company and to "recommend policies."

An indication of the increased emphasis on improved risk management is that the CEO now routinely reports to the board of directors on any matters "that might reasonably be considered to pose a material risk to UGG." UGG's approach to risk is not just to integrate risk financing into a common program but also to integrate the control of risk into its management structure and practices.

UGG has made considerable progress in risk management. Commenting on the early phase of establishing an enterprise-wide risk management system, Cox states, "We didn't really know enough about the methodology for looking into the whole range of risks we faced." Later, he recognized how much had been accomplished: "What we've done is overlaid all the techniques and the quantitative discipline with a process." Cox comments further on that risk process:

> The value added to the process is to convey a consistent approach. We're now more aware at the executive level and audit level what all the risks are and we're beginning to communicate more clearly throughout the organization what our level of risk tolerance is, not leaving it to line managers to assume it. We're not all the way there yet, but that's where we're headed.

UGG attributes much of its success to the cohesiveness of its senior management team and its ability to both recognize its need for outside expertise and work effectively with creative consultants. McAndless provides this further insight:

> I think the real secret was two major factors. First, senior management had bought into the process early. Second, we worked well as a team and were able to bring different disciplines together effectively.

# Case Summary

UGG could not operate its business without risk management. The company's environment is inherently risky. Its business, competition, and regulatory frameworks are all changing. It sees enterprise-wide risk management as a tool to improve its competitive advantage. McAndless notes,

> I think when everything is said and done, it will be recognized that risk management is something that should be taught to and internalized by every manager. It can't be "Oh, we've got a risk manager who looks after the company's risks over there in the corner of the office." It doesn't happen that way. It's like budgeting or any other staff process. You have somebody to develop and facilitate the process, but the process has to be actively carried out by operations managers throughout the organization.

As a result of the process it has gone through, UGG knows its principal risks better than it ever did. The company validated them with a cross section of employees, ranked them for significance, and then focused on validating a short list of risks by rigorous quantitative analysis. UGG now understands these risks and their significance more clearly and has been able to lay off a significant amount of risk that it had previously considered unavoidable. It took UGG three years to get through the first part of the process and establish its Integrated Risk Financing Program.

Although the future will be the ultimate test of its enterprise-wide risk management process, UGG can make better and more consistent decisions than before. Better information on risk-adjusted returns facilitates capital allocation. The company has been able to integrate risks, previously transferred through a number of insurance policies or not insured at all, into one insurance program and capture the resulting savings. It knows that an integrated view is necessary to determine the optimal mix of risk management strategies. It knows whether the risks it is taking are tolerable in the context of the company's entire risk portfolio. It has confirmed or improved the appropriateness of some of its risk control measures. The results have also shown that managing risk more appropriately can lead to a lower total cost of risk, protect the company from excessive downside risk, reduce earnings volatility, increase leverage capacity, and lower the cost of capital—all of which have the potential to increase shareholder value.

UGG realizes that the work is not over and perhaps has just begun. Brown notes, "The 47 risks may already be outdated. We are in the process of conducting exposure reviews to determine the most important risks outstanding today." However, UGG now has the infrastructure in place to help it continually identify and manage those risks. CEO Hayward sums it up: "My job is to protect the corporation so that we're in business the next day."

## People Interviewed

Brian Hayward, CEO

Peter G. M. Cox, CFO

George Prosk, treasurer

Brian G. Brown, manager, corporate audit services

Michael J. McAndless, corporate risk manager

## Reference

*Guidance on Control* (Toronto, Ontario: Canadian Institute of Chartered Accountants, 1995).

# Unocal Corporation

*We had a pretty comprehensive loss control program that certainly was right in the fairway of loss control programs of industrial corporations. But it was still very much a compliance-based system—meaning you had X number of things you had to do from an operational standpoint, almost a series of checks. And the operations folks learned what those checks were and went through and ensured they were in compliance for those loss control guidelines.*

*[Now we've had] an organizational shift to saying, "Look, the only way we're really going to get our line people to truly embrace safe operations, effective operations, control operations as a huge part of their job is to take away the crutch of [overreliance on] staff support and, at the same time, go from a compliance-based loss control system to a more commitment-based system—here is how you run your business, and by the way, if you run your business in an effective way, the loss control numbers should follow."*

*[We're taking] an integrated way of looking at risk. But I think sometimes when we say "risk," we tend to try to segment risk as something different than just running our business. To me, running a business is all about managing risk and managing returns, whether on the financial side or balance sheet side, or running a field operation. If you analyze the real drivers of loss control, or just the drivers of economics, you will quickly see that the same drivers from a loss control standpoint tend to be pretty much the same drivers of how you make money in this business.*

Tim Ling, CFO of Unocal and executive vice president,
North American Operations[1]

# Company Background

U nocal Corporation is the world's largest investor-owned oil and gas exploration and production company.[2] Formerly known as Union Oil Co. of California,[3] Unocal traces its roots to one of the pioneers of the oil and gas industry, Lyman Stewart. Stewart began his career in the oil business in northwestern Pennsylvania during the 1850s. The teenaged Stewart would search for oil by riding the countryside on horseback and "sniffing gopher holes." Stewart originally planned to become a missionary and thought he could finance this pursuit with money from the fledgling oil business. At that time, oil was used mainly for "cure-all" medicines marketed in apothecary shops. It was considered too odorous to be used for lighting—whale oil was then the predominant fuel for lighting. (Locomotives and steamships were powered by burning wood and, later, coal.) But in 1859, the realization that oil could be refined into kerosene (by then a viable fuel for lighting buildings and streets) touched off an oil boom.

Stewart began working in the Pennsylvania oil business full time, becoming an active partner in a series of drilling ventures. By the 1880s, he had accumulated a comfortable net worth but had grown tired of the vagaries and tough competition that characterized the business in Pennsylvania. He decided to move his family to California, where the oil industry was in its infancy. With W. L. Hardison, one of his Pennsylvania partners, Stewart began drilling for oil in untapped Ventura County, north of Los Angeles. Most of his efforts resulted in dry holes, almost bankrupting him. Finally in 1887, Stewart and Hardison struck a gusher. This success set them on firm footing and allowed them to transform their Hardison & Stewart partnership, along with two oil ventures of others, into Union Oil Co. of California.

Stewart proved to be a very astute oil man, guiding Union Oil over the years into one of the industry's most striking success stories. He accumulated massive holdings of valuable oil land and leases, helped pioneer the conversion from coal-powered to oil-powered engines, and shrewdly capitalized on the emergence of gasoline as the main driver of profits in the industry.[4]

Today, Stewart's legacy is reflected in Unocal in several important ways that affect the company's approach to risk management.

- The company has remained an "independent." In the early years, Stewart fended off repeated attempts by larger oil companies to acquire Union Oil. The most serious was a tough 1922 proxy fight waged by Royal Dutch Shell, based in the Netherlands but controlled by British interests. Stewart and his allies narrowly averted a takeover amid a national concern about foreigners controlling U.S. oil. In 1985, T. Boone Pickens attempted a hostile takeover of Unocal but was unsuccessful. However, the battle left the company with a heavy debt load.[5]

- The company prides itself on being the low-cost oil driller in the industry.[6] It is clear that company culture reflects the economic lessons learned by the highly efficient, no-frills, resourceful Lyman Stewart back in his wildcatting days.

- Of late, the company has focused on its primary strengths of exploration and production, which Stewart pioneered a hundred years ago. In 1997, Unocal sold its refining and marketing operations, including the Union 76 retail trademark. This has allowed the company to direct its capital deployment toward its core strengths.

In 1890, Union Oil came into existence with equity capital of $5 million. In early 2000, Unocal had a market capitalization of some $7 billion. A timeline of significant events in Unocal's history appears in figure 7.1. Figure 7.2 shows Unocal's stock price from 1979 to May 2000.

## Unocal in 2000

Lyman Stewart would hardly recognize the Unocal of 2000. Although the company still maintains its corporate headquarters in Southern California, once the nexus of Unocal's operations, all the California oil properties have been exhausted or sold. The company's energy assets are now centered in the Gulf of Mexico (Spirit Energy 76[7]) and the Far East, with lesser holdings in other areas of the United States, principally Alaska, and countries such as the Netherlands and the Congo. Overall, almost 60 percent of company revenues derive from oil production and about 30 percent from natural gas production. Table 7.1 shows the

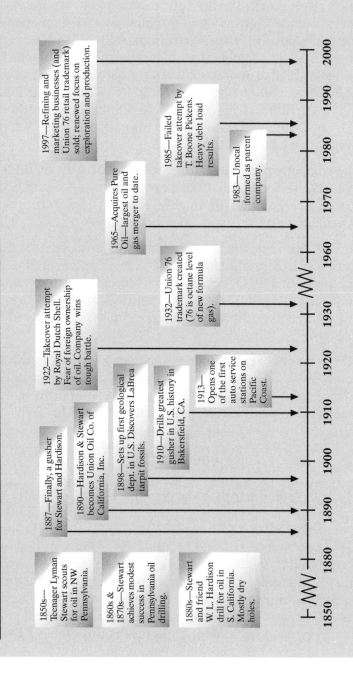

*Figure 7.1*
*Unocal Timeline*

1850s—Teenager Lyman Stewart scouts for oil in NW Pennsylvania.

1860s & 1870s—Stewart achieves modest success in Pennsylvania oil drilling.

1880s—Stewart and friend W. L. Hardison drill for oil in S. California. Mostly dry holes.

1887—Finally, a gusher for Stewart and Hardison.

1890—Hardison & Stewart becomes Union Oil Co. of California, Inc.

1898—Sets up first geological dept. in U.S. Discovers LaBrea tarpit fossils.

1910—Drills greatest gusher in U.S. history in Bakersfield, CA.

1913—Opens one of the first auto service stations on Pacific Coast.

1922—Takeover attempt by Royal Dutch Shell. Fear of foreign ownership of oil. Company wins tough battle.

1932—Union 76 trademark created (76 is octane level of new formula gas).

1965—Acquires Pure Oil—largest oil and gas merger to date.

1983—Unocal formed as parent company.

1985—Failed takeover attempt by T. Boone Pickens. Heavy debt load results.

1997—Refining and marketing businesses (and Union 76 retail trademark) sold; renewed focus on exploration and production.

1850   1880   1890   1900   1910   1920   1930   1960   1970   1980   1990   2000

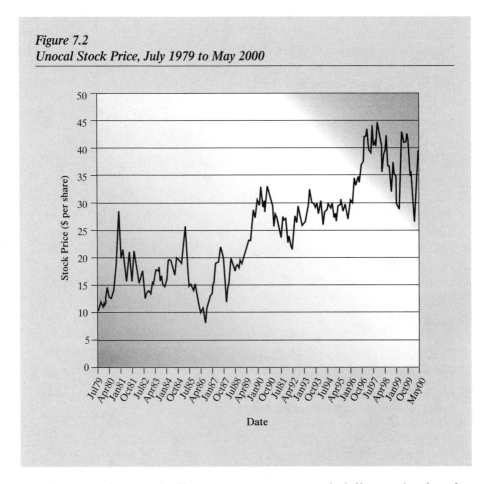

*Figure 7.2*
*Unocal Stock Price, July 1979 to May 2000*

breakdown of proved oil and gas reserves and daily production for 1997–1999.

The producing units "sell" most of their oil and gas output to Unocal's global trade business unit, which in turn sells the output in outside markets. The global trade unit is also responsible for conducting hedging activities to dampen the economic impact of commodity price swings. Table 7.2 displays Unocal's revenue by segment, income, and balance sheet highlights for 1995–1999.

*Table 7.1*
*Unocal Proved Reserves and Daily Production*

## Net Proved Reserves at Year End

| | 1999 | 1998 | 1997 |
|---|---|---|---|
| **Crude oil and condensate (million barrels)** | | | |
| United States | 175 | 182 | 209 |
| Far East | 193 | 190 | 158 |
| Other international | 178 | 158 | 166 |
| Equity affiliates | 4 | 2 | — |
| Worldwide | 550 | 532 | 533 |
| **Natural gas (billion cubic feet)** | | | |
| United States | 1,665 | 1,919 | 2,120 |
| Far East | 4,171 | 3,955 | 4,189 |
| Other international | 686 | 226 | 241 |
| Equity affiliates | 96 | 22 | — |
| Worldwide | 6,618 | 6,122 | 6,550 |

## Daily Production

Net quantities of the company's crude oil and condensate, natural gas, and natural gas liquid production per day, including the company's proportionate shares of production of equity affiliates, were as follows:

| | 1999 | 1998 | 1997 |
|---|---|---|---|
| **Crude oil and condensate (thousand barrels)** | | | |
| United States | 67 | 73 | 76 |
| Far East | 73 | 80 | 95 |
| Other international | 35 | 31 | 26 |
| Worldwide | 175 | 184 | 197 |
| **Natural gas (million cubic feet)** | | | |
| United States | 880 | 928 | 993 |
| Far East | 847 | 853 | 795 |
| Other international | 109 | 45 | 60 |
| Worldwide | 1,836 | 1,826 | 1,848 |
| **Natural gas liquids (thousand barrels)** | | | |
| United States | 13 | 14 | 12 |
| Far East | 5 | 5 | 6 |
| Other international | 1 | — | — |
| Worldwide | 19 | 19 | 18 |

Source: Unocal 10-K Report for 1999.

*Table 7.2*
*Unocal Selected Segment Information ($ millions)*

| | 1999 | 1998 | 1997 | 1996 | 1995 |
|---|---|---|---|---|---|
| **Revenue data** | | | | | |
| Sales | | | | | |
| Crude oil and condensate | $3,511 | $2,208 | $2,707 | $2,495 | $1,964 |
| Natural gas | 1,646 | 1,823 | 1,857 | 1,482 | 1,031 |
| Geothermal steam | 153 | 166 | 119 | 131 | 120 |
| Natural gas liquids | 73 | 66 | 105 | 95 | 97 |
| Petroleum products | 209 | 32 | 13 | 16 | 84 |
| Minerals | 35 | 67 | 106 | 97 | 95 |
| Other | 124 | 142 | 319 | 161 | 58 |
| Total sales revenues | 5,751 | 4,504 | 5,226 | 4,477 | 3,449 |
| Operating revenues | 91 | 123 | 116 | 108 | 169 |
| Other revenues | 215 | 476 | 283 | 227 | 278 |
| Total revenues from continuing operations | 6,057 | 5,103 | 5,625 | 4,812 | 3,896 |
| Discontinued operations | 313 | 376 | 439 | 4,787 | 4,529 |
| Total revenues | $6,370 | $5,479 | $6,064 | $9,599 | $8,425 |
| **Earnings data** | | | | | |
| Continuing operations | $113 | $93 | $515 | $358 | $175 |
| Discontinued operations | 24 | 37 | 4 | (322) | 85 |
| Extraordinary item | — | — | (38) | — | — |
| Net earnings | $137 | $130 | $581 | $36 | $260 |
| **Balance sheet data** | | | | | |
| Current assets | $1,631 | $1,388 | $1,501 | $3,228 | $1,576 |
| Current liabilities | 1,559 | 1,376 | 1,160 | 1,622 | 1,316 |
| Working capital | 72 | 12 | 341 | 1,606 | 260 |
| Total assets | 8,967 | 7,952 | 7,530 | 9,123 | 9,891 |
| Total debt and capital leases | 2,854 | 2,558 | 2,170 | 3,058 | 3,706 |
| Trust convertible preferred securities | 522 | 522 | 522 | 522 | — |
| Total stockholders' equity | 2,184 | 2,202 | 2,314 | 2,275 | 2,930 |
| Return on average stockholders' equity: | | | | | |
| Continuing operations | 5.4% | 4.3% | 26.8% | 13.8% | 6.1% |
| Including discontinued operations and extraordinary item | 6.5% | 6.0% | 25.3% | 1.4% | 9.1% |

Source: Unocal 10-K Report for 1999.

# The Nature of Risk at Unocal

The earth has been picked over for hydrocarbons. Companies have been looking everywhere since the late part of the last century and this century. All of the obvious deposits have been found. The only thing that's left is what's been excluded from exploration because of some political or technological hurdle that's yet to be overcome.

Mike Bell, vice president,
Gulf of Mexico Deepwater, Unocal Corporation

It doesn't take a sophisticated risk analysis to understand that oil exploration is an ultimate big-stakes gamble: Find oil or go broke. Rags-to-riches-to-rags tales of oil barons and wildcatters have been the stuff of popular entertainment for decades. Paraphrasing a theme from the first Clinton-Gore campaign, Mike Bell explains, "'It's the oil, stupid.' Our greatest risk is not finding sufficient volumes of hydrocarbons to develop, and develop at what would be attractive returns for us."

## Replacing the Factory

John Donohue, Spirit Energy 76's president, likens the oil business to a very unusual factory:

You know, this is a funny business. [In the past] I've worked in manufacturing, which is straightforward: here are my manufacturing costs and my transportation costs, and here's what I can sell the product for; here are my margins. The difference with oil is that you deal in a business in which you have to rebuild a big portion of your factory every year.

I can't think of another way of putting it—we have to replace a third of our factory every year. Say that on January 1 we start with 170,000 barrels a day. If we do nothing during the year, we'll end up with only about 110,000 to 120,000 a day by the end of the year. A third of our production will be gone. So we've got to rebuild that factory every year while the factory's running. It's kind of like going across the Atlantic in a 747 and saying you have to go out and fix the engine while it's flying. And that's what we do—go out and fix it, keep it running, keep it full.

Our manufacturing environment is highly unusual. This is like research, this is like taking a risk on pharmaceuticals and new drugs. Tremendous research goes into them, but only some of them pay off. In fact the majority of them do not. You've got to pay for the majority with the minority success ratio.

Ken Butler is vice president for the mature regions profit center of Spirit Energy 76. He manages assets, primarily in the Gulf of Mexico area, to maintain or increase production from known resources and to expand that resource base through additional exploration opportunities. Butler describes the problem of replenishing the company's reserves:

I've got to be taking a lot of shots out there to bring reserves in, so I've got to manage that. Can't slow it down. But if I get too risk averse and pull back on it, I'm not going to get the reserves coming in, and the pipeline will get shut off. I get into a new pool of oil or gas and I deplete that pool very, very rapidly. If I make a new discovery, a new pocket of gas, I generally will deplete that within three years.

There are two reasons for that. One is the rocks—they're very porous and very permeable, so the liquids come out at very high rates. The other reason is that we're dealing with a mature environment. There's been a lot of drilling and a lot of production [in the mature fields], so when we find something new it generally tends to be a smaller package today than it was 10 or 20 years ago.

A lot of the Middle East reservoirs are very, very thick in their hydrocarbons. The flow rate's more modulated, so once they hook them on, they're going to maintain their flow rates for 50, 60, 70 years. You come back to this environment, and what keeps me up at night is keeping the machine going. So if we find something in the morning, we've got to be figuring out that afternoon how to replace it. It's very, very repetitive.

Given limited capital for exploration, the search for oil involves decisions about which projects to pursue and which to defer. Since there is nothing approaching certainty in any of these decisions, understanding the trade-offs is critical. Tim Pownell, the director of strategic planning for Spirit Energy 76, explains:

> We have a finite amount of resources. If we're going to do X, ultimately we're not going to do Y. We need to understand what that Y is and the trade-off we're making. Is X a better project than this thing we're deferring (which really means it's not going to happen)? We have a finite amount of resources today, and we're not going to have an infinite amount next year. So if we have to defer something this year, something has to be different for that same thing not to be deferred next year. As long as we can make sure decisions are being made with everybody's eyes wide open, then I think that's the best we can do.

Understanding the risk–reward characteristics of projects is a major element in effective management of oil and gas exploration. The strategic planning unit has been experimenting with analytical tools adapted for use with the unique risk set confronting an exploration and production company. Truett Enloe, a manager in Spirit's strategic planning unit, describes one approach:

> What we're working with right now is an economic analysis software package that allows us to use Monte Carlo analysis[8] to better understand the risk and return attributes of our projects. We can do a complete risk analysis that includes reserve uncertainty, capital requirements uncertainty, and performance uncertainty. We can then use the optimization features of the software to build efficient portfolios with varying risk and return components.

A key success indicator for oil and gas companies is the replenishment of reserves. For 1999, Unocal increased its worldwide proved oil reserves by 18 million barrels, or about 3 percent. But this was possible only because the company purchased reserves of 38 million barrels, compared with 31 million barrels discovered. In that year, discoveries were only 48 percent of production. For 1996, 1997, and 1998, Unocal worldwide oil reserve replacement from discovery was 68 percent, 157 percent, and 121 percent, respectively.

## Incidents

The Exxon *Valdez* oil spill serves as a vivid reminder of another major risk of the oil business—accidents (which the industry calls "incidents") that damage the environment, result in human casualties, or cause significant property damage. In its long history, Unocal, like every other company operating in this complex and dangerous industry, has had its share of incidents, including the industry nightmare, petroleum fires. In April 1926, lightning struck a company tank farm storage facility in San Luis Obispo, California, and ignited four one-million-barrel reservoirs. A day later, lightning from the same storm struck another company tank farm in Brea, California. All told, eight million barrels of oil were destroyed (the equivalent of one-eighth of Unocal's 1999 production). At the time, the double calamity was dubbed the greatest fire loss since the San Francisco fire of 1906.

Unocal may be the low-cost oil driller, but discussions with company management make it clear that safety is never sacrificed for economic reasons. D. J. Ponville, Spirit Energy 76 drilling manager, describes his feelings about safety:

> We will risk dollars but not people. If I overspend on a well, if we perform poorly on a project, that won't keep me awake at night. My biggest fear would be for us to have a fatality on one of our jobs. Where somebody would lose a dad or someone would lose a spouse. I'm convinced that going into the new millennium, we've progressed to a point where we ought to be able to send everyone back home to their families with all their digits intact and in the same condition as when they left.

But even with strong safety programs in place, serious incidents can occur without warning. One recent incident on an offshore drill platform (operated by a company other than Unocal ) started out with fluid leaking on a mechanical brake. At the time, the brake was holding up drilling gear that weighed one and a half million pounds. The slipping brake was generating an enormous amount of heat, and it actually caught fire. The equipment operator had only a few seconds to respond with a particular sequence of actions. He did not succeed, and the gear crashed through the drill floor and fell 5,000 feet to the sea bottom. The gear, valued at tens of millions of dollars, now lies buried in the mud of the seabed, probably lost forever. One person who saw a photograph of the damage to the drill floor commented, "It was a good thing none of the workers were there at the time because nobody would have lived who had been there."[9]

## Hedging Prices

Unocal sells its oil and gas output on the open market, typically as soon as it is produced. Like any player in a commodity-based business, Unocal is subject to the risk of price fluctuations, which in the oil business can be extreme. The company actively uses futures contracts, swaps and options, and other hydrocarbon derivative financial instruments to hedge exposure to price fluctuations. Even so, its net average worldwide oil selling price (after hedging gains or losses) went from $17.71 per barrel in 1997 to $11.67 per barrel in 1998 (a 34 percent drop) to $15.38 per barrel in 1999 (a 32 percent increase). Also, the use of derivatives limited the company's ability to enjoy price upswings such as that of mid- to late 1999.

## Political Risk

Political risk is another significant factor. Most of Unocal's U.S. drilling is offshore, much of it not far from desirable recreational beach properties. This drilling is possible only with the permission and oversight of the federal government. Unocal oil and gas operations in the Far East and other parts of the world are highly dependent on the goodwill of cooperative governments.

## Sensitivity Analysis

Oil prices and drilling success rates have a highly significant impact on Unocal's earnings. As shown in table 7.3, a $1 change in worldwide oil prices per barrel would lead to an estimated $33 million change in net income and a $0.14 change in earnings per share. A 10 percent change in the exploratory drilling success rate would lead to a $27 million change in net income and an $0.11 change in earnings per share. Given the instability of oil and gas prices and the uncertainty of exploratory drilling success rates, Unocal faces significant income exposure from these two factors.

*Table 7.3*
*Unocal Earnings Sensitivity, 2000 Full Year Impact*

| | Change in Pretax $ million | Change in After-Tax $ million | Change per Share |
|---|---|---|---|
| **Prices** | | | |
| Worldwide oil per $1 change | $47 | $33 | $0.14 |
| Lower-48 gas per $.10 change | $28 | $18 | $0.07 |
| **Exploratory drilling** | | | |
| 10% change in overall success rate | $44 | $27 | $0.11 |

Source: Presentation by Tim Ling.

# Deepwater Operations

There's a time-honored principle that oil exploration has in common with the "vote early–vote often" tales of Chicago politics. It's a principle that favors companies that enter frontier areas early and drill aggressively. Late entry generally leads to value destruction. When the industry started in the deep water in the Gulf of Mexico 15 years ago, the area outboard of 1,500 feet was very lightly explored. To find that sort of lightly drilled territory now, we would have to go out beyond 5,000 feet. A fair amount of our acreage is in 3,000- to 4,000-foot water depths, but we've been focusing our efforts in acreage we hold in between 5,000 and 10,000 feet of water, which presents a unique set of challenges and a unique set of risks that are distinct from the ones in shallower water depths.

Mike Bell

As the earth is depleted of its oil, exploration companies must look harder and spend considerably more money to find what remains. With dwindling resources in the mature fields, the industry is staking a good portion of its future on deepwater exploration, a drag on current reported earnings that carries a whole new array of risks. Two converging factors made deepwater oil exploration economically feasible in the late twentieth century: the availability of vastly improved seismic data to locate the oil efficiently, and technological improvements to drill deepwater wells and bring the oil to the surface.

But deepwater drilling is risky and expensive. The seismic information is costly because of the complexity of data gathering and analysis, which must be done by specialty companies. Mike Bell explains,

> These are massive ships, 400 feet long, that are pulling a dozen six-kilometer-long cables behind them and several tons of air guns that are going off and generating enough information to swamp a supercomputer. These vessels churn through the ocean, acquiring vast quantities of information, which is transmitted via satellite to shore for in-depth analysis.

> Some of the other technologies include positioning and drilling technologies that allowed us to get drilling equipment out in deeper and deeper water; anchor-handling technologies; and remote vehicles, like the ones used to retrieve airline black boxes, that we use on a routine basis for maintaining the well head on the ocean floor. These remote vehicles are controlled by operators carrying out precision maneuvers from 7,000 feet above the wellhead.

Deepwater drilling in the Gulf of Mexico, where Unocal has a large stake, began in the mid-1980s, and the first significant discovery there was the Mars field, a joint venture of Shell and BP in the late 1980s. Since then, there has been a flurry of activity in the deepwater Gulf of Mexico. Developing and exploiting these fields is a capital-intensive undertaking that magnifies the traditional risks of oil exploration. Unocal also has deepwater interests in Indonesia, Gabon, and Brazil.

Drilling ships developed in the mid-1970s were 500 feet long and could drill in 7,000-foot water depths. The new deepwater drilling ships are 900 feet long (roughly the length of the *Titanic*), carry two drilling rigs, and can drill in 10,000-foot depths. Moreover, they are 30 to 50 percent more efficient than the older generation. Bell states, "We now have the seismic data to see where we're drilling, the drilling capability to get the drill bit down there, and an understanding of the subsurface, plus all of the breakthrough production technologies, such as tension leg platforms, that have begun to appear."[10]

Unocal's deepwater drill ship, the *Discoverer Spirit,* came on line in the third quarter of 2000. The cost to operate it is a staggering $210,000 per day. Unocal's success in the deepwater Gulf of Mexico has been mixed so far: The company has had success with wells in which it had a joint venture interest, but the four wells it drilled in 1999, although achieving records in terms of speed and cost containment, were not geological successes. The company anticipates more favorable results after the *Discoverer Spirit* is deployed. So far, Unocal has some $500 million invested in its deepwater Gulf of Mexico operation. The impact of deepwater exploration on Unocal's reported net income is highly significant. Figure 7.3 shows that in 1999, sustaining properties such as the Gulf of Mexico shelf generated pretax earnings of $831 million, while emerging deepwater business generated a pretax loss of $342 million. Year 2000 estimates predict that the loss on the emerging business segment will shrink to $250 million, and Unocal expects this positive trend to continue.

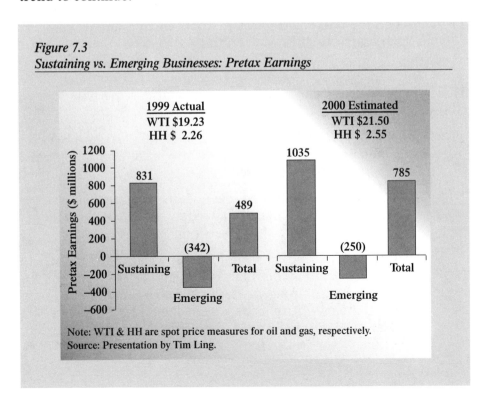

*Figure 7.3*
*Sustaining vs. Emerging Businesses: Pretax Earnings*

Note: WTI & HH are spot price measures for oil and gas, respectively.
Source: Presentation by Tim Ling.

Deepwater exploration is risky for another reason: Its economic feasibility is highly sensitive to the volatile price of oil. Bell explains,

> Deepwater developments are billion-dollar investments, and forecasting commodity prices over the typical 20- to 30-year timeframe is difficult to do. The risk profile for such a development is unique. It's very different from a more typical project in shallow waters, where the time from development to reservoir depletion is much shorter, making commodity price forecasting less risky.

## Origins of Enterprise-wide Risk Management

> I think you will see almost all companies over the next few years moving in the same direction [as we are], really trying to integrate the notion of risk management with the notion of just business management. Because to me, it is the same thing. You let your risks get out of control, you have losses that are out of control, and you know your stock is going to suffer, your bottom line is going to suffer.
>
> Tim Ling

Three circumstances came together at roughly the same time to lead Unocal toward enterprise-wide risk management:

- Karl Primm became head of internal audit after leaving a Big Five accounting firm. Primm moved quickly to make Unocal's internal audit approach more risk-based.

- The company had matured beyond its existing compliance-focused health, environment, and safety (HES) audit program, known informally as the "800 Questions."

- Tim Ling arrived as CFO from McKinsey and Company, where he had worked as a consultant with Unocal management for seven years. Ling's strong views on risk management can be summarized as follows: Risk management should be a line function, not a staff function, and a good manager is a good risk manager.

## Internal Audit

When I came here, we had something like 1,500 audit units, however you want to define "unit." I don't even know how it was defined. It was a huge network; it was more than competitors much larger than Unocal. So I knew there had to be a better way to do it.

After I had been here a few months, we were getting ready to make the presentation to the audit committee about what we were going to do for next year, which we do every July. So the audit managers went back and risk-rated the audit units. I said we ought to have a framework that we can hold up to the audit committee. Where are the problems, where are the risk areas? It was interesting when the audit managers did the risk ratings and we looked at the audits of the previous three or four years: we weren't hitting any of the problems, any of the riskier areas.

When they grade [the units], they also estimate the number of hours expected [for the audit], and develop/update a rotation schedule: Riskier units every other year, the less risky units once in five years to create a fairly even level of effort over the five-year period. This approach is very traditional and used by many internal audit groups. So that's what we did initially as I stepped into this role.

But still we had a huge number of audit units that didn't make any sense. We stepped back again and started looking at the COSO framework.[11] We showed [our results] to the audit committee, and said, "Here are the areas, and [in the past] we've been working on all the low-risk stuff and none of the high-risk stuff."

Karl Primm

In today's business environment, it has become tougher and tougher to justify expanding the budgets of internal audit functions that focus on the traditional audit approach of compliance with existing controls. Increasingly, companies are adopting the view that an internal audit should be a value-added activity; it should examine the root causes of problems and lead to workable solutions. Under the COSO framework, risk assessment is a fundamental component of internal control. Basically, the organization has to know the nature of its risk exposures to be able to control them.

Primm recognized that the internal audit department he inherited was less than effective because it concentrated on examining whether traditional controls such as segregation of duties were being followed and ignored most of the fundamental business risks facing Unocal. Internal audit was not spending its resources well, and Unocal was getting very little return on this investment.

## Risk Profiles

[This executive] really didn't want to meet with us about risk assessment. We're sitting in this building talking to him and suddenly I see something out of the corner of my eye. Two big turkey vultures come—I mean huge—and sit on his window ledge and peer in at us. And they start pecking on the window. And that's the way our interview went.

Kim Timber, internal audit risk assessment manager

Kim Timber came to Unocal in 1998 as risk assessment manager and reports to Karl Primm in internal audit. Previously, she had worked with Unocal in early risk assessment efforts as a consultant with a Big Five firm that had expertise in enterprise-wide risk management and that Unocal had hired to assist in developing a risk assessment process with its internal audit structure.

Internal audit performed three pilot studies of its risk assessment concept, resulting in Unocal's first real risk profiles. Management chose the first two studies, while internal audit initiated the third. The first study was specific to a particular project: Should Unocal buy a unique operating asset or not? Although the study demonstrated the department's risk assessment techniques and identified additional risks to the proposed acquisition, because of its single-project nature it could not be considered even a rudimentary integrated risk assessment, by Unocal's own admission. The second study was more conducive to a comparison of risks across the company and paralleled a concept Unocal refers to as a portfolio approach. This study consisted of evaluating the risks associated with six of the company's international joint venture operations,[12] or as Unocal calls them, partner operated ventures (POVs). The POV study allowed for more free-form thinking (see table 7.4).

*Table 7.4*
*Tailored POV Risk Factors (selected)*

**Financial**

1. Inability to prevent the renegotiations and/or reinterpretation of contract terms.
2. Failure to address Foreign Exchange Risk.

**Sociopolitical**
4. Failure to address government regulations.
5. Failure to manage interference by officials.
6. Potential confiscation of assets by foreign governments.
7. Inability to identify the specific government entity that has control over a geographical area (ministries, institutes, governments, etc.).
8. Failure to export in a reasonable timeframe (5–7 years).
9. Failure to develop effective business continuity plans.

**Construction**
11. Failure to meet construction timelines and/or schedules.
12. Failure to develop appropriate costs, resulting in capital costs overruns.

**Operating**
14. Failure of people and technology to perform as required.
16. Failure to appropriately insure for property damage/losses.
17. Inability to forecast fluctuations/volatility in the feedstock or fuel supply.
18. Failure to anticipate appropriate costs, resulting in operating cost overruns.

**Revenue**
19. Failure to develop export solutions in concert with timely field development to maximize net present value.
20. Failure to perform adequate market analysis and develop alternative marketing opportunities.
21. Failure to provide for offtake defaults.
22. Failure to maintain competitive position in the marketplace.
23. Failure to manage pending or threatened litigation.
24. Failure to meet schedules and projections of product output.

**Appraisal**
25. Failure to appropriately estimate the presence of the resource.
26. Failure to appropriately estimate the quantity, quality, and deliverability of the resource.
27. Failure to deliver quality of the resource under current contract.

The POV operations managers, one for each of the selected ventures, worked with internal audit representatives to develop a high-level, concise list of key business risks these ventures faced. They then discussed each venture individually in relation to the list of risks and produced a Risk Matrix Status Board showing which risks affected which ventures to what degree (see figure 7.4).

POV operations managers and internal auditors discussed, for a sample of risks, each risk's likelihood and its potential impact on the company (see figure 7.5). They identified the root causes of the risks with the greatest exposure, discussed potential mitigating controls, and determined action items (see table 7.5). Finally, they developed "signposts" or indicators of a change in the risk profile. They planned to develop these signposts from all POV operations so every POV operations manager could monitor his or her operations for the signposts as an early warning signal of a change in the operation's risk profile.

The results of these early efforts to instill a risk management and assessment mentality in Unocal's line managers were decidedly mixed. The level of skepticism was high. Primm explains,

> Unocal's audit history, whether financial, operational, information technology, or HES, has been very heavy on compliance. This is what managers were used to and many of them were reluctant to change. They were very concerned about what standards they were going to be audited against. Combine that with the fact that the internal audit department rarely looked at anything outside the finance area, and it's easy to see why these meetings raised huge perception questions. Managers had trouble understanding that we no longer wanted to be the policemen pointing out what was done wrong. With the operations people, the classic dialogue was:
>
> "So in other words, you're going to be telling me where I ought to be putting my drill bit?"
>
> "Well, no, that's not what we said."
>
> "Well, what *are* you saying?"
>
> It was and still is a difficult concept for many people to accept audit as a support function willing to assist in analyzing processes for potential improvements versus blowing the whistle on their failures.

*Figure 7.4*
*Risk Matrix Status Board*

| | Financial | Socio-political | Construc-tion | Operating | Revenue | Resource |
|---|---|---|---|---|---|---|
| Project A | 1) M | 5) M/H 7) M 9) M | 12) L | 14) L | 20) H 21) H 24) M 19) H | 26) M |
| Project B | 2) M | 5) H 7) H 8) H | 11) H 12) L | 14) L 16) L | 20) H 22) H | 26) L |
| Project C | 1) M/H | 9) H | 11) L | | 21) H | 26) M 27) L |
| Project D | 2) L | 4) L | 12) M | 14) M 17) L 18) L | 20) M | |
| Project E | | 6) M 9) L | | 14) L | 23) M | 25) L |
| Project F | 1) L | 9) M | 11) L | | | |

H = high
M = moderate
L = low

In spring 1999, internal audit initiated the third pilot study with the cooperation of Spirit Energy 76. Internal audit's objective was to prepare an initial process map or framework of Unocal's exploration and production operations with Spirit as the model and risk-rate each of the primary processes and subprocesses. (A discussion of the risk profile at Spirit appears in a later section.) At about the same time, senior Unocal management required all business units to perform a risk assessment as part of the corporation's new operations management system (OMS), described in the next section. The first unit to complete this risk assessment was Unocal Geothermal Indonesia, a small unit of fewer than 200

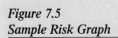

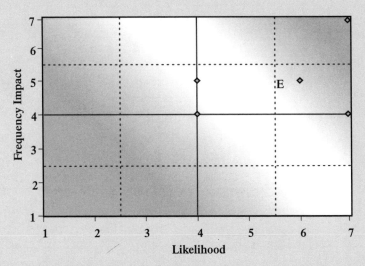

*Figure 7.5*
*Sample Risk Graph*

E = Failure to export in 5 to 7 years

Note: The five diamonds indicate where each manager involved in rating this risk plotted the risk on the matrix. The "E" shows the average of the five diamonds. (This was done using off-the-shelf voting technology.)

employees. A description of this effort follows the Spirit Energy 76 pilot study discussion.

As Unocal's internal audit department developed the risk assessment process, its HES audit function was also undergoing major changes that closely paralleled internal audit's efforts in the approach to risk.

The story of the shift from 800 HES-based questions to a new risk-based, operations-focused paradigm in a large, mature, successful company like Unocal speaks volumes about the dynamics of cultural change toward a focus on risk. This shift was essential for effective management not only of Unocal's health, environmental, and safety concerns, but also of its core exploration and production operations. The OMS protocols were an outgrowth of the company's strong loss-control

*Table 7.5*
*Causes, Mitigants, Action Items, and Signposts for Sample Risk Item*

**Country Risk: Sociopolitical. Government regulations/interference, expropriation, government's limited control over geographic area**

**Risk Statement: 8. Failure to export on a reasonable timeframe (5–7 years).**

| Causes | Mitigants |
|---|---|
| A) Inability to influence government policy Government unwilling to give up resources to other countries. Possessiveness of government for fear of running out (cultural issue) | A) Seek to export value-added projects such as power. Sell gas, power, and saturate domestic markets. Influence key decision makers. Meet local needs first. Build reserve bubble. Control and minimize investment to milestones. Apply to most of the causes. |
| B) Insufficient proven resource | B) Export consortium in planning stage. |
| C) Lack of trust of neighboring countries | C) Support a study that will address overcoming future disaster, showing them they can afford to pay for infrastructure development through exporting. Gathering a collection of World Bank and other multilateral agency (MLA) studies. These are showing them how to spend their money by fuel substitution and other macro-economics forces to better utilize resources. |
| D) Timing is the real issue. How long will it take to start exporting to neighboring countries and the rest of the world? | D) We have a program with the Asian Development Bank (ADB) and the World Bank on export programs. International Finance Corporation (IFC) as potential partner. Country is on the dole and the World Bank is a major influence. |

### Action Items and Champions

**What can you do to improve the way this risk is being managed?**

— Minimize the number of initiatives by partnering with the MLAs
— Lead a group with a flood effort to be good neighbors in the community (work with non-government organizations)
— Try to use existing right of ways to minimize the landowner conflicts
— Create a research bubble
— Use MLAs as leverage with the government

Champions:
Manager of Gas Exports and Country Manager

### Signpost/Indicators

— The reserve bubble does not grow by 2000.
— The reserve bubble does grow by 2000 but no movement by government to support export.
— No political support.
— Change of political party, opposition is more nationalistic.
— Market captured by gas from other exporters.
— IOCs get paid for gas. Current account balance decrease
— Sanctions on neighboring countries

program and clearly reflect senior management's belief in the parallels between management of the business and management of risk.

## 800 Questions

I think to understand [the origin of the new system] we need to go back about 10 years when a decision was made to implement the International Safety Rating System, ISRS, at Unocal. Like many decisions of that type, it was made following a terrible accident, which was in our Chicago refinery. Top management's response was that we just had to do a better job on safety.

The principles behind ISRS are very sound in my mind because they really are as simple as "know your business, know what the risks are, put good programs in place to minimize those risks, and periodically evaluate how things are going." What we found at Unocal was that while the principles are sound, the system itself embodies a set of questions, rather than a set of standards. It's all questions. Partially because of that, the system puts more emphasis on how things are documented than it does on how things are being implemented.

George Walker, vice president,
public policy and health, environment, and safety

Health, environmental, and safety concerns are paramount at Unocal, as they are at any responsible oil and gas company. A problem has been to ensure that the most relevant, up-to-date practices and procedures are being followed as a part of everyday business. Unfortunately, it is common for businesses to appear to be reactive to these issues. Following the calamitous 1926 storage tank fires, Unocal formed a groundbreaking fire safety unit that researched the best practices for avoiding and containing petroleum fires. The reason that two of the worst fires in the industry occurred 74 years ago is that Unocal and other companies learned from them.

The ISRS system described above was considered state-of-the-art in 1990, but it had originally been built around safety issues in a manufacturing environment. Unocal had to modify the system heavily for its own specialized use. Even then, it was strictly compliance based. An auditor from the HES unit would simply check off yes or no answers for some 800 questions relating to safety and environmental concerns. Each question was assigned a numerical score, and it was all or nothing; there was no partial credit. Predictably, operating management became focused on achieving acceptable scores on this instrument. But what the company really wanted was a culture of concern and attention to environmental and safety issues that would permeate everything management did—not a separate check-up system to be dealt with in preparation for the HES auditor's visit.

Ling describes what senior management was looking for:

> We had built up a pretty significant staff in the health, environmental, and safety group—such that there were 15 to 20 staff safety and compliance people within each of our big operating business units, as well as pretty significant staff at corporate. I have a real bias—I think that a lot of people in this company do, and my boss certainly does—that when you get people in a room and you ask who is in charge of safety, if you have a lot of staff people who are safety guys, they tend to raise their hands and the line guys don't. And, ultimately, if we are to have in-control operations that are safe and environmentally effective, the people who should be raising their hands are the [line managers such as] field foremen, the asset managers, the field superintendents.

Senior management was not the only group unhappy with ISRS. The line managers themselves recognized its flaws. Drilling Manager D. J. Ponville describes his view of ISRS: "We used to be 'points driven' and had to do things that, quite honestly, if it were your own company, it may not have made business sense to do." Unocal is now implementing the operations management system: risk based and developed by an internal task force. George Walker, one of the leaders in the development of OMS, explains how it came about:

> There was always some unhappiness with the 800 questions; some of that was valid and some of that was—in my experience—that line people are always complaining about auditors. So as far as I can tell, if a line person is not complaining about the audit staff, then he's probably not alive anymore. There were some legitimate concerns and there was some whining.

In response to the unhappiness, Unocal engaged another Big Five consulting firm to evaluate the HES audit practices. The consultant reported back to Walker and his colleagues, "The principles are sound but unless the very first thing you do is identify and evaluate the risks in your operations, then the chances are that your effort [at improvement] will be misdirected."

Walker continues,

And we [started] working on that, but those recommendations were not nearly as radical as changing the system completely to the [eventual] OMS system. At one point we had some serious accidents in Southeast Asia, some very large losses of assets. We were extremely lucky that there was no injury or loss of life involved. But they were big accidents; no one got hurt, but we lost production, we lost fields, and we lost one drilling rig.

So that was a great concern to our CEO, and to me of course. He felt that we needed to do some thinking outside the box. He grabbed a well-respected senior oil and gas line manager to look into this. His team was to look at the management of change implications because the thought was that at least part of what was behind one of the accidents was a failure in the management of change process. But as he began to look at things around the world, he naturally expanded his own charter and looked at the whole system.

The oil and gas industry is undergoing rapid change, much of it driven by new technology—technology that, like what came before, can be dangerous or even deadly. Unocal management seemed right on target in assessing that ISRS was not up to the challenge. Only a risk-based system would be able to deal effectively with the rapid change. Instead of worrying about 800 check marks in an auditor's workpapers, management would, through dynamic self-assessment, identify the areas of greatest risk and devise steps to manage them. The auditor's role would shift toward a greater degree of consulting and facilitating and away from the pure compliance aspect.

Walker describes how the new risk-based approach would fit the specific needs of each local unit:

Suppose a very small operation has two low-pressure relief valves. A couple of people write on their desk calendars when to test those valves, and they have done it effectively that way. So you conclude, "All right, looks like that's working." But for plants with hundreds and hundreds of relief valves, many of them for high-pressure toxic materials and in situations where equipment runs for long periods of time and is only out of service for a few weeks in a year, you need an organized risk program to check the relief valves.

We are not going to write that into the worldwide standard. We're going to say, "You need to assess what the risk is and determine what kind of program you need for your relief valves." We had a hard time getting people to understand that because many people in smaller and simpler facilities had felt for years that ISRS required them to put a whole bunch of busy work in place that probably didn't help a lot and was more appropriate for a larger facility.

We had a hard time getting people to understand that we had spent a lot of time writing the program so that it would only require them to do what made sense. There was no longer anything in there that said, "You have to do this, whether it makes sense or not." It just said, "Figure out what makes sense and then do what makes sense and do it well."

But changing the mind-set of line managers who had worked under the old system for a long time was not going to be easy. To managers of large operations, the new system looked particularly onerous. Walker disagrees:

People's reaction was "Oh you're putting a huge new burden on us." We replied, "No, we're not. In fact, really if you'll look at it with us and work through it with us, this is going to be easier for you. If you're a big, high-risk facility and you haven't been properly addressing all the risks then yes, it will be harder, but it's also going to be real important."

Much of the resistance to the change stemmed not so much from concerns about extra work as from the old view of health, environmental, and safety issues: Let the staff people worry about them. Walker explains the real difficulty in acclimating line managers to the new approach:

## 7

It's kind of old thinking, but there certainly are people around who will say, "Well look, we have to run the business, and over here we'll have the safety stuff, but we have to run the business first." And that doesn't work. You don't need work procedures and safety procedures, you need safe work procedures.

OMS is being implemented through pilot "consultations" and required business-unit self-assessments. The consultation teams consist of former HES auditors and experienced line managers. Walker wants these visits to be seen as peer reviews rather than as audits, just as the company wants the system to be more risk based and less compliance based. One of the first such consultations took place at the Spirit Energy 76 operation based in Lafayette, Louisiana, in late 1999. Walker candidly admits that this will be an evolutionary process:

> We just did our first trial on it. Kim [Timber] just participated in one down in Spirit Drilling. I think there is still too much emphasis on the HES part and I'm a little disappointed in that. But I think it's only natural that this has happened this way. We do need to work to continue to shift this toward its being more of a peer review than an audit by professional auditors.

As the program rolls out in 2000 and the consultations are staffed, another reminder of the old mind-set shows up. Walker explains,

> We started to contact business units to supply key line managers to work on audits of other facilities in the year 2000. From some people, the first reaction was "Why don't you ask my HES manager?" It is an ongoing issue to go back and say, "No, remember OMS is much broader than HES and we're looking for a line manager here. How about your maintenance man? How about one of your production foremen? That sort of thing." So I think that is still very much still evolving. It's going to be awhile before people really get it.

### Spirit Energy 76 Risk Profile

Internal audit brought the Big Five consultants back in, and Timber was already on duty to assist with the Spirit risk profile. Forty-two employees, most from Spirit Energy 76 but some from the corporate office, were interviewed during April and May 1999. These employees came from three groups: senior Spirit executives, Unocal managers who provide support services (e.g., internal audit, HES), and Spirit managers responsible for key processes (process owners). Their interview responses were entered into a database as they were interviewed.

Some key findings of the project are presented in Appendix 7.1, which shows selected slides from a June 1999 presentation about the project. The risk profile contains a summary analysis of the following:

- Certainty of achieving Spirit's objectives

- Significant issues identified

- Emerging opportunities

- The key processes at risk

- Spirit's readiness to respond to risks

An important result is the risk map on the slide entitled "The Significance and Certainty of Achieving Spirit's Objectives." Culled from all responses, this map shows how the managers assessed the probability of Spirit's attaining its five key business objectives. They ranked objective C, "Create/Seize Opportunities" as the most important. Yet they gave this objective only a 50 percent probability of achievement. They ranked objective A, "Continuously Improve Capital Efficiency," second highest and gave it a 65 percent probability of achievement. They ranked objective B, "Drive Down Costs While Growing" lowest, but gave it a 70 percent probability of achievement. With respect to the risk map, internal audit concluded, "The results of this analysis demonstrate management believes the objectives are important but the issues/risks presented in this document, if not resolved, will likely prevent Spirit from reaching its objectives."

The final slides in Appendix 7.1 show the Process Risk Ranking and Level of Concern by Interview Category. The risk profile describes process risk ranking as follows (Note the discussion of deepwater opportunities. The term "exploitation" refers to deriving benefits from the company's oil and gas properties.):

The assessment approach used for this profile provided an opportunity to obtain the perspective of both Senior Management and the Process Owners regarding their level of concern with Spirit's key processes. Generally, the assessment of concern by the Process Owners was in alignment with that of Senior Management....

Although there was substantial alignment between perspectives of Senior Management and the Process Owners, a lesser concern for the overall process of exploitation by Senior Management than seems warranted based upon the greater concern expressed by the Process Owners for the exploitation subprocesses was noted. This is generally attributable to issues raised by the Process Owners over future developments in technology and preparing facilities and markets for the finds coming from the current exploration opportunities in Deepwater. While most of these concerns were ranked high and will actually have an impact 3–5 years from now, the Process Owners generally believed that they were on track to address the issues as they arise in the future.

## Unocal Geothermal Indonesia

The risk assessment performed for Unocal Geothermal Indonesia (UGI)...looked at [risk] from a pretty high level and focused on what they believed to be their top 39 risks.

Clearly UGI's relationship with the government is key. UGI produces steam from geothermal wells, sells some of the steam to the government power company (PLN) for them to produce electricity, and uses the rest of the steam in its own power plants to produce electricity, which is then sold to PLN. While Unocal has some differences with PLN, we also have other geothermal steam fields in the country that we are trying to develop but that have been put on hold since the Asian currency crisis began. We cannot pursue further development without government approval.

Two years ago, I asked the general manager of UGI what his three biggest risks were. He responded, "PLN, PLN, PLN." Given that, UGI's high-level risk focus may be appropriate.

Karl Primm

The first risk assessment done under the new OMS guidelines was completed in early 2000. (The Spirit Energy 76 risk assessment was performed under the aegis of internal audit.) Appendix 7.2 shows excerpts from the instrument used to gather information for the risk assessment, and Appendix 7.3 shows excerpts from the risk profile evaluation.

The instrument in Appendix 7.2 suggests that participants assign ratings on four-point scales for probability and severity of a master list, developed by the participants, of "issues or events to prioritize." Participants are instructed not only to consider HES issues but also to include other risks such as purchasing practices and relations with clients. The risk profile evaluation (Appendix 7.3) displays the results.

One outcome of the assessment is a matrix of risks classified according to probability of occurrence and severity. Figure 7.6 displays the risk matrix for the UGI field operation without a detailed description of specific risks.

*Figure 7.6*
*Risk Matrix UGI Field Operation*

| PROBABILITY OF OCCURRENCE | | 1 | 2 | 3 | 4 |
|---|---|---|---|---|---|
| | 4 Almost Certain | | V | | |
| | 3 Probable | | D | D | |
| | 2 Maybe | | L | E, F, R | E |
| | 1 Improbable | | | M | R |
| | | 1 Minor | 2 Moderate | 3 Significant | 4 Major |

SEVERITY OF CONSEQUENCES

D = Natural disaster      M = Damage to critical warehouse stock
E = Environmental issue   R = Regulatory infringement
F = Equipment failure     V = Vehicular accident
L = Labor dispute

Source: Adapted by the researchers from Unocal Report.

# Risk Management as Cultural Change

RCLs (real change leaders) use whatever works, but they seldom start with structure. They recognize that changing structure alone seldom leads to performance improvement. Doing so also carries a high price in terms of internal disruption. Instead, they use informal, *ad hoc* networks and find ways to cross functional boundaries and hierarchical levels by focusing on action flows and objectives, not on functions and positions.[13]

*Real Change Leaders,* Jon R. Katzenbach et al.

Unocal is committed to instilling in its entire organization the sense that risk management is a component of good management, not an adjunct to it. The company's risk management philosophy can be seen in a presentation that Ling made to a conference in fall 1999, which is excerpted in figure 7.7. A central theme of Ling's presentation is that companies face an overall business risk that can be broken down into component risks but should be managed through an integrated program. The integrated management of business risk is possible only when line managers understand the company's objectives and how the various risks can stand in the way of accomplishing those objectives.

Unocal has not viewed integrated risk management as just another corporate program to be imposed from headquarters. Instead, integrated risk management has emanated logically from internal audit and HES, two areas where risk management should have been a prime focus but was not until recently. Senior management's refusal to view integrated risk management as another "program" makes perfect sense to Primm: "The old method was very prescriptive; you have to do this. People don't want another corporate initiative. But they recognize that there's a benefit to risk assessment."

Ling was coauthor of the *Real Change Leaders* study while he was at McKinsey and Company. The quote from the book captures Unocal's risk management implementation strategy: Focus on "action flows and objectives, not on functions and positions." Primm elaborates,

All along we wanted structure in terms of a consistent framework to capture and report on risks as well as a degree of consistency in

*Figure 7.7*
*Unocal's View of Risk Management*

**AN EMERGING VIEW OF RISK**

| From | To |
|------|-----|
| Separate types of risk | Business risk |
| Multiple mitigation programs | Integrated business risk management |
| Compliance | Commitment |
| Staff-driven | Line-driven |
| Audits | Self-assessment |

**RISK (OBJECTIVES) – CONTROL = EXPOSURE**

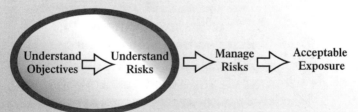

Understand Objectives ➟ Understand Risks ➟ Manage Risks ➟ Acceptable Exposure

Think of risk as . . .

- anything that gets in the way of the achievement of objectives
- inevitable and a function of our objectives and the way we do business
- anything that threatens diminution of the company's assets or franchise

*Figure 7.7*
*Unocal's View of Risk Management (Continued)*

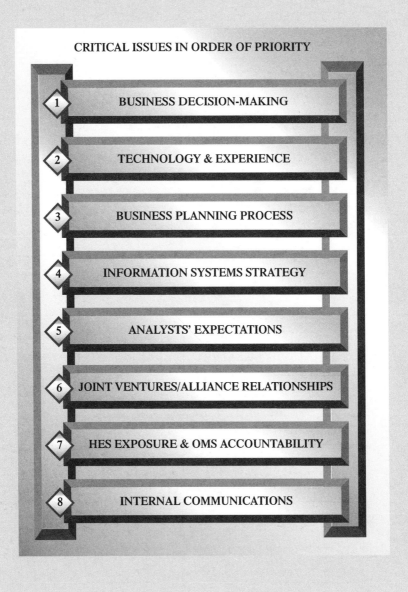

CRITICAL ISSUES IN ORDER OF PRIORITY

1. BUSINESS DECISION-MAKING
2. TECHNOLOGY & EXPERIENCE
3. BUSINESS PLANNING PROCESS
4. INFORMATION SYSTEMS STRATEGY
5. ANALYSTS' EXPECTATIONS
6. JOINT VENTURES/ALLIANCE RELATIONSHIPS
7. HES EXPOSURE & OMS ACCOUNTABILITY
8. INTERNAL COMMUNICATIONS

*Figure 7.7*
*Unocal's View of Risk Management (Continued)*

---

### SUMMARY

- Integration of *all* risk types *is* business risk

- Business risk must be controlled by understanding business objectives and risk and managing for an acceptable risk profile given required performance levels

- Increasingly, risk management should be considered a line function

- Technology will make this easier and more effective over time

Source: Presentation by Tim Ling.

evaluating risks to ensure their comparability for management purposes. However, we recognized that you cannot force a structure onto someone. Thus we are trying to be flexible in attempting to achieve our longer term goals of a consistent framework and methodology. Risk management is not new. Managers have been doing this since the beginning of time. An integrated approach, however, does shed new light and benefits on the process.

The OMS guidance is, by design, somewhat vague to avoid the concept of "another corporate initiative" or more "stuff" from corporate. We [auditing and OMS personnel] have made a significant investment in speaking with individuals at varying levels of the organization, crossing both functional and hierarchical boundaries to build support for risk assessment.

# Case Summary

From its humble beginnings with wildcatter Lyman Stewart to its current position as the world's largest investor-owned oil and gas exploration and production company, Unocal has had to manage the high-stakes risks of finding oil and producing it economically and safely. Failure to manage these risks would have spelled ruin for the company.

But only recently has Unocal embraced the notion that risks should be managed on an integrated, enterprise-wide basis—not left for staff people in various areas to deal with risk by risk. Risk management is a line function, Unocal management believes, and that means it must permeate everything the company does.

Starting in the internal audit and health, environmental, and safety units, a focus on risk assessment and control is beginning to affect all business units. A cultural change like this takes time, but Unocal is committed to the effort, and its progress to date is substantial.

# People Interviewed

Tim Ling, CFO of Unocal Corporation and executive vice president of Unocal's North American Operations (currently president and COO of Unocal Corporation)

Mike Bell, vice president, Gulf of Mexico Deepwater, Unocal Corporation

George Walker, vice president, Public Policy & Health, Environment & Safety, Unocal Corporation

Karl Primm, general auditor, Unocal Corporation

Kimberly Timber, internal audit risk assessment manager, Unocal Corporation

## Spirit Energy 76 Unit

John Donohue, president, Spirit Energy 76

Ken Butler, vice president, mature regions profit center, Spirit Energy 76

D. J. Ponville, drilling manager, Spirit Energy 76

Tim Pownell, director, strategic planning, Spirit Energy 76

Truett Enloe, manager, strategic planning, Spirit Energy 76

# References

Katzenbach, Jon R., Timothy Ling, et al., *Real Change Leaders* (New York: Times Business, 1996).

Koepp, Stephen, "A Shark Loses Some of Its Teeth," *Time* (June 3, 1985): 58.

McNamee, David, and Georges Selim, "The Next Step in Risk Management," *Internal Auditor* (June 1999): 35–38.

Waddell, Paul R., and Robert F. Niven, *Sign of the 76* (Los Angeles: Union Oil Co. of California, 1976).

# Endnotes

1. Since this section was written, Ling has become president and COO of Unocal Corp.

2. The largest energy companies, such as Royal Dutch Shell and Exxon Mobil, are integrated. Their operations include exploration, production, refining, and marketing to end users.

3. Technically, Union Oil Co. of California still exists as a subsidiary of Unocal. But the company is generally known in the business world by the Unocal name.

4. Automobiles were scarce in the early 1900s, so gasoline production was low priority. A visitor to Ventura County from Santa Barbara was once told he would have to wait a few days for his return trip so that gasoline could be made to fill his gas tank. Later, the first service stations featured individual 50-gallon storage tanks for individual motorists, which the company would keep filled. A driver would pull his automobile up to his own tank and "fill 'er up" himself.

5. To thwart Pickens, Unocal offered to buy back a portion of its common stock at $72 per share compared with Pickens' tender price of $54. But the offer excluded Pickens' shares—he could not sell them back to the company at a profit, as had been his custom in other corporate "raids." Pickens sued, and Unocal won a landmark court decision affirming the legality of its buyback offer. Pickens lost an estimated $100 million on the takeover attempt, but Unocal incurred $4.1 billion in additional debt to finance the stock buyback (see Koepp, 1985).

6. A Dodson Benchmarking Database study showed Unocal with 1998 drilling costs in the Gulf of Mexico shelf of $202 per foot, the lowest of 11 companies in the study. The next lowest cost was $234 per foot, and the highest was $651 per foot.

7. Spirit Energy 76 is Unocal's "lower 48" U.S. exploration and production operation. By definition, Spirit Energy 76 does not include Alaska operations.

8. Monte Carlo simulation involves generating a large number of trials to determine the distribution of possible outcomes. It was developed during World War II when a team of mathematicians was trying to evaluate the feasibility of the atomic bomb. This secret project was code-named *Monte Carlo*.

9. See also "Texaco, Marathon Oil Project Faces Delay by Deck Module Fall," *The Wall Street Journal* (December 7, 1998).

10. Traditional offshore oil platforms are not suited for deepwater development: The fixed steel configurations would be unstable at those depths. Instead, deepwater rigs float on the surface. With a tension leg platform, 4,000- to 5,000-foot-long tendons extend from the platform to a foundation in the seabed. The tendons pull the platform down below its natural buoyancy and stabilize it. The result is a much lighter, more stable structure.

11. COSO is the Committee of Sponsoring Organizations of the Treadway Commission on fraudulent financial reporting. Traditional internal auditing is focused on examining controls while the COSO framework views risk as a justification for the importance of controls (see McNamee and Selim, 1999).

12. The oil and gas industry is unusual in the degree to which competitors work together on exploration and production projects. Because of the technological complexity of these operations, combined with the huge capital outlay and the myriad of risks to be overcome, it is not uncommon for several companies to participate in the development of an oil and gas field, usually with one company selected as the operator.

13. See Katzenbach et al., 282.

*Appendix 7.1*
*Spirit Energy 76 Risk Profile (excerpted)*

## Objective of the Risk Profile

The primary objective of this risk profile is to enable the Unocal Internal Audit team to better understand the risk issues and emerging opportunities facing Spirit Energy (Spirit) so their efforts may be more clearly focused on the success of Spirit. This project was designed to identify issues, not to provide recommendations or solutions.

This profile summarizes the results of the assessment conducted at Spirit in April and May of 1999 and is based on the analysis of information collected and the results of interviews with key Spirit personnel. This profile contains a summary analysis of the certainty of achievement of Spirit's objectives, the significant issues identified, emerging opportunities, the key processes at risk, and Spirit's readiness to respond to risks.

Significant effort was given to maintaining the anonymity of the interviewees' specific contributions to this assessment.

## Overview of Approach

A series of structured interviews was held with three groups of employees: Spirit Senior Executives and other Unocal management that provide support services (e.g. HES, Audit, etc.) to Spirit (collectively, Senior Management), and Spirit managers responsible for key processes (Process Owners).

Senior Management from Spirit Energy were interviewed to understand their assessment of significant risk issues and emerging opportunities facing Spirit.

Senior Management was given a pre-interview package to complete. Within that package were a series of categories and thought starters to help them identify and prioritize their concerns. This interview approach facilitated identification of issues/risks by focusing on business issue categories from various perspectives of the organization. Senior Management were asked to identify and rank issues/risks in the following seven categories:

| External Relations | Customers | Employees | Operations | Information | Technology | Corporate Infrastructure |
|---|---|---|---|---|---|---|

Additionally, management was asked to rank their level of concern regarding key processes, the risk readiness (culture), and the significance and certainty of the Spirit Energy objectives (as stated in the 1999 business plan).

During the interview, the level of concern was recorded on the scale Very High, Medium, Low, Very Low. Average results presented in this report are based on a scale of (1 to 5) where 5 is a Very High concern rating. The following color code is used throughout the report to indicate the relative level of concern.

| ■ High Concern 1st Quartile | ■ Medium Concern 2nd Quartile | □ Low Concern 3rd/4th Quartile |
|---|---|---|

## Overview of Approach

Interviews with Process Owners were also conducted during April and May; however, a separately tailored interview package structure was used for these interviews. These interviewees were asked to identify key processes or activities within their area of responsibility, rank those processes as to risk (very low to very high) and then provide specific issues/risk associated with those processes they ranked H and VH. In those interviews, the focus was on the process risks and their impact on the achievement of process objectives, versus the use of broad business categories. These responses provided a greater level of detail to the issues identified by Senior Management and also assisted in determining if there was an alignment of the issues facing Spirit as seen from both Senior Management and the Process Owners (collectively Management). Process Owners were also asked to identify key objectives for their area of responsibility and discuss the alignment of those objectives with those of Spirit (as noted in the 1999 business plan) and to assess the Control Environment.

All interviewees focused on understanding the "why" or the reason(s) for the concern and related emerging opportunities. An emerging opportunity was defined as something that could be done to reduce the identified risks and increase the likelihood of achieving stated objectives. An issue/risk-centric database was used to capture all relevant information for this assessment process. All opportunities/risks (along with noted management activities and contributing factors) are linked in the database to relevant categories, processes, and functions. In order to maintain the anonymity of the individuals and their contributions to the assessment, access to the database is restricted.

For all interviews or discussions, a definition for the term "risk" was first discussed in order to emphasize the desire to understand all issues which Spirit faces in achieving its objectives.

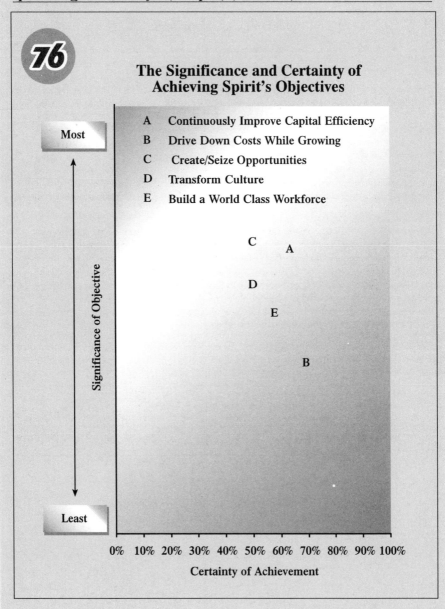

**76**

## The Significance and Certainty of Achieving Spirit's Objectives

A    Continuously Improve Capital Efficiency
B    Drive Down Costs While Growing
C    Create/Seize Opportunities
D    Transform Culture
E    Build a World Class Workforce

Most

Least

Significance of Objective

0% 10% 20% 30% 40% 50% 60% 70% 80% 90% 100%

Certainty of Achievement

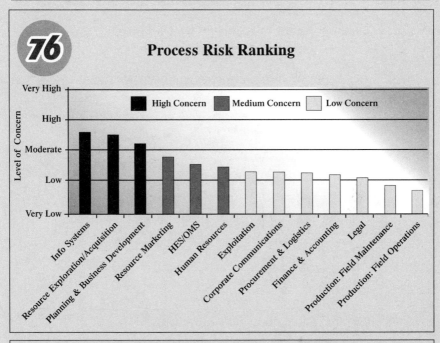

## Process Risk Ranking

## Level of Concern by Interview Category

The table that follows depicts the results of the category ranking used to direct the Executive and Senior Management interviews. These rankings indicate the level of concern expressed by Senior Management when discussing issues within the categories.

As you might expect, there is a strong correlation between the category rankings presented here and the critical issues presented earlier in this document. Not only did the risk categories provide a comprehensive structure to the interview, they highlight management's concern in specific categories. As noted before, this information and other information collected during the interviews were the basis for the overall critical issues identified.

In addition to these rankings, a listing of selected concerns by category can be found in the Appendix. That listing includes the issues discussed in the body of this profile along with certain other issues identified. These issues (and related data) are contained in the database used to capture the assessment information.

*Appendix 7.1*
*Spirit Energy 76 Risk Profile (excerpted)  (Continued)*

# Level of Concern by Category

### TRUST RESPONSIBILITIES TO STAKEHOLDERS

- External Relations
- Customers
- Employees

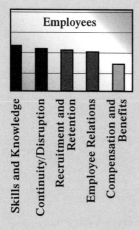

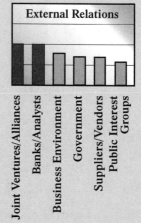

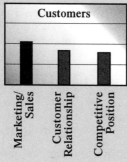

*Appendix 7.1*
*Spirit Energy 76 Risk Profile (excerpted) (Continued)*

## Level of Concern by Category, continued

PERFORMANCE RESPONSIBILITIES OVER
ASSETS AND BUSINESS PROCESSES
- Operations
- Information & Technology
- Infrastructure/Support Svc.

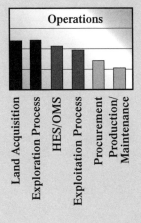

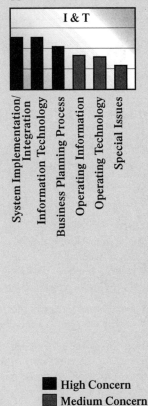

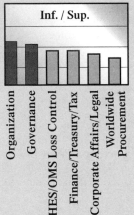

High Concern
Medium Concern
Low Concern

*Appendix 7.2*
*Planning and Risk Profile Evaluation, Unocal Geothermal Indonesia (excerpted)*

# Unocal Geothermal, Indonesia Business Unit

| GO-2.0 | Planning and Risk Profile Evaluation | Good Operations Management Standard |
|---|---|---|

**Revision History**

| Rev. | Date | By | Reviewed | Approved | Description |
|---|---|---|---|---|---|
| 0 | 8/6/99 | DI | LCC | | Good Operations Management System |
| 1 | | | | | |
| 2 | | | | | |
| 3 | | | | | |

**Purpose**

This element standard provides guidelines for effective management of Planning activities and Risk Profile Evaluation, as part of the Unocal Indonesia Business Unit (UIBU) Good Operations Program.

The Planning is divided into two main activities: Long range strategic planning and Short term operation planning.

The objective of Long-range strategic planning is to formulate a business strategy that will enable the business unit to compete in the market successfully. A well prepared long range plan is necessary to achieve the business unit's objectives efficiently and will provide adaptability and foster growth to the business unit in the midst of rapid changes in the environment.

The objective of Short term planning is to formulate a program to guide the Business unit operation within the time frame of one year,

The objective identification and evaluation of risk is critical to safe, efficient and environmentally responsible operations. Risk Profile is a necessary tool to assist in identifying priority issues for additional management system control.

*Appendix 7.2*
*Planning and Risk Profile Evaluation, Unocal Geothermal Indonesia (excerpted)*
*(Continued)*

**RISK PROFILE**

**Establishment of Risk Profile**

The General Manager of UIBU will ensure that a systematic review of risks is conducted to establish the Risk Profile.

— The Risk Profile should not focus only on Health, Environmental and Safety (HES) risks. There might be other risks in areas other than HES that have significant impact to the Business Operation that needs to be addressed.

— The General Manager of UIBU will ensure that an appropriate/representative cross function of the business unit is involved in the establishment of the Risk Profile.

— The Planning and Valuation manager will lead the Risk Profile evaluation.

**Procedure for Establishing the Risk Profile**

The General Manager of the UIBU shall ensure that the procedure, developed to provide guidance on the establishment of the Risk Profile, is followed.

The steps for establishing the Risk Profile should include:

1. Establish a team consisting of personnel from appropriate cross section of the business unit. The team, consisting of the Loss Control Coordinator, the Element Coordinator and one representative from every department, is responsible for developing the risk profile.

2. Conduct a systematic listing of issues or events to prioritize. Issues and events should not be limited to those relating to Health, Environmental and Safety issues. The process need also to identify and evaluate non-HES issues and business processes, which may include risks associated with issues such as:

   — processes and equipment
   — contractor activities
   — non-compliance with regulations
   — personnel exposures
   — impact of surrounding community
   — environmental impact
   — aviation safety
   — marketing practices
   — purchasing practices
   — relations with clients

*Appendix 7.2*
*Planning and Risk Profile Evaluation, Unocal Geothermal Indonesia (excerpted)*
*(Continued)*

3. Assign each issue a rating based on the following definitions of probability and severity:

**PROBABILITY**

| Rating | Probability of occurrence |
|---|---|
| 4 | Almost Certain |
| 3 | Probable |
| 2 | Maybe |
| 1 | Improbable |

**SEVERITY**

| Rating | Severity of Consequences |
|---|---|
| 4 | Major. Possibly impacting the entire corporation. Losses would be major and not easily recoverable |
| 3 | Significant. Affecting primarily the specific Business Unit. Significant temporary losses that can, over an extended period of time, be recovered |
| 2 | Moderate. Temporarily disrupting to business, but recovery can be made |
| 1 | Minor. Temporarily distracting but recovery can be made quickly, with no long term negative impact |

4. Construct a matrix and assign each issue into one of the boxes

**PROBABILITY RATING**

| | | | | |
|---|---|---|---|---|
| (4) Almost Certain | (4,1) | (4,2) | (4,3) | (4,4) |
| (3) Probable | (3,1) | (3,2) | (3,3) | (3,4) |
| (2) Maybe | (2,1) | (2,2) | (2,3) | (2,4) |
| (1) Improbable | (1,1) | (1,2) | (1,3) | (1,4) |
| | (1) Minor | (2) Moderate | (3) Significant | (4) Major |

*Appendix 7.2*
*Planning and Risk Profile Evaluation, Unocal Geothermal Indonesia (excerpted)*
*(Continued)*

### SEVERITY RATING

The exercise is not intended to assign quantitative values or risk factors to specific issues or events. The matrix number should therefore not be used as absolute numbers, but as a guide to ranking risks.

The resulting Risk Profile is then used to evaluate any existing controls the Business Unit may already have in place to mitigate the high priority risks. If the residual risk is unsatisfactory to the business unit, then additional management controls are to be created and implemented to reduce the risk exposure. This may result in additional Elements, standards or procedures being needed beyond the current Unocal Good Operations Management System.

### Integration into the Management System

The General Manager of UIBU will ensure that the outcomes from the Risk Profile are actually integrated into the management system priorities and processes.

Reasonable management controls/action plans must be set in motion to reduce the risk, to include the following:

— Establishment and implementation of personal performance standards

— Establishment and implementation of procedures

— Initiation of corrective action or prevention projects

### Annual Review of the Risk Profile

The General Manager of UIBU will ensure that the Risk Profile is reviewed annually involving cross section representatives of the business unit, and the Good Operations Standards is amended if needed.

There is no need to duplicate the original work. A team similar in composition to the original team should examine the existing Risk Profile and evaluate whether significant changes have occurred in the business unit's operation or exposures that necessitate modifications to the profile.

If significant changes are identified, modifications to the Risk Profile should be followed by modifications to the Good Operations Standards.

*Appendix 7.3*
*Risk Profile Evaluation, Unocal Geothermal Indonesia (excerpted)*

## Unocal Indonesia
## Geothermal and Power Operation
# Year 2000
# RISK PROFILE EVALUATION
## February 24, 2000

### Risk Profile Evaluation

**Objective:** To identify priority issues for additional management system control. The intent, as required by OMS, is to consider a broad range of risks, to include

- Processes and equipment
- Contractor activities
- Noncompliance with regulations
- Personnel exposures
- Impact to surrounding communities
- Environmental impacts
- Marketing practices
- Purchasing practices

*Appendix 7.3*
*Risk Profile Evaluation, Unocal Geothermal Indonesia (excerpted) (Continued)*

# Risk Profile Evaluation

### Steps Taken in 2000 Risk Profile Evaluation:

- Established the team consisting of personnel from all the different departments.

- Conducted systematic listing of issues or events to prioritize, assigned rating to each issue and reviewed whether the list reasonably reflects the risks faced by the business unit.

- Integrated result into the goals of the relevant departments.

  – Evaluate existing control in the management system to mitigate the high priority risks.

  – Create and implement additional management controls to mitigate the risk exposure not yet covered.

# Risk Profile Evaluation

### Current Status

| | | |
|---|---|---|
| • Team established | | mid December 1999 |
| • Meetings: | December 20, 1999 | brainstorming and systematic listing of key risks |
| | January 24, 2000 | discussion of mitigation plan |
| | February 1, 2000 | Review by GOC |
| • Accomplished so far: | | Key Risk Profile and action plan—Approved |
| • Next Risk Profile Review | | August 2000 before AOP process |

*Appendix 7.3*
*Risk Profile Evaluation, Unocal Geothermal Indonesia (excerpted) (Continued)*

## Results of First Meeting:

- The severity criteria include dollar amounts associated with the risk:
  - Minor:        more than $500 but less than $25,000
  - Moderate:     more than $25,000 but less than $500,000
  - Significant:  more than $500,000 but less than $5,000,000
  - Major:        more than $5,000,000

The evaluation coverage was not limited to risks in the year 2000 only.
We also looked into those relevant in the next 3 to 4 years.

| Department/Section | No. of risks evaluated |
|---|---|
| Operation | 14 |
| Reservoir engineering/Geoscience | 7 |
| HELC & government relations | 22 |
| P&L | 5 |
| Finance/commercial | 17 |
| IS | 6 |
| HRD and other | 7 |
| TOTAL | 78 |

## Results of Second Meeting:

- Evaluated Key Risks with Probability of Occurrence and Severity Ratings
  of 3 and 4.

| Department/Section | No. of risks evaluated |
|---|---|
| Operation | 10 |
| Reservoir engineering/Geoscience | 8 |
| HELC & government relations | 5 |
| P&L | 0 |
| Finance/commercial | 11 |
| IS | 1 |
| HRD and other | 4 |
| TOTAL | 39 |

# Conclusion

*The high-risk society is not going to disappear. If anything, it is going to intensify.*

Michael Mandel, *The High Risk Society*[1]

*Risk management is an essential element of effective control.*

CICA Criteria of Control Board,
*Learning about Risk: Choices, Connections and Competencies*[2]

**A** major question for boards of directors and senior management is how to manage risk and create value in today's high-risk society. Businesses operate in an environment where forces such as the Internet, technology, globalization, deregulation, restructurings, and consumer expectations are creating much uncertainty and prodigious risks. How senior management responds to these and other forces to build an organization that manages all the risks may very well determine the profitability and sustainability of that organization.

In 1992, COSO introduced a control framework that was much broader than the traditional accounting control model and included risk assessment. Since the COSO framework was released, a number of professional bodies have issued documents that expanded the risk assessment component of control, giving rise to a new paradigm for risk management.

This new paradigm views risks from an enterprise-wide perspective and sees the task as managing the uncertainties that could influence achievement of the organization's objectives. The goal of this integrated and broadly focused perspective is to create, protect, and enhance shareholder value. A management process that identifies all the business risks and assesses their potential impact and likelihood of occurrence should be a welcome addition to the arsenal of management practices.

# The Study Companies

The five study companies in this project have started down the long road to implementing an enterprise-wide risk management system, and each has had success along the way.

Chase has a well-organized committee structure to oversee its risk management activities, which begins at the board of directors level and flows into operating committees. Chase's management of market and credit risk is strong and innovative, using sophisticated techniques such as value at risk (for market risk) and stress testing. The development of operational risk management is progressing but is not nearly as advanced as market and credit risk management. Chase introduced a shareholder value-added metric to give decision makers incentives to incorporate risk considerations into their decisions.

In its approach to enterprise-wide risk management, DuPont has established risk policies, guidelines, and line management strategies and procedures. It has a risk management committee and a risk framework with top-level executive involvement. DuPont believed that more sophisticated tools were required to manage its risk. Accordingly, together with consultants, it developed an earnings at risk measure, which provides a common language for risk management that all managers understand. This new tool will allow DuPont to better manage earnings volatility and preserve margins.

Microsoft's approach has focused on financial risk and business risk. A risk management group, headed by the treasurer, oversees both types. Financial risk focuses on market risks, and the group uses VAR and stress testing to quantify the risks. The group uses scenario analysis to identify nonfinancial risks. It disseminates best practices in risk management via the company's intranet and uses face-to-face contact with operating management to convey the importance of risk management in decision making.

UGG identified its risks with a cross section of key employees. The company then focused on a short list of risks that affected 50 percent of the variability in revenues and learned that the main risk affecting the earnings was not the weather but grain-handling volume. With the assistance of consultants, UGG quantified its risks rigorously and has been able to integrate risk management and see significant savings.

A risk management committee oversees the enterprise-wide risk management effort.

Unocal's initiative began in the internal audit and health, environmental, and safety units. Together, these units, with assistance from outside consultants, have designed a risk assessment and control process that is being implemented in all Unocal business units. The essence of the effort is embedded in the belief that a good manager at Unocal is a good risk manager.

## Elements of Risk Management

Most of the major elements for an enterprise-wide risk management system are in place at the case study companies. Each company has identified a broad array of risks it is seeking to manage. In some instances, the company has also analyzed and measured the risks in terms of significance and impact. In some areas, such as financial risks, VAR and stress testing have provided sophisticated measures. Another measure, earnings at risk, has also been introduced. Also, the relationship between the risks and their revenues, cash flows, and earnings (including the likelihood of achieving earnings per share targets) has been included. Finally, some companies looked across the portfolio of risks facing them and found inefficient allocation of capital, inconsistencies in the level of risks assumed, potential savings, and pockets of risk that were either over- or undermanaged.

Some case-study companies used a combination of the risk response strategies of accept, transfer, and mitigate. Each company has, in its own way, drilled risk management into lower levels of the organization. Linking risk management with incentives is one way to drill into the organization the importance of risk management. Other techniques include using the company's intranet and ongoing face-to-face contact between operating management and risk management leadership.

Senior management leadership is a prerequisite to implementing enterprise-wide risk management. Each company has developed a risk management infrastructure in the form of risk committees or a risk management group to monitor the effort. The CFO's participation in enterprise-wide risk management is essential.

# The Future

What's next in the evolution of enterprise-wide management? An area that seems to need the most development is measurement. While EAR, VAR, and stress testing are sophisticated measures for financial risk, such measures do not yet exist for nonfinancial risk. Since many of the events in the nonfinancial risk area are random, it is difficult to build models that offer predictability. Nevertheless, as companies gain experience, they should be able to set up methodologies that provide insights on how to approximate a measure for such risks.

CFOs in the future will need to be well informed on best practices in enterprise-risk management and know how to use that information in the context of their companies. The need for such knowledge provides an opportunity for business educators to develop materials to teach enterprise-wide risk management to future CFOs. Such materials could be incorporated into existing graduate or undergraduate courses or used in a new course devoted to the subject.[3]

## Assessing Your Organization

To assess your organization's risk management strategy, take the quiz in figure 8.1. After completing the quiz, ask yourself the following questions:

- Does management agree on what the risks are for your organization?
- Does management agree on the importance of these risks?
- Does management know the real level of importance and significance of these risks?
- For risks that are undermanaged, does your organization have a plan in place to improve the management of these risks?
- For risks that are overmanaged, does your organization have a plan in place to reallocate resources?
- Does your organization take inconsistent levels of risks?
- Is risk management an integral part of your organization? If not, why not?

*Figure 8.1*
*Risk Management Quiz*

| Three Most Important Risks | Importance 10=highly important | Management Effectiveness 10=highly effective | Gap Importance minus effectiveness |
|---|---|---|---|
| 1. | | | |
| 2. | | | |
| 3. | | | |

**Instructions:**

- List the three most important risks your organization faces. (If you do not know your important risks or if you get different answers from different managers within your organization, you may have even more risk than you realized.)

- Assess each risk according to how important it is to your organization. Use a scale of 1 to 10, with 10 being highly important risks.

- Ask yourself how effective management is at managing that risk. Again, use a scale of 1 to 10, with 10 implying that the risk is managed extremely well and 1 implying that the risk is not managed at all.

- Finally, determine the gap, or the difference between the importance of the risk and the effectiveness of its management. Simply subtract the third column from the second to get the gap. The gap can indicate many things, but a positive gap generally indicates that risks are undermanaged, and a negative gap may indicate that risks are overmanaged.

# 8

## Summary

In the ever-changing business environment of the twenty-first century, managers cannot be lax or undisciplined about risk management. When a risk disaster happens, punishment is swift and unmerciful. One look at the daily newspaper gives evidence of this. Stakeholders have little patience with managers who respond, "I didn't realize it was **that** serious" or "We didn't think **that** would happen." At a minimum, managers must know their risks and be prepared to deal with them effectively.

While successful organizations tend to manage individual risks well, the future is with those farsighted managers who take risk management to higher levels—who adopt an enterprise-wide approach. These managers will benefit from a full awareness of their key business risks and the satisfaction of knowing plans are in place for managing those risks in a coordinated, sophisticated way. Effective risk management is not optional in the twenty-first century: Stakeholders will demand it and the best managers will embrace it.

## Endnotes

1. Michael Mandel, *The High Risk Society* (New York: Times Business, 1996): 198.

2. Canadian Institute of Chartered Accountants Criteria of Control Board, *Learning about Risk: Choices, Connections and Competencies* (Toronto, Canada: CICA, 1998): 26.

3. Risk analysis and control was one of the areas recommended in a recent report on improving the accounting curriculum. See W. Steve Albrecht and Robert J. Sack, *Accounting Education: Charting the Course through a Perilous Future,* Accounting Education Series, Volume 16 (Sarasota, FL: American Accounting Association, 2000): 63. For a description of a risk assessment course, see Paul L. Walker and William G. Shenkir, "Teaching a Risk Assessment Course," *Advances in Accounting Education,* (2000): 33–56.

# Enterprise-wide Risk Management Interview Protocol

**1   Company Background, History, and Environment**

1.1   How did you become aware of the potential advantages of adopting an enterprise-wide risk management approach?

1.2   Why did you decide to initiate an enterprise-wide risk management approach? Were you motivated by a single event or circumstance?

1.3   Whose idea was it to try to move to an enterprise-wide risk management system?

1.4   When did your company begin the enterprise-wide risk management initiative? Please describe the status of your company when you began this endeavor.

1.5   How far along are you in your enterprise-wide risk management plan? Please describe the various stages of your enterprise-wide risk management implementation plan.

1.6   What are your goals for the enterprise-wide risk management system?

1.7   What documents relating to the enterprise-wide risk management system could be made available to the researchers?

**2   Organization Structure**

2.1   Describe the organization structure for your enterprise-wide risk management initiative.

2.2　　Do you have a risk officer? To whom does he/she report? What is the risk officer's job description?

2.3　　Do you have appropriate resources—human and technological—for managing risk?

## 3　Assess Risks (identify, source, prioritize)

3.1　　How do you identify risk? Describe the process you followed to identify your comprehensive risk language, and describe any risk frameworks you use. (For example, risk might be classified as strategic, operating, or information risk.)

3.2　　Do you have an agreed-upon set of objectives and have you identified the risk related to each objective?

3.3　　With respect to the identification of risk—Is it the responsibility of one overall group or of each department?

3.4　　With respect to the identification of risk—Is it done for every department, division, and product?

3.5　　Do you use a risk checklist or questionnaire to assist in identifying risk? If so, describe.

3.6　　Have you used consultants to help you in the identification of risk? If so, what was their expertise and can you describe how they assisted you?

3.7　　Have you considered risk for each step in your value chain? The value chain is the sequence of business functions in which utility or usefulness is added to the products or services of an organization.

3.8　　Have you benchmarked your company to know if you've identified all significant risks? For example, have you compared the risk you've identified with those of any other organizations?

3.9　　Do you look at recent changes in your business to see if new risks have surfaced (e.g., new sales policies, new products, etc.)?

3.10    For each significant process in your company, have you determined the risk level and the level of controls in that process?

3.11    Are your risks communicated throughout the company? If so, how?

3.12    After identifying a given risk, have you sourced and measured it?

3.13    Is your risk measurement quantitative or qualitative?

3.14    Do you assess the significance of the risk? If so, how do you perform the assessment? Who is responsible for the assessment?

3.15    Do you assess the dollar impact of the risk? If so, how do you perform the assessment? Who is responsible for the assessment?

3.16    Do you assess the likelihood of the risk? If so, how do you perform the assessment? Who is responsible for the assessment?

**4    Develop Risk Strategies (avoid, transfer, control, accept)**

4.1    Have you evaluated how effectively you're managing your risks? Are you overmanaging or overcontrolling? For any risks that you're undermanaging, what changes have you made?

4.2    Do you use any form of a risk scorecard or a balanced scorecard?

4.3    What controls have you implemented to ensure you manage a given risk?

4.4    Once a given risk has been identified, how do you manage it?

4.5    What software do you use to help you manage risks?

4.6    What other tools do you use to help you manage risk?

4.7    Who is responsible for ensuring risks are managed?

## 5  Measure/Monitor Risk Processes

5.1   In general, are your risks increasing or decreasing?

5.2   How often do you update your identified risks?

5.3   How often do you update your assessment of risks?

5.4   How often do you review your controls and information gathering system based on your risks?

5.5   Do you have a summary metric or a series of metrics that identify your risk level?

5.6   Can you give the researchers examples of information you use to monitor risk?

5.7   Is monitoring and measurement linked to your assessment and prioritization of risks?

5.8   Describe key performance indicators you use and how they assist you in managing risk.

## 6  Role of Key Executives and Committees

6.1   What are the responsibilities of key executives (e.g., chairman, CEO, CFO, chief legal counsel, operations VP, marketing VP, human resources VP, chief internal auditor, etc.) in your company with respect to the enterprise-wide risk management system?

6.2   Are there special skills required of an executive when a company initiates an enterprise-wide risk management system? If so, please describe.

6.3   What training courses have you attended or offered on risk management?

6.4   Are incentive plans and pay linked to risk management?

6.5   Does the Audit Committee of the Board of Directors receive regular reports on the company's enterprise-wide risk management system? If so, describe the information shared with the audit committee.

## 7 Implementation Issues

7.1     What do you do differently now that you have an enterprise-wide risk management system?

7.2     In your experience, what are the most significant obstacles to a successful implementation of an enterprise-wide risk initiative?

7.3     What type of support is needed from top management for an enterprise-wide risk initiative?

7.4     What do you consider the best way to implement an enterprise-wide risk management system?

7.5     What would you do differently if you were initiating an enterprise-wide risk management system again?

7.6     What are your "best practices" for managing risks? Best practices are leading edge techniques that other companies might find useful.

## 8 General

8.1     What risks are of the most concern at the present?

8.2     What possible future risks are of concern?

8.3     What actions have you taken with respect to those current and future risks?

8.4     Do you allocate capital requirements or resources based on your assessment of risk?

# References

American Institute of Certified Public Accountants, Special Committee on Assurance Services. *Report of the Special Committee on Assurance Services.* New York: AICPA, 1997.

American Institute of Certified Public Accountants and Canadian Institute of Chartered Accountants. *Managing Risk in the New Economy.* New York: AICPA, 2000.

Arthur Andersen. *Operational Risk and Financial Institutions.* London: Risk Books, 1998.

Augustine, N. R. "Managing the Crisis You Tried to Prevent." *Harvard Business Review* (November–December 1995): 147–158.

Banham, R. "Kit and Caboodle: Understanding the Skepticism about Enterprise Risk Management." *CFO* (April 1999): 63–70.

Bernstein, P. L. *Against the Gods—The Remarkable Story of Risk.* New York: John Wiley & Sons, Inc., 1996.

Bolon, M., and A. Weber. *Benchmarking: A Manager's Guide.* New York: Coopers & Lybrand Publishing Division, 1995.

Boulton, R. E. S., B. D. Libert, and S. M. Samek. *Cracking the Value Code: How Successful Businesses Are Creating Wealth in the New Economy.* New York: HarperBusiness, 2000.

Brown, G., and D. Chew (editors). *Corporate Risk: Strategies and Management.* London: Risk Books, 1999.

Canadian Institute of Chartered Accountants Criteria of Control Board. *Guidance on Control.* Toronto, Ontario: Canadian Institute of Chartered Accountants, 1995.

___. *Learning About Risk: Choices, Connections and Competencies.* Toronto, Ontario: Canadian Institute of Chartered Accountants, 1998.

___. *Guidance for Directors—Dealing with Risk in the Boardroom.* Toronto, Ontario: Canadian Institute of Chartered Accountants, 2000.

Committee of Sponsoring Organizations of the Treadway Commission (COSO). *Internal Control—Integrated Framework.* New York: AICPA, 1992.

Coopers & Lybrand (U.K.). *GARP, Generally Accepted Risk Principles.* London: Coopers & Lybrand International, 1996.

Davis, S., and C. Meyer. *Future Wealth.* Boston: Harvard Business School Press, 2000.

DeLoach, J. W. *Enterprise-wide Risk Management: Strategies for Linking Risk and Opportunity.* London: Financial Times, 2000.

Deloitte & Touche LLP. *Perspectives on Risk for Boards of Directors, Audit Committees, and Management.* Wilton, CT: Deloitte Touche Tohmatsu International, 1997.

Drake, L. L. "What Your CEO Wants to Know about Managing Risk. *Financial Executive* (September/October 1997): 25–27.

Economist Intelligence Unit, written in cooperation with Arthur Andersen & Co. *Managing Business Risks—An Integrated Approach.* New York: The Economist Intelligent Unit, 1995.

Economist Intelligence Unit, written in cooperation with Arthur Andersen & Co. *Managing Business Risks in the Information Age.* New York: The Economist Intelligent Unit, 1998.

Financial and Management Accounting Committee of the International Federation of Accountants (IFAC), prepared by Pricewaterhouse-Coopers. *Enhancing Shareholder Wealth by Better Managing Business Risk.* New York: International Federation of Accountants, 1999.

Internal Control Working Party. *Internal Control: Guidance for Directors on the Combined Code.* London: The Institute of Chartered Accountants in England & Wales, 1999.

Joint Australia/New Zealand Standard, prepared by Joint Technical Committee OB/7 Risk Management. *Risk Management (revised draft)*. Strathfield NSW, Australia: Standards Association of Australia, 1999.

Kaplan, R. S., and D. P. Norton. "The Balanced Scorecard—Measures that Drive Performance." *Harvard Business Review* (January–February 1992): 71–79.

Kaplan, R. S., and D. P. Norton. "Putting the Balanced Scorecard to Work." *Harvard Business Review* (September–October 1993): 134–147.

Mandel, M. *The High Risk Society.* New York: Random House, 1996.

McNamee, D., and G. M. Selim. *Risk Management: Changing the Internal Auditor's Paradigm.* Altamonte Springs, FL: The Institute of Internal Auditors Research Foundation, 1998.

Nottingham, L. *A Conceptual Framework for Integrated Risk Management,* Members' Briefing Publication 212–97. Ottawa, Ontario: The Conference Board of Canada, 1997.

O'Kelly, E. "A Checkup for Your Treasury Policy." *Financial Executive* (September/October 1995): 40–44.

Puschaver, L., and R. G. Eccles. "In Pursuit of the Upside: The New Opportunity in Risk Management. *PwC Review* (December 1996): 1–10.

Risk Management Association. *Operational Risk—The Next Frontier.* Philadelphia: Risk Management Association, 1999.

Rusate, D. A., E. Harris, P. Collier, and A. J. Kearney. "The Reins on Risk." *Financial Executive* (July/August 1995): 18–23, 57–58.

Sammon, A. E. *Assurance Services: Risk Assessment.* Jersey City, NJ: The American Institute of Certified Public Accountants, 1997.

Scherzer, M. H., and R. Mackay. "Risky Business." *Financial Executive* (September/October 1998): 30–33.

Simons, R. L. *Levers of Control.* Boston: Harvard Business School Press, 1995.

___. "Control in an Age of Empowerment." *Harvard Business Review* (March–April 1995): 80–88.

___. "How Risky Is Your Company?" *Harvard Business Review* (May–June 1999): 85–94.

Steering Group on the Financial Reporting of Risk. *No Surprises: The Case for Better Risk Reporting.* London: The Institute of Chartered Accountants in England and Wales, 1999.

Stewart, T. A. "Managing Risk in the 21st Century." *Fortune* (February 22, 2000): 202, 206.

Uzumeri, M. V., and C. A. Snyder. "Information Technology and Accelerated Science: The Case of the Pentium Flaw." *California Management Review* (Winter 1996): 44–63.

Walker, P. L., and W. G. Shenkir. "Teaching a Risk Assessment Course," *Advances in Accounting Education* (2000): 33–56.

Zweig, P. L. "Managing Risk," *Business Week* (October 31, 1994): 86–92..

# Annotated Bibliography

## Books and Reports

American Institute of Certified Public Accountants, Special Committee on Assurance Services. *Report of the Special Committee on Assurance Services.* New York: AICPA, 1997.

This committee, known as the Elliott Committee after its chairman, Robert Elliott, identified many potential assurance services for CPAs, including risk assessment. The report indicated that risk assessment includes three tasks: identification and assessment of primary potential risks, independent assessment of risks, and evaluation of systems for identifying and limiting risks. The report discusses categories of risk, why CPAs should provide risk assessment services, and the potential market for this service.

American Institute of Certified Public Accountants and Canadian Institute of Chartered Accountants. *Managing Risk in the New Economy.* New York: AICPA, 2000.

A joint AICPA and CICA Risk Services Task Force produced this report for CPAs and chartered accountants who provide or plan to provide risk services to their clients. While recognizing that various approaches to risk management exist, the report identifies the following steps: establishing a context, identifying risks, analyzing and assessing risks, designing strategies for managing risk, implementing and integrating risk management, and measuring, monitoring, and reporting.

Arthur Andersen. *Operational Risk and Financial Institutions.* London: Risk Books, 1998.

This book focuses on operational risks for financial institutions and does not cover credit risk or market risk. It contains 12 essays written by a variety of experts. Operational risks have become increasingly important to financial institutions in recent years. The book presents an overall framework of risk to show how operational risk fits into the risk universe. The essays deal with such issues as implementing new approaches to operational risk management and recent developments in quantifying operational risk.

Bolon, M., and A. Weber. *Benchmarking: A Manager's Guide.* New York: Coopers & Lybrand Publishing Division, 1995.

This how-to book for managers offers guidance on how to benchmark, which is one way to identify risk in a business. The authors define benchmarking, suggest how to select benchmarking partners, and describe how to write survey questionnaires. They also discuss collecting and interpreting the data.

Boulton, R. E. S., B. D. Libert, and S. M. Samek. *Cracking the Value Code: How Successful Businesses Are Creating Wealth in the New Economy.* New York: HarperBusiness, 2000.

This book, written by three Arthur Andersen partners, focuses on how organizations are creating value in the New Economy. The authors define a value dynamics framework, which consists of five classes of assets: physical, financial, customer, employee and supplier, and organization. The authors give case examples of companies that are creating value in new ways in each of the five classes of assets. Of particular relevance to enterprise-wide risk management is chapter 10, which focuses on risk management. Using the Arthur Andersen Business Risk Model with three categories of risk—environment, process, and information for decision making—the authors identify a company that is creating value by managing risk in each of those areas.

Brown, G., and D. Chew (editors). *Corporate Risk: Strategies and Management.* London: Risk Books, 1999.

This book contains 30 essays organized around four themes: the theory of corporate risk management, the practice of corporate risk management, evidence on corporate risk management, and case studies in corporate risk management. The essays represent a wide range of approaches to financial risk management for nonfinancial corporations. Financial risk is defined as any risk that can be managed with a financial instrument. The case studies of financial risk management include Dell, McDonald's, Merck, Metallgesellschaft, Microsoft, and Western Mining.

Canadian Institute of Chartered Accountants Criteria of Control Board. *Learning About Risk: Choices, Connections and Competencies.* Toronto, Ontario: Canadian Institute of Chartered Accountants, 1998.

The Criteria of Control Board issued this document to spark thought and discussion that might lead to a better understanding of the nature of risk and the process of risk identification and assessment. The nature of risk is examined, and seven risk models are introduced that can be used to recognize, assess, and act on risk. Each of the models is discussed using excerpts from news articles, annual reports and books, and quotations from senior executives. The report gives 11 propositions about risk, such as the following: "The most significant risk for an organization is the possible loss of reputation." Several appendices, including a case study, provide a variety of helpful aids.

Canadian Institute of Chartered Accountants Criteria of Control Board. *Guidance for Directors—Dealing with Risk in the Boardroom.* Toronto, Ontario: Canadian Institute of Chartered Accountants, 2000.

This document looks at broad concepts of risk and control to assist boards of directors in carrying out their responsibilities. The board of directors plays a key role in an organization's success by appointing the CEO, approving strategy, and evaluating performance and competence of senior management. The document provides sample questions for the board to explore with the CEO and senior management as well as questions for individual directors to ask themselves as they assess their thoughts and feelings about the CEO and senior management.

# APPENDIX C

Committee of Sponsoring Organizations of the Treadway Commission (COSO). *Internal Control—Integrated Framework.* New York: AICPA, 1992.

The COSO report is in four parts: an executive summary, a Framework volume, a Reporting to External Parties volume, and an Evaluation Tools volume. COSO radically changed the concept of control, defining it as a process affected by an entity's board of directors, management, and other personnel, designed to provide assurance regarding the following categories: effectiveness and efficiency of operations, reliability of financial reporting, and compliance with applicable laws and regulations. The COSO framework identifies five interrelated components of internal control: control environment, risk assessment, control activities, information and communication, and monitoring.

Coopers & Lybrand (U.K.). *GARP, Generally Accepted Risk Principles.* London: Coopers & Lybrand International, 1996.

This document presents risk management practices and controls for banks, securities houses, and other financial institutions engaged in "dealing" in the capital markets. It distills and codifies major principles developed from guidance issued by regulators, practitioners, and other advisors to establish a comprehensive framework. The framework consists of 89 core principles classified under five categories.

Davis, S., and C. Meyer. *Future Wealth.* Boston: Harvard Business School Press, 2000.

The authors, who are part of the Ernst & Young Center for Business Innovation, develop three themes: risk as opportunity, financial markets for human capital, and higher wires, stronger nets. They look at how these themes affect individuals, companies, and society in the connected economy. The five chapters that focus on companies are relevant to the topic of enterprise-wide risk management. One interesting concept is a strategic risk unit, which would identify, evaluate, differentiate, package, and trade the various risks a company faces.

DeLoach, J. W. *Enterprise-wide Risk Management: Strategies for Linking Risk and Opportunity.* London: Financial Times, 2000.

This book is a comprehensive treatment of enterprise-wide risk management by a partner of Arthur Andersen, who also co-authored the 1995 study, *Managing Business Risk: An Integrated Approach* (see below). Enterprise-wide risk management is described as a journey that includes these steps: adopt a common risk language; establish overall risk management goals, objectives, and oversight structure; assess risk and develop risk management strategies; design and implement risk management capabilities; continuously improve strategies, processes, and measures for individual risks; aggregate multiple risk measures; link aggregate measures to enterprise performance; and formulate enterprise-wide risk strategy. The author sees risk management as an integral part of an organization's overall strategy that aligns strategy, processes, people, technology, and knowledge to manage the uncertainties that a business faces as it creates value. The book presents case studies of six companies that have begun implementing enterprise-wide risk management.

Deloitte & Touche LLP. *Perspectives on Risk for Boards of Directors, Audit Committees, and Management.* Wilton, CT: Deloitte Touche Tohmatsu International, 1997.

This booklet is a brief general overview of risk assessment. An appendix provides a business risk framework containing four categories of risk—strategic, operating, financial, and information. Broad changes introduce new opportunities and carry business risks. To illustrate, the booklet examines three phenomena—increase in globalization, increase in intangible assets, and emergence of the virtual organization—as new opportunities and discusses the new risks they present. The booklet describes a risk assessment model that includes the following steps: set business objectives, identify key business risks, assess potential impact and likelihood of occurrence, choose a course of action for each business risk, and monitor the internal and external environment for changes in conditions and compliance with controls.

# APPENDIX C

Economist Intelligence Unit, written in cooperation with Arthur Andersen & Co. *Managing Business Risk: An Integrated Approach.* New York: The Economist Intelligent Unit, 1995.

The research upon which this report is based began with the hypothesis that businesses realize the complexity of the risks they face and are searching for a more comprehensive approach to managing them. The results from in-depth personal interviews with 40 senior executives and from a questionnaire (response rate not indicated) supported this hypothesis. The questionnaire used in this research is presented in an appendix. The forces for change call for an integrated, enterprise-wide approach for dealing with business risks, which is defined as the threat that an event or action will adversely affect an organization's ability to achieve its business objectives and execute its strategies successfully. An integrated system for controlling business risks starts with identifying risks and pinpointing their sources. Next, companies should take steps to avoid, transfer, or reduce a risk to acceptable levels. Companies must then measure and monitor risks and, finally, conduct an ongoing assessment of the performance of their risk control processes. The Arthur Andersen Business Risk Model identifies three major risk categories: environment, process, and information for decision-making risks. Under each category, numerous specific risks are identified. The report concludes with six case studies.

Economist Intelligence Unit, written in cooperation with Arthur Andersen & Co. *Managing Business Risks in the Information Age.* New York: The Economist Intelligent Unit, 1998.

A survey of 150 firms of various size in North America, Europe, and Asia and interviews with 50 senior executives were conducted to

- Identify the types of business risk related to information technology (IT)
- Understand how firms are identifying and managing technology-related business risks
- Describe the best practices of managing information technology risks

This report uses the Arthur Andersen Business Risk Model to illustrate how IT sits at the heart of the risk framework. IT risk can be successfully managed only if IT strategies are integrated within the firm's overall business risk strategies. Failure to do so makes it difficult to identify the links between business processes and business risks that result from the use of IT. Technology plays a critical role in many firms now and is expected to extend its influence to virtually all firms in the near future. Even so, most firms do not have a formal process in place to either identify potential critical risks or assess the sources of risk. The most worrisome IT risks relate to information, not the technology itself, and include integrity, availability, and relevance risks. An appendix defines IT risk and elaborates upon its elements. Eleven case studies serve as examples of best practices in the field of business risk management.

Financial and Management Accounting Committee of the International Federation of Accountants (IFAC), prepared by Pricewaterhouse-Coopers. *Enhancing Shareholder Wealth by Better Managing Business Risk.* New York: International Federation of Accountants, 1999.

This report defines risk as uncertainty over future events that could influence achievement of the organization's objectives. Risk is seeking the upside of opportunities while managing the downside of threats and hazards. IFAC's framework focuses more on the upside of opportunities and recommends that organizations emphasize the relationship of risk management to shareholder value. Firms should analyze their activities and ask, "What are the drivers of value and which are the key risks associated with them?" Answers can be secured by mapping processes that drive value and by identifying and analyzing risks and how to respond to them. Risk is divided into three components, each of which tends to be the particular concern of certain management levels: (1) risk as opportunity (senior management and the planning staff); (2) risk as uncertainty, with risk management attempting to reduce the variance between anticipated outcomes and actual results (CFO and line managers responsible for operations); and (3) risk as hazards (internal auditors and insurance administrator). Risk management has traditionally concentrated on the latter two categories. Instead, they all should be linked to the idea of sustainable shareholder value and, therefore, to achieving the firm's stated objectives.

Internal Control Working Party. *Internal Control: Guidance for Directors on the Combined Code.* London: The Institute of Chartered Accountants in England & Wales, 1999.

This pronouncement was issued with the support and endorsement of the London Stock Exchange, which has stated that listed companies will have to comply with the principles or explain why they have not. A company's system of internal control plays a key role in the management of risks that are significant to the fulfillment of its business objectives. The internal control system should be imbedded within operations and form part of the company's culture, be able to adapt to new risks, and be customized to each company's unique situation. This document is divided into the following sections: an introduction, maintaining a sound system of internal control, reviewing the effectiveness of internal control, the board's statement on internal control, internal audit, and an appendix containing a series of questions for assessing the effectiveness of the company's risk and control processes. In establishing and maintaining a sound system of internal control, a company must ensure that its policies manage risks effectively.

Joint Australia/New Zealand Standard prepared by Joint Technical Committee OB/7—Risk Management. *Risk Management (revised draft).* Strathfield NSW, Australia: Standards Association of Australia, 1999.

This draft is a revision of an earlier pronouncement, also entitled *Risk Management.* Its objective is to provide a generic framework for establishing the context, identification, analysis, evaluation, treatment, communication, and ongoing monitoring of risks. A risk management process is viewed as being generic and independent of any specific industry or economic sector. Risk management is an integral part of good management and should be inculcated into an organization's culture—including its philosophy, practices, and business plans. Risk management is an iterative process consisting of well-defined steps, taken in sequence, that support better decision making and encompass both negative outcomes and positive opportunities. The report provides several appendices for detailed guidance.

Mandel, M. *The High Risk Society.* New York: Random House, 1996.

The author, economics editor of *Business Week,* describes the new economic era in which we are living as the "high-risk society." Open markets and free trade, deregulation, business restructuring, and technological change are some of the forces contributing to growth and prosperity, while at the same time causing economic turbulence. All of this is painted against a historical backdrop of security and stagnation that has preceded these times. The author argues that the real economy is increasingly looking like the financial markets and compares them using four characteristics: uncertainty of rewards, ease of entry, widespread availability of information, and rapid reaction to profit opportunities.

McNamee, D., and G. M. Selim. *Risk Management: Changing the Internal Auditor's Paradigm.* Altamonte Springs, FL: The Institute of Internal Auditors Research Foundation, 1998.

This research study includes case studies of 29 organizations (15 to derive a model and 14 to validate the model) and a literature search. It discusses how the presence of a risk management system influences the practice of internal auditing. The paradigm shift described in this study is based on viewing the business process through a focus on risk instead of controls. Internal auditors are participants in this shift and, as a result, are employing a new approach to their audits on both the micro (individual audit assignments) and macro (the annual audit planning process) levels. This study looks at macro risk assessment from the internal auditor's viewpoint. The authors suggest using scenarios to develop and rank risk factors and then concentrating the annual audit plan on a hierarchical ranking of risk factors.

Nottingham, L. *A Conceptual Framework for Integrated Risk Management, Members' Briefing Publication 212–97.* Ottawa, Ontario: The Conference Board of Canada, 1997.

This report describes a conceptual framework to aid in developing an enterprise risk management system. Risks that a company faces come from multiple fronts and call for a coordinated, organization-wide response—that is, an integrated approach to risk management that stretches across the enterprise. As such, risk management is an anticipatory, proactive process that is a key part of strategy and planning and results in minimizing uncertainty and maximizing opportunities. The author asserts that no single methodology exists for a risk management system. However, certain elements that surfaced during the course of conducting research for this study constitute the broad conceptual framework. Throughout the document, the author draws examples from leading firms that have risk management systems in place. The author states that risk management must become a core competency of all employees.

Risk Management Association. *Operational Risk—The Next Frontier.* Philadelphia: Risk Management Association, 1999.

PricewaterhouseCoopers served as the consultant for this study for the British Bankers Association, the International Swaps and Derivatives Association, and the Association of Lending and Credit Risk Professionals. The study is based on the results of a survey of 55 financial institutions. While financial institutions have focused on credit and market risks, operational risk as a separate discipline has received attention primarily during the past three years. Operational risk is defined as the risk of direct or indirect loss resulting from inadequate or failed internal processes, people, and systems or external events. This study excludes business risk, such as competitive positioning, economic cycles, changes in market profit margins, and restructuring of a market. The study focuses on these aspects of operational risk: management structure, tools for assessing operational risk, insurance strategies, senior management reporting, operational risk capital, and future trends. The study indicates that methodologies are evolving to quantify operational risk capital.

Sammon, A. E. *Assurance Services: Risk Assessment.* Jersey City, NJ: The American Institute of Certified Public Accountants, 1997.

This continuing professional development course was written to enable independent accountants to develop and offer risk assessment as a new kind of assurance service. The course draws on a number of different studies to explain risk assessment. A risk identification questionnaire provides a lengthy list of queries grouped by categories to assist in identifying an organization's risk.

Steering Group on the Financial Reporting of Risk. *No Surprises: The Case for Better Risk Reporting.* London: The Institute of Chartered Accountants in England and Wales, 1999.

This steering group published a paper on "Financial Reporting of Risk: Proposals for a Statement of Business Risk" in December 1997, which showed that listed companies already report a lot of information about risk. The current report accepts the proposition that risk reporting is well on its way to reality and takes as its theme "Do you want to do a better job of reporting on risk?" The report, which has eight chapters and a series of appendices, aims to help companies obtain capital at the lowest possible cost by disclosing information about risks faced, actions to manage them, and relevant measures. Risk is defined in terms of uncertainty and volatility and consequently includes opportunities (upsides) and threats (downsides). Several companies were examined for their risk disclosures in prospectuses and annual reports. Five of them are used to illustrate disclosures using the Arthur Andersen Business Risk Model.

# Articles

Banham, R. "Kit and Caboodle: Understanding the Skepticism about Enterprise Risk Management." *CFO* (April 1999): 63–70.

This article explores the use of an enterprise risk management approach in several pioneer companies. The author defines enterprise risk management as combining traditional insurable risks with other exposures such as financial, commodity, legal, and environmental risks. The author explains how a natural hedge is created when these unrelated risks are combined into a basket of risks. The author also presents a step-by-step process for enterprise risk management.

Puschaver, L., and R. G. Eccles. "In Pursuit of the Upside: The New Opportunity in Risk Management." *PwC Review* (December 1996): 1–10.

This article focuses on managing risk using a three-part definition of risk, which requires managers to evaluate risk as opportunity, uncertainty, and hazard. The authors illustrate how managing risk from these three perspectives will allow organizations to obtain optimal results. The authors created a Business Risk Continuum to illustrate how different functional areas and employees can contribute to the risk management process under the three-part definition of risk. They interviewed 19 companies from a variety of industries to obtain a broad perspective of attitudes toward risk management in today's business environment.

Simons, R. L. "How Risky Is Your Company?" *Harvard Business Review* (May–June 1999): 85–94.

This article identifies the negative impact that success may have on management's concern about risk. The author created a "risk exposure calculator" that allows managers to calculate their internal risk exposure based on certain pressure points within their organizations. Critical pressure points are those that come from growth, culture, and information management. Within these three categories of pressure points, the author provides a guide to evaluating a company's level of internal risk exposure. After managers have calculated their level of internal risk exposure, the author provides a chart to aid with the interpretation of the score. The author also created a "levers-of-control" model that allows managers to align the existing controls in the company with the business strategy.

Zweig, P. L. "Managing Risk." *Business Week* (October 31, 1994): 86–92.

This article examines recent changes in risk management techniques by many large U.S. corporations. The article identifies several major changes, including creation of a high-level risk manager, declining use of complex derivatives, restructuring of foreign exchange risk, and promoting a risk-sensitive corporate culture. The article highlights several individuals for their innovative approaches to risk management.

# ABOUT THE AUTHORS

**Thomas L. Barton** is Kathryn and Richard Kip Professor of Accounting and KPMG Research Fellow of Accounting at the University of North Florida. He holds a Ph.D. in accounting from the University of Florida and is a certified public accountant (CPA). Dr. Barton has over 35 professional publications, including research articles in *Barron's, Decision Sciences, Abacus, Advances in Accounting, CPA Journal,* and *Management Accounting.* He coauthored the 1998 Financial Executives Research Foundation study, *Open Book Management: Creating an Ownership Culture.* He received the Lybrand Silver Medal for his article, "A System Is Born: Management Control at American Transtech." Dr. Barton is the creator of the Minimum Total Propensity to Disrupt method of allocating gains from cooperative ventures. This method has been the subject of several articles in *Decision Sciences.* He is also a recognized expert in the application of management controls to highly creative activities. Dr. Barton has taught over 100 professional development seminars and has extensive consulting experience with a wide cross section of organizations in the public and private sectors. Dr. Barton is the recipient of several teaching awards for his undergraduate and graduate work. He was a winner of the State University System of Florida's prestigious Teacher Incentive Program award in 1994, the program's inaugural year.

**William G. Shenkir** is the William Stamps Farish Professor of Free Enterprise at the University of Virginia's McIntire School of Commerce. He served as dean of the school from 1977 to 1992. His teaching and research interests are in management accounting, business risks and controls, and accounting policy. He has produced more than 50 professional publications in leading academic and practitioner journals, made more than 70 presentations before professional and academic organizations, and edited or coauthored five books, including *Open Book Management: Creating an Ownership Culture.* From 1973 to 1976, he served as a technical advisor and project director at the Financial Accounting Standards Board. Dr. Shenkir has served as president of the American Assembly of Collegiate Schools of Business and as a vice president of the American Accounting Association. He has been on numerous committees of the American Accounting Association, American Institute of Certified Public Accountants, Financial Executives Institute, Institute of Management Accountants, and the Virginia Society of CPAs. He was a member of the Board of Directors of Dominion Bankshares Corporation, the Deloitte & Touche Academic Advisory Board, and First Union National Bank—Mid-Atlantic Region. He is currently on the board of directors of ComSonics, Inc. He has taught executive development programs for personnel from industry, government, and accounting firms. He is a CPA and has consulted with a variety of organizations. In 1995 he received the Virginia Outstanding Educator Award from the Carman Blough Chapter of the IMA, and in 1997 he was recognized as one of the 10 University of Virginia Distinguished Professors in the students' yearbook, *Corks and Curls*.

**Paul L. Walker** is an associate professor of accounting at the University of Virginia's McIntire School of Commerce. He obtained his Ph.D. from the University of Colorado and is a CPA. He has professional experience as both an auditor and systems auditor for a Big Five accounting firm. He also worked in securities, internal auditing, and lending at a major U.S. corporation. Professor Walker has also served as a consultant to entities such as Ernst & Young and COSO (the Committee of Sponsoring Organizations of the Treadway Commission). He is a member of the AICPA, the AICPA Risk Task Force, and the American Accounting Association. He teaches courses on accounting information systems, auditing, risk management, and financial accounting. Professor Walker's articles have appeared in *The Accounting Review, Decision Sciences, Auditing: A Journal of Practice and Theory, Research in Accounting Regulation,* and *Review of Accounting Information Systems*.

# ACKNOWLEDGMENTS

The authors have benefited enormously from the help of a number of people. They are indebted to the executive officers, chief financial officers, treasurers, directors of internal audit, and all the others in the five companies in this study for sharing their views on risk management and information about their companies' efforts to develop enterprise-wide risk management.

Tom Barton would like to recognize the following students at the University of North Florida, who ably assisted him in this study: Mandy Brady, Danny Simmerman, Huan Ye, and Monica Broughton. Mandy Brady prepared material for the value at risk sidebar in chapter 2 (figure 2.1), and Danny Simmerman did extensive research for the company timelines. Rosa Price contributed her excellent design work for the timelines. He also thanks Pat Cagnassola for her diligence in transcribing some of the interview tapes. He is especially grateful to Earle Traynham, dean of the College of Business Administration, and John MacArthur, chairperson of the Department of Accounting and Finance at the University of North Florida. They have demonstrated strong and unwavering support for his research program.

Bill Shenkir and Paul Walker are grateful for the financial support they received in 1996 from the Coopers & Lybrand Foundation (now PricewaterhouseCoopers) to develop a new graduate course in business risk and control, which they have team taught for the past three years. This research study has benefited immensely from the spirited class discussions with the McIntire graduate students who took the course, as well as from the excellent speakers who shared their consulting experiences on enterprise-wide risk management with the students. They thank Cynthia Hoeffer, who did an excellent job of transcribing most of the interviews for the five companies. Also, they appreciate the support of Dean Carl Zeithaml of the University of Virginia's McIntire School of Commerce, who enabled them to team teach the business risk and control course and supported them in this research project and in their research program. Over the past four years, the following McIntire graduate students have been supported by the McIntire School as they worked as research assistants on enterprise-wide risk

# ACKNOWLEDGMENTS

management: Latoria Alexander, Duane Carling, Tom Contiliano, Stephen Hunn, Melanie Paris, and Amber Wilkinson. They also thank Tracy Berman for her assistance on this study.

Finally, Bill Shenkir thanks his wife, Missy, for her moral support and always good humor and for her constant encouragement on all of his professional activities. And Paul Walker thanks his family for their love and continuous support throughout the project.

The authors are most grateful to the Financial Executives Research Foundation staff and the Project Advisory Committee for their support and assistance. At the outset of the project, Jim Lewis was very helpful in securing two of the case study companies. Bill Sinnett, as the project manager, was with us from the beginning to the end of the project and was always available to provide assistance. Gracie Hemphill worked with us as the project was nearing completion. The Project Advisory Committee, led by Arnold Kaplan, was very supportive and readily available whenever we needed assistance.

# INDEX

# INDEX

# INDEX

# The *Financial Times* delivers a world of business news.

## Use the Risk-Free Trial Voucher below!

To stay ahead in today's business world you need to be well-informed on a daily basis. And not just on the national level. You need a news source that closely monitors the entire world of business, and then delivers it in a concise, quick-read format.

With the *Financial Times* you get the major stories from every region of the world. Reports found nowhere else. You get business, management, politics, economics, technology and more.

Now you can try the *Financial Times* for 4 weeks, absolutely risk free. And better yet, if you wish to continue receiving the *Financial Times* you'll get great savings off the regular subscription rate. Just use the voucher below.

# 8 reasons why you should read the Financial Times for 4 weeks RISK-FREE!

To help you stay current with significant
developments in the world economy ...
and to assist you to make informed business
decisions — the Financial Times brings you:

**❶** Fast, meaningful overviews of international affairs ... plus daily
briefings on major world news.

**❷** Perceptive coverage of economic, business, financial and political
developments with special focus on emerging markets.

**❸** More international business news than any other publication.

**❹** Sophisticated financial analysis and commentary on world market
activity plus stock quotes from over 30 countries.

**❺** Reports on international companies and a section on global investing.

**❻** Specialized pages on management, marketing, advertising and
technological innovations from all parts of the world.

**❼** Highly valued single-topic special reports (over 200 annually)
on countries, industries, investment opportunities, technology and more.

**❽** The Saturday Weekend FT section — a globetrotter's guide to
leisure-time activities around the world: the arts, fine dining, travel,
sports and more.

*For Special Offer See Over*

**FT FINANCIAL TIMES**
World business newspaper

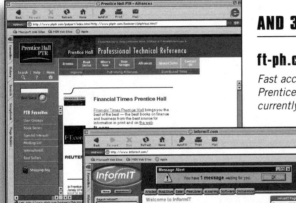